ANATOMY AND EMBALMING

LECTOR HOUSE PUBLIC DOMAIN WORKS

ANATOMY AND EMBALMING

ALBERT JOHN NUNNAMAKER, CHARLES OTTO DHONAU

ISBN: 978-93-89821-82-6

Published: 1913

LECTOR HOUSE LLP
E-MAIL: lectorpublishing@gmail.com

ANATOMY AND EMBALMING

A TREATISE ON THE SCIENCE AND ART OF EMBALMING, THE LATEST AND MOST SUCCESSFUL METHODS OF TREAT MENT AND THE GENERA ANATOMY RELA TING TO THIS SUBJECT.

BY

ALBERT JOHN NUNNAMAKER, A. B.
AND
CHARLES O. DHONAU

PROFESSORS OF ANATOMY AND SANITARY SCIENCE AT
THE CINCINNATI COLLEGE OF EMBALMING,
CINCINNATI, OHIO.

ILLUSTRATED

1913

**DEDICATED TO
THOSE WHO ARE ADVANCING THE STANDARDS OF
THE PROFESSION**

PREFACE

This book is the result of many years of contact with embalmers in training and in practice. We have included in this work a crystallization of essential information without which, the embalmer must be poorly equipped to carry out the many duties incident to his calling in a manner satisfactory to his patrons and to himself.

Having been thrown in contact with the many problems surrounding the education of the embalmer, the authors have gained many ideas as to just how to place the information before the embalmer so that the result will be reflected in an increased capacity for good work on the part of the individual embalmer.

In prescribing information for the embalmer in this manner, we know clearly just what is to be expected from the application of the sciences herein described, and wish for the novitiate and practitioner the same enthusiasm for actual knowledge that has helped us thus far in arranging the information.

In **Part One**, we have chronicled, from the word of historians and men of the present day, a condensed, yet complete exposition of the funeral customs relating to the care of the dead, giving our readers a better understanding of present methods by reason of an opportunity to compare them with those of the past.

In **Part Two**, we have placed the ground work or foundation for the securing of the proper education in embalming. The work on Anatomy, which, if mastered by the student or practitioner, is by far the greatest lever in helping him to master his lifework.

In **Part Three**, we have placed the practical application of the principles of modern embalming, tempered by the use of the sciences of pathology, bacteriology, and chemistry in our own application of the work and in its transcription to these pages.

In formulating the technical part of the work, we have been greatly assisted by many authorities among whom are:—Green, Howell, Thomas, Piersol, Gray, Spalteholz, Myers, Barnes, Renouard, Clarke, and those authors who have from time to time contributed articles to the current embalmers journals. We are deeply indebted to these men for the results of their work.

We have based the treatments given herein on the following classification of embalming fluid as expressed in the percentage strength of formaldehyde gas contained within the fluid.

½ strength	= standard fluid of 5% diluted to 2½%
¾ strength	= standard fluid of 5% diluted to 3¾%
Normal strength	= standard fluid 5%
1¼ strength	= standard fluid of 5% raised to 6¼%

As the existence of a calling or profession depends on a constant assimilation of newly discovered information counterbalanced by the throwing off of that which has been found faulty, we commend this book to the embalmer and hope that it will meet with all the requirements of the higher education, for which we are constantly battling.

THE AUTHORS.

CONTENTS

PART I.
HISTORY OF EMBALMING

PART II.
ANATOMY

PART III.
EMBALMING

**PART IV.
TREATMENTS**

LIST OF ILLUSTRATIONS

ANATOMY AND EMBALMING

PART I.
HISTORY OF EMBALMING

ANCIENT EMBALMING

CHAPTER I.

HISTORY OF EMBALMING.

GUANCH EMBALMING.

—The Guanches with the Egyptians are the only nation among whom embalming had become national, and there exists in the process and mode of preservation of both such striking analogy, that the study of the Guanch mummies is, probably, the surest means of arriving at some positive notions of their origin and relationship. The details known of the mode of embalming among the Guanches will enlighten and complete the descriptions that ancient authors have left to us of the Egyptian processes. They were silent on desiccation in the act of mummification, but it is to be regarded as a simple omission on their part. This desiccation was continued during the seventy days of preparation, and it constituted the principle part of the process adopted.

The details that I am about to give are extracted from the work of M. Bory de Saint Vincent on the fortunate Isles.

"The arts of the Guanches were not numerous, the most singular without doubt is that of embalming. The Guanches preserved the remains of their relations in a scrupulous manner and spared no pains to guarantee them from corruption. As a moral duty each individual prepared for himself the skins of goats, in which his remains could be enveloped, and which might serve him for sepulture. These skins were often divested of their hair, at other times they permitted it to remain, when they placed indifferently the hair side within or without. The processes to which they resorted to make perfect mummies, which they named *xaxos*, are nearly lost.

With the Guanches, the embalmers were abject beings; men and women filled this employment respectively, for their sexes; they were well paid, but their touch was considered contamination; and all who were occupied in preparing the xaxos lived retired, solitary, and out of sight.

There were several kinds of embalming, and several different employments for those who had charge of it. When they had need of the services of the embalmers, they carried the body to them to be preserved, and immediately retired. If the body belonged to persons capable of bearing the expenses, they extended it at first on a stone table, the operator then made an opening in the lower part of the belly with a sharpened flint, wrought into the form of a knife and called *tabona*; the intestines were withdrawn, which other operators afterwards washed and cleaned; they also washed the rest of the body, and particularly the delicate parts, as the eyes, interior of the mouth, the ears, and the nails, with fresh water saturated with salt. They filled the large cavities with aromatic plants; they then exposed the body to the hottest sun, or placed it in stoves, if the sun was not hot enough. During the exposition they frequently endued the body with an ointment, composed of goats' grease, powder of odoriferous plants, pine bark, resin, tar ponce stone, and other absorbing material.

On the fifteenth day the embalming should be completely terminated; the mummy should be dry and light; the relatives send for it and establish the most magnificent obsequies in their power. They sew up the body in several folds of skin, which they had prepared while living, and they bind it with straps.

The kings and the grandees were besides placed in a case or coffin of a single piece, and hollowed out of the trunk of a juniper tree, the wood of which was held as incorruptible.

They then finally carried the xaxos, thus sewed and encased, to inaccessible grottoes consecrated to this purpose.

EGYPTIAN EMBALMING.

—The Egyptians embalmed their dead, and the processes which they employed were sufficiently perfect to secure them an indefinite preservation. This is a fact which the pyramids, the cavern, and all the sepultures of Egypt offer us irrefragible proof. But what were the causes of the origin of this custom? We have in answer only hypothesis and conjecture. In the absence of valid documents, each one explains according to the bias of his mind, or the nature of his studies, a usage, the origin of which is lost in the night of time. One of the ancients informs us that the Egyptians took so much pains for the preservation of the body, believing that the soul inhabited it so long as it subsisted. Cassien, on the other hand, assures us that they invented this method because they were unable to bury their dead during the period of inundation. Herodotus, in his third book, observes, that embalming had for its object the securing of bodies from the voracity of animals; they did not bury them, says he, for fear they would be eaten by worms, and they did not burn them, because they considered fire like a wild beast that devours everything it can seize upon. Filial piety and respect for the dead, according to Sicculus, were the sentiments which inspired the Egyptians with the idea of embalming the dead bodies. De Maillet, in his tenth letter upon Egypt, refers only to a religious motive as the origin of embalming: The priests and sages of Egypt taught their fellow citizens that, after a certain number of ages, which they made to amount to thirty or forty thousand years, and at which they fixed the epoch of the grand revolution when the earth would return to the point at which it commenced its existence, their souls would return to the same bodies which they formerly inhabited. But in order to arrive, after death, to this wished for resurrection, two things were absolutely necessary; first that the bodies should be absolutely carefully preserved from corruption, in order that the souls might re-inhabit them; secondly, that the penance submitted to during this long period of years, that the numerous sacrifices founded by the dead, or those offered to their names by their friends, or relation, should expiate the crimes they had committed during the time of their first inhabitation on earth.

With these conditions exactly observed, these souls separate from their bodies, should be permitted to re-enter at the arrival of this grand revolution which they anticipated—remember all that had passed during their sojourn, and become immortal like themselves. They had further the same privilege of communicating this same happiness to the animals which they had cherished, provided that their bodies inclosed in the same tomb with themselves, were equally well preserved. It is in virtue of this belief that so many birds, cats, and other animals are found embalmed with almost the same care as the human bodies with which they have been deposited.

Such was the idea of perfect happiness which they hoped to enjoy in this new life. Surely superstition alone, it could scarcely be believed, would induce men to save from destruction the mortal spoils of individuals whom they had loved whilst living. We much prefer looking for the source of this usage in the sentiment which survives a cherished object snatched from affection by the hand of death. Since death levels all distinctions—respecting neither love nor friendship—since the dearest and most sacred ties are relentlessly broken asunder, it is the natural attribute of affection, to seek to avoid in some degree, a painful separation, by preserving the remains of those they loved and by whom they were beloved. This according to Saint Vincent. Volney and Paraset write as follows as to the probable cause of the origin of the custom: In a numerous population, under a burning climate, and the soil profoundly drenched during many months of the year, the rapid putrefaction of bodies, is a leaven for plague and disease. Stricken by these numerous pests, Egypt at an early day, struggled to obviate them; hence have arisen, on the one hand a custom of burying their dead at a distance from their habitations; and on the other an art so ingenious and simple to prevent putrefaction by embalming. One individual may be induced to embalm the bodies of his relatives and friends by motives of superstition; another from egotism and personal interest; a third from motives of salubrity or common interest; another is impelled to perform the sacred duty of preserving the remains of those who were dear to him by an instinctive affection. Caylus says that the Egyptians, according to appearances owe the idea of their mummies, to the dead bodies which they found buried in the burning sands which prevail in some parts of Egypt, and which, carried away by the winds, bury travelers and preserve their bodies, by consuming the fat and flesh without altering the skin.

The mourning, embalming and funerals were conducted as follows: When a man of consideration dies, all the women of his house, cover the head and even the face with mud; they leave the deceased in the house, girdle the middle of their bodies, bare the bosom, strike the breast, and overrun the city, accompanied by their relations. On the other side, the men also girdle themselves, and strike their breasts; after this ceremony they carry the body to the place where it is to be embalmed.

Certain men according to the law have charge of the embalming, and make a profession of it. When a body is brought to them, they show the bearers models of the dead in wood. The most renowned represents, they say, *Him whose name I am scrupulous to mention*. This model was probably the figure of some divinity. To be prepared after this model would cost one talent, (about nine hundred dollars of our money). They show a second which is inferior to the first, and which is not so costly, twenty mina, (or about three hundred dollars in our money). They also show a third of lower price, the price of which was considered by Herodotus as a trifle, which we would infer to mean from fifty to seventy-five dollars of our money. The exhibition of models on the part of the embalmers, had reference to the richness of the work demanded, and to the expense of the chosen form. They demand after which of the three models they wish the deceased to be embalmed. After agreeing about the price, the relatives retire; the embalmers work alone and proceed as follows, in the most costly embalming.

They first withdraw the brain through the nostrils, in part with a curved iron instrument, and in part by means of drugs, which they introduce into the head. They now make an incision in the flank with a sharp Ethiopian stone. The body is extended upon the earth, the scribe traces on the left flank the portion to be cut out. He who is charged with making the incision cuts with an Ethiopian stone, as much as the law allows; which, having done, he runs off with all his might, the assistants follow, throwing stones after him, loading him with imprecations, as if they wished to put upon him this crime. They regard, indeed, with horror, whoever does violence to a body of the same nature as their own.

They withdraw the intestines through this opening, clean them, and pass them through palm wine, place them in a trunk; and among other things they do for the deceased, they take this trunk, and calling the sun to witness, one of the embalmers on the part of the dead, addresses that luminary in the following words, which Euphantus has translated: "Sun and ye too, Gods, who have given life to men, receive me, and grant that I may live with the eternal Gods: I have persisted all my life in the worship of those Gods, whom I hold from my fathers, I have ever honoured the Author of my being, I have killed no one, I have committed no breach of trust, I have done no other evil: if I have been guilty of any other fault during life, it has not been on my own account, but for these things." The embalmer in finishing these words, shows the trunk containing the intestines, and afterwards casts it into the river. As to the rest of the body when it is pure they embalm it.

Afterwards they fill the body with pure bruised myrrh, with cannella and other perfumes, excepting incense, it is then sown up. When that is done they salt the body by covering it with natrum for seventy days. The natrum carries off and dries the oily, lymphatic, and greasy parts. After the seventy days the body is not permitted to remain longer in the salt. The seventy days elapsed, they wash the body and entirely envelope it in linen and cotton bandages, soaked with gum Arabic. The relatives now reclaim the body, they have made a wooden case for the human form, in which they enclose the corpse, and put it in a chamber destined for this purpose, standing erect against the wall. Such is the most magnificent method of embalming the dead.

Those who wish to avoid the expense, choose this other method; they fill syringes with an unctious liquor which they obtain from the cedar, with this they inject the belly of the corpse without making any incision, and without withdrawing the intestines; when this liquor has been introduced into the cavity, they cork it; the body is then salted for the prescribed time. The last day they draw off from the body the injected liquor, it has such strength that it dissolves the ventricles and intestines, which come away with the liquid. The natrum destroys the flesh, and there remains of the body only the skin and the bones. This operation finished, they return the body without doing anything further to it.

The third kind of embalming is only for the poorer classes of society, they inject the body with a fluid called surmata, they put the body in natrum for seventy days, and they afterwards return it to those who brought it.

As to the ladies of quality, when they are dead, they are not immediately sent to the embalmers, any more than such as are beautiful or highly distinguished; they are reserved for three or four days after death. They take this precaution lest the embalmers might pollute the bodies confided to their care.

The relatives now fix the day for the obsequies in order that the judges, the relations, and the friends of the dead may be present, and they characterize it by saying that he is going to pass the lake; afterwards the judges, to the number of more than forty arriving, place themselves in the form of a semicircle beyond the lake. A bateau approaches, carrying those who have charge of the ceremony, and in which is a sailor whom the Egyptians name in their language, Charon. Before placing in the bateau the coffin containing the body of the deceased, it is lawful for each one present to accuse him. If they prove that he has led a sinful life, the judges condemn him, and he is excluded from the place of his sepulture, if it appear that he has been unjustly accused, they punish the accuser with severity. If no accuser presents himself or if the one who does so is known to be a calumniator, the relatives, putting aside the signs of their grief, deliver an eulogism, on the deceased without mentioning his birth, because they consider all Egyptians equally noble. They enlarge on the manner in which he has been schooled and instructed from his childhood; upon his piety, justice, temperance, and his other virtues since he attained manhood, and they pray the Gods of hell to admit him into the dwelling of the pious. The people applauded and glorified the dead who were to pass all eternity in the abodes of the happy. If any one has a monument destined for his sepulture, his body is there deposited; if he has none, they construct a room in his house, and place the bier upright against the most solid part of the wall. They place in their houses those to whom sepulture has not been awarded, either on account of crimes, of which they are accused, or on account of the debts which they may have contracted; and it happens sometimes in the end that they obtained honorable sepulture, their children or descendants becoming rich, pay their debts or absolve them.

The Egyptian embalmers knew how to distinguish from the other viscera, the liver, the spleen, and the kidneys, which they did not disturb; they had discovered the means of withdrawing the brain from the interior of the body without destroying the bones of the cranium; they knew the action of alkalies upon animal matter, since the time was strictly limited that the body could remain in contact with these substances; they were not ignorant of the property of balsams, and resins to protect the bodies from the larvae of insects and mites; they were likewise aware of the necessity of enveloping the dried and embalmed bodies, in order to protect them from the humidity, which would interfere with their preservation.

The preceding is a description of ancient Egyptian embalming as given by Herodotus, and has been the subject of numerous commentations, discussions and researches. It is almost a positive fact that Herodotus has omitted desiccation, and that it naturally took place during the time consecrated to preparation. From the mummies examined it is believed now that the body was first salted for seventy days, then dried, and that it was not until after this desiccation that the resinous and balsamic substances were applied. A simple inspection of the mummies is sufficient to confirm this opinion and besides what use would have been these resinous matters, with which the alkali of the natrum would soon form a soapy mass, which the lotions would have carried off, at least in great part? It is much more reasonable to suppose that these balsamic and resinous substances were not applied to the bodies until after they were withdrawn from the natrum.

All the ancients agree, in saying that the Egyptians made use of the various aromatics to embalm the dead; that they employed for the rich myrrh, aloes, canella, and cassia lignea; and for the poor, the cedria, bitumen, and natrum. The natrum was a mixture of carbonate, sulphate, and muriate of soda. It was a fixed alkali, which acted after the manner of quicklime; despoiling the bodies of their lymphatic, and greasy fluids, leaving only the fibrous and solid parts. The odoriferous resins and bitumen not only preserved from destruction, but also kept at a distance the worms and beetles which devour dead bodies.

The embalmers, after having washed the bodies with palm wine, and having filled them with odoriferous resins or bitumen, they place them in stoves, where by means of convenient heat these resinous substances united intimately with the bodies, and these arrive in a very little time to that state of perfect preservation which we find them at the present day. This operation of which no historian has spoken, was, without doubt, the principle and most important part of their embalming.

CHAPTER II.

EMBALMING FROM EGYPTIANS DOWN TO CIVIL WAR.

Here facts are almost entirely wanting and the history of the art we are studying, can only be followed in the recitals of historians, to control whose veracity we have no longer those monuments which Egypt offers us in such great numbers. Among the Jews, the Greeks, the Romans, and all modern nations, we see the honors of embalming accorded to Kings, Princes and men of distinction, but no tomb that has been opened, has rendered a single mummy so perfect, as those which we admire among the Egyptians.

JEWS.

—The Jewish people, who, like others, testified their respect for the dead, never admit the care of embalming the body as a common usage. Thus Abraham purchased the field where Sarah was buried; Joseph had the body of his father magnificently embalmed; Moses only carried away the bones of Joseph; David praised the people of Gilead, for having buried with pomp Saul and his sons, etc. In most of these examples, no mention is made of embalming; nevertheless, the body of Jesus Christ was embalmed. It is written that Joseph of Arimathea, a secret disciple, and Nicodemus, ministered unto him, after the crucifixion, and that 100 lbs. of myrrh and aloes were used. In this action the greatest secrecy had been observed, for "when the Sabbath was over, very early on the first day of the next week, came the faithful women who had loved him, with spices and ointment they had prepared where with to annoint him, not knowing that, already, this loving service had been performed by the hand of pious affection."

The following is nearly the method used by the Jews: Each sex took care of its dead; they first of all, close the mouth and eyes of the exposed person, afterward they washed the body and then rubbed it with perfumes, tied it with bands, and then bandaged it in several cloths of very fine linen or woolen; and finally, they put it into the sepulture. It is thought that the myrrh and aloes which they employed had very little virtue to resist putrefaction, and that the great quantities of aromatics which they consumed, was rather for pomp, than for the long preservation of the subject. They took no pains to dry the body; they did not take away the intestines, and in spite of all these odoriferous drugs, decomposition must have soon revealed itself as was testified by the body of Lazarus when resurrected.

PERSIANS.

—Neither did the Persians possess a very great knowledge of preservation. Cyrus, King of Persia, said to his children: "when I have ceased to live, place my body neither in silver nor in gold, nor in any other coffin, but return it immediately to the earth, etc." It will be perceived that Cyrus, in forbidding that any care should be taken with his body, does not allude to embalming, which, of all other means, would have been the most efficient in preventing its elements from returning to the Common Mother.

BABYLONIANS.

—The Babylonians, anointed the bodies of their dead with honey, after which, they were immersed in the same substance. It is highly improbable that this process was successful for long time preservation, for the preservative power of honey was only equal to its ability to keep the air from the body.

SCYTHIANS.

—The Scythians coated the bodies of their dead with wax. This process could not have been successful excepting to retard decomposition through shutting off all communication between the body and the air.

ETHIOPIANS.

—The Ethiopians coated the bodies of their dead with waxy covering called parget. The same comment given on the Babylonian and Scythian processes must also be used here.

ROMANS.

—The disposition of the dead among the Romans embraced the following treatment: the deceased was first washed with hot water varied with oil, at intervals, for seven days; was dressed and embalmed with the performance of a variety of singular ceremonies. Cremation was then the means of ultimate disposal of the dead, the ashes being gathered and placed in urns and then the urns, in turn, were placed in tombs.

GREEKS.

—Homer describes cremation, as an honorable mode of sepulture practiced in the heroic ages. Later from their many conquests, the Greeks acquired the art of embalming patterned after the Arabian and Assyrian-Persian methods, of which we have no record.

NORSEMEN.

—It appears from the sages that a form of cremation was used by the early Norsemen, who used to place the viking in his ship and send him "flaming out to sea." Later it became the custom to place him, with all his belongings, in his vessel set on an even keel, and entomb him beneath a mound of earth.

HINDOOS.

—Suttee (from Sati-a virtuous wife), an Indian custom, involving the burning of widows on the same funeral pyre as the husband, was the rule until 1829 A. D.

FRENCH AND BELGIANS.

—Paleolithic cave dwellers of France and Belgium buried their dead in natural caves or crevices, like those in which they lived. Later stone-age people throughout Europe buried in chambered barrows or cairns. Bronze age people buried in unchambered barrows or in cemeteries of stone cists set in the ground often on a natural eminence, and surrounded by circles of standing stones. The cist was formed of a double row of stones covered with rude stone slabs.

BRITAINS.

—Neolithic tribes in Britain buried either in caves or in chambered tombs, probably representing the huts of the living. Some of these barrows are very elaborate and massive; that of West Kennett is said to be 350 feet long. The dead were buried in the British tombs as they died, or in a contracted posture, probably due to their habit of sleeping in this position, and not at full length on a bed. Many cleft skulls are found in these tombs, suggesting human sacrifice, which as Caesar tells us, was prevalent among the Gauls. The bronze age usages were divided between burying and cremation. In burying, the contracted posture was followed. In cremation, the body was placed in a coffin made of the hollow trunk of an oak, split in two. In cremation, the ashes were collected in a funeral urn, twelve to eighteen inches high and were placed in a chamber. Articles of daily use were thrown into the fire.

PERUVIANS.

—The aborigines of the western continent were familiar with embalming. Prescott's "Conquest of Peru" tells that the royal "Incas" of Peru, were preserved by some process which did not give evidence of an external application. These bodies were then secreted under mounds of earth and in the interior of the temples. Prescott presents highly interesting pictures of these embalmed Peruvian monarchs sitting "natural as life," in the chairs of the temples of the sun, at Cusco. They were clothed as in life, the raven black hair on their heads was still unchanged, and their hands were crossed upon their bosoms in the grim dignity of death.

AZTECS.

—The Aztecs, who were highly civilized, and were one of the most interesting and powerful tribes of early America, inhabited Mexico. The Aztecs were conquered by Cortez in 1519. Their history has been traced back to the twelfth century. The bodies of their dead, especially of those who could claim royal descent, were embalmed. It is related in Aztec legends how, after the deluge, seven persons came forth from the tomb to which their mummified bodies had been committed, and, in renewed existence, repeopled the earth.

NORTH AMERICAN INDIANS.

—Even our own North American Indians knew the art of embalming. Mummies remarkably well preserved have been found among the Flat Heads, Dakotas and Chinooks; and the Florida and Virginia Indians preserved the bodies of their Kings in the same way. The Kentucky caves have given up some remarkable specimens of this kind. The bodies of a woman and child were, in 1899, found in a cave in the Yosemite valley, and which, on account of its size (six feet and eight inches), some authorities believe to be a relic of the lost tribe of the stone age, possibly antedating the Christian era 3,000 years.

EARLY CHRISTIANS.

—For a time the early Christians embalmed the bodies of their dead, using these forms with which they were familiar in Palestine. After a time, however, they gave up the practice. It has been said that they feared by the continuation of the process to cast discredit upon the power of God to call together the scattered dust of the body which had returned to its native element, and present it, like unto Christ's own glorious body, on the morning of the resurrection. No word spoken by Jesus, would indicate that he disapproved of methods, with which he as a Jew was familiar, to preserve the body from decay. During the first four centuries of the Christian era, the catacombs at Rome were used for burial. These catacombs consist of subterranean excavations, long horizontal passages with recesses on either side, arrayed in tiers for the reception of bodies, closed in by slabs bearing inscriptions and emblems of the faith.

LATER EUROPEAN EMBALMING.

—After the previous discussion of the care of the dead affecting prehistoric as well as the earliest historic usages, we are brought forward to the seventeenth century. All embalming processes of the earlier days having been forgotten during the dark ages. The slow but sure development of the medical profession having manifested a dire necessity for the preservation of anatomical material, this necessity was first met by Dr. Frederick Ruysch, who occupied the chair of anatomy at Amsterdam, Holland, during the close of the seventeenth and early years of the eighteenth century (1665-1717).

Dr. Ruysch was probably the first to practice a successful system of arterial injection, in order that his anatomical specimens might resist the processes of decay. The reader should understand that embalming as a convenient process for preserving human dead bodies for funeral purposes had not been thought of at this time, and the principal interest in embalming was for its successful preservation of anatomical specimens. The method followed by Dr. Ruysch, was first an arterial injection, then allowing the diffusion of the fluid for some hours, after which, he proceeded to open the body as in making a postmortem examination, removing the viscera, cleaning them and replacing them surrounded with a preservative solution. Dr. Ruysch died, leaving his secrets buried with him, and they were lost to science.

Dr. William Hunter, an eminent Scottish physician, anatomist and physiologist of the eighteenth century (1718-1783) is given credit by many as being the original inventor of the injection system, for he published his plan of injection in minute detail, so that science might benefit thereby. The artery usually selected by Dr. Hunter was the femoral and his solution was composed of oil of turpentine five pints; Venice turpentine, one pint; oil of lavender, two fluid ounces; oil of rosemary, two fluid ounces; and vermillion. This was forced into the vessel until it reached over the whole body, giving the skin a general reddish appearance. As in Dr. Ruysch's method, the body was left untouched for a time, and was then opened, the viscera being treated and placed back again. After treating the exterior of the body in some cases, a coffin was prepared and the body was placed on a bed of dry plaster of paris in order that desiccation might set in. The body was then left for four years and if dryness had not set in by that time, was placed upon another bed of plaster of paris. Some of Hunter's specimens are to be seen today in the museum of the Royal College of Surgeons, London.

Dr. John Hunter, a younger brother of William, was also very active in experimentation along these lines, and his work was little less renowned along the same lines. The Hunterian method was used for years by English anatomists with little if any alteration.

M. Boudet, attempted to use the Egyptian form of procedure in embalming, using as preservative agents corrosive sublimate, tan, salt, asphalt, Peruvian bark, camphor, cinnamon, and other aromatics. He completely enveloped the body in bandages, varnish being coated over the body and cavities and outer bandages.

M. Franchini, injected the common carotid artery with a solution made up of eight decigrams of arsenious acid, combined with a small quantity of cinnabar, dissolved in nine kilograms of spirits of wine. By this method bodies could be kept odorless and natural in color for sixty days, after which desiccation set in.

Jean Nicholas Gannal, and his son Dr. Gannal of Paris, injected chloride of alumina with success, J. N. Gannal, had previously, a formula containing arsenic, which the French Government compelled him to discontinue by prohibiting the sale of the arsenic. In addition to the above treatment the body was placed in a lead coffin and four or five litres of various essences were poured over the body and the casket was soldered. In this way preservation was said to be indefinite.

M. Sucquet, injected a solution of chloride of zinc arterially, and in one body which was taken up after being buried 14 months achieved remarkable success, the incident being the result of a contest between M. Gannal, M. Dupre, and M. Sucquet. This led to the use of the zinc salts in fluid, not only in Europe but in this country as well.

M. Falcony, desiccated the body in a mixture which was composed of saw dust and powdered zinc sulphate. Bodies so preserved remained flexible for about forty days, after which they dried up, although still retaining their natural color.

Franciolli, used arsenic acid, four ounces; carbonate of potash, two ounces; powdered alum, eight ounces. He completely eviscerated the body and then injected it in all directions, afterwards replacing the organs and surrounding them with liquid preparation composed of corn starch, water, alcohol, and corrosive sublimate, which after hardening, would prevent the sinking of the parts.

Many processes are noted in the various histories of the art, all using the arterial injection, which by this time had become universally accepted as the only true way of reaching the body tissues completely. The reader has noted absolutely nothing as to embalming being the most convenient process for funeral purposes. This is left to the following matter which begins with the embalming done by Dr. Thomas Holmes during the civil war (1861-1865 A. D.)

CHAPTER III.
EMBALMING IN AMERICA AFTER THE CIVIL WAR.

HOLMES

Dr. Holmes was authorized by the U. S. Government to prepare the bodies of slain troops, so that they could be transported to their former homes. The practice of embalming for funeral purposes received its greatest impulse during the regime of Dr. Holmes, and it opened up an era of unprecedented discovery and success in preserving the dead body.

BILLOW

After Holmes, the man who cared for the dead began to feel that his was a professional work worthy of the name. The average undertaker, at the time just after the civil war, was a cabinet maker, whose chief function was to make the coffin or casket for the body, take the casket to the house and place the body in it. Then the larger undertakers in the larger cities found that they were compelled to preserve some of the bodies in some way so that distant relatives could reach the scene before the funeral. This probably was the result of betterments in transportation facilities which led people to travel more. Along with this, travelers frequently died away from home and had to be shipped. The baggage men rightfully objected to remaining in the same enclosed space with an unembalmed body and, altogether, a condition arose in which it was necessary to have some way to preserve the body.

As evolution is always a slow process, we cannot as we would like to do, chronicle the introduction of chemical embalming at this time, for refrigeration was the first thing thought of. The ice box, was the means by which bodies were kept for several days; the body being covered and left that way until a few hours before the funeral. This became so unsatisfactory specially when the sensibilities of the undertaker became sharpened, that they immediately looked about for a more convenient way to handle the situation. Spurred on by this demand, several concerns came into the market with preservative solutions with an arsenical base, and which were used principally for external application and cavity injection. All kinds of instruments were used with which to introduce the fluid into the body cavities until Captain George Billow, of Akron, Ohio, a civil war veteran, and at present a member of the Ohio State Board of Embalming examiners, contrived the pen point trocar, which is still in use among the profession.

With the introduction of the trocar, and the campaigns of the fluid manufacturers, trade periodicals and traveling men, cavity embalming became the means of preservation, until its limitations were learned.

CLARKE

Joseph Henry Clarke, who first traveled for fluid houses, and who was interested in the anatomy of the human body, since his connection with the U. S. hospital service in the Civil war, determined to introduce the arterial injection as the means of placing the fluid through the body. In collaboration with Dr. C. M. Lukens, the occupant of the chair of Anatomy at the Pulte Medical College of Cincinnati, Prof. J. H. Clarke opened a school of embalming naming it the Cincinnati School of Embalming. This took place during the year 1882.

RENOUARD

Prof. Auguste Renouard of Denver, Colorado, came into the field about the same time. Thus we have the beginning of the greatest revolution of all times in the care of the dead human bodies.

SULLIVAN, MEYERS, BARNES

After Prof. Clarke and Prof. Renouard, came Prof. Frank Sullivan, and from time to time the list was augmented by the addition of others, a few of whom being Dr. Eliab Meyers, of Springfield, Ohio, Dr. Carl L. Barnes of Chicago, etc. With the efforts of all these men, the undertakers were led to use the arteries more and more until now, at the present time, this form of embalming is used exclusively through the United States, and Canada; European countries not having, as yet progressed as rapidly in that direction. The additions to the work from the time just previous to the start given to it by Prof. Clarke, number all the methods which we use today, including, the injection of any large artery in the body; the drainage of blood to further the obtaining of a complete circulation; the various processes by which discolorations are prevented and cured; the various processes by which bodies are disinfected; the various processes by which features are restored and many other of the vital operations of the present time. The undertaker having progressed from the cabinet maker, to a man of professional bearing having a good knowledge of all things pertaining to the dead human body, is now a man in whom the greatest reliance may be placed. Where previously, he was uneducated and uncultivated in matters pertaining to the body, he is now an authority to a great extent.

As a part of this historical contribution, we cannot overlook the very great advance made in the nature and composition of the preservative solutions used today. When formaldehyde was introduced, the high cost of it prevented its immediate use; but, later on, improved methods of manufacture brought the cost down to such a point where it became an essential ingredient in the fluids. Later when, on medico-legal grounds, arsenic was prohibited in the fluid (this action paralleling the action taken by France in the case of J. N. and Dr. Gannal), formaldehyde was depended upon for the maximum preservative action. Thus it still remains the base of most of the modern fluids. Several compounders have discontinued its use, preferring phenol, creosote, etc., but these chemicals have not as yet, made much progress against the formaldehyde.

In the early days, when the fluids were likely to be inadequate to care for certain conditions, the question as to which fluid is to be used was the principal care of the embalmer. Today, when the standard fluids are of the highest possible efficiency, it is a question of knowledge and technic on the part of the embalmer; it being a recognized fact that there is only about 1 chance in 1,000 for a standard fluid to contain inferior elements. In this way we may state that the burden of obtaining success has been shifted from the fluid, to the man using it; and it is then unnecessary to state that the best preparation along the line of education for the embalmer is advised, so that by his knowledge, he may do what he is expected to do by the people whom he is serving.

PART II.
ANATOMY

ANATOMY

The word anatomy is derived from two Greek words, meaning, to cut apart, which literally means dissection.

Anatomy is used to indicate the study of the physical structure of organized bodies.

Anatomy is the science of organization or the science of organic structure.

Human anatomy is divided into two great divisions, known as (a) general or descriptive anatomy and (b) surgical or regional anatomy.

Descriptive anatomy deals with the separate parts of the human body.

Histology is that part of descriptive anatomy where the separate parts of the human body are studied by means of the microscope.

Osteology is that part of descriptive anatomy describing the number, form, structure and uses of bone.

Myology is that part of descriptive anatomy which treats of muscles.

Neurology is that part of descriptive anatomy which treats of nerves.

Syndesmology is that part of descriptive anatomy which treats of ligaments.

Angiology is that part of descriptive anatomy which treats of the blood-vessels and lymphatics.

Surgical or regional anatomy describes the relation which certain parts,—muscles, nerves, arteries, etc.,—bear to each other.

CHAPTER IV.

HISTOLOGY.

DEFINITION.

—Histology is that part of descriptive anatomy which treats of the intimate structure of the tissues as seen under the microscope.

Histology as taught in most professional schools constitutes a one year's course, but for the embalmer this is not entirely necessary and with the short term of schooling now existing it is quite impossible, but certain of the fundamental principles of histology are important. For this reason a few of the more important tissues have been discussed, not, however, in great detail, but only superficially, merely to have the embalmer acquainted with them.

A CELL.

—A cell is defined as a nucleated mass of protoplasm endowed with the attributes of life.

Protoplasm is the name applied to the semi-fluid, granular substance contained within the cell.

The simplest forms of animal life are organisms consisting of only one cell which are called *protozoa*.

Cells having similar shape and similar functions are grouped to form tissues.

Tissues are grouped together to form organs.

Every cell consists of a cell body and a nucleus. The cell body consists of a substance known as protoplasm. The nucleus is the essential part of a typical cell and is the controlling center of its activity.

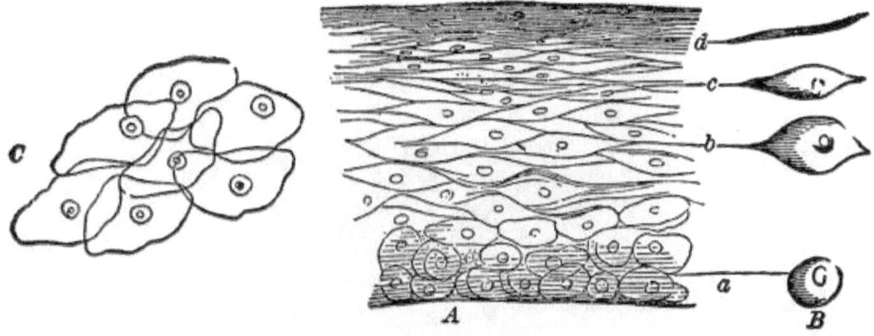

**FIG. 1—A, A VERTICAL SECTION OF THE CUTICLE; B, THE LAT-
ERAL VIEW OF THE CELLS; C, THE FLAT SIDE OF SCALES LIKE
(D) MAGNIFIED 250 DIAMETERS.**

Cells divide or reproduce themselves by means of direct or indirect division. In direct division the nucleus and the cell wall simply divide into two equal divisions and results in the formation of two new cells. In indirect division the process is much more complicated, and several stages must be passed through before there is a complete division.

The process of fertilization consists in the conjugation of two sexual cells. The male sexual cell is called the spermatazoon, and the female sexual cell is called the ovum.

The nucleus of the ovum in its earlier development stages is known as the germinal vessicle.

In the living organism many cells are destroyed during the various physiologic processes and are replaced by new ones. When a cell dies, changes take place in the nucleus which result in its gradual disappearance. This process is known as chromatolysis.

TISSUES.

—A *tissue* is an aggregate of cells all having a common function.

Those important tissues with which the embalmer should be more or less acquainted are the following:

Skin, nails, hair, superficial fascia, deep fascia, lymphatics, glands, cartilage, bone, teeth, nerves, muscles, tendons, aponeuroses, ligaments, fat, mucous membranes, serous membranes, synovial membranes, arteries, veins and blood.

THE SKIN.

—The skin or integument (intego, to cover) is the outside covering of the human body. It is the first tissue that is cut when operating upon the body.

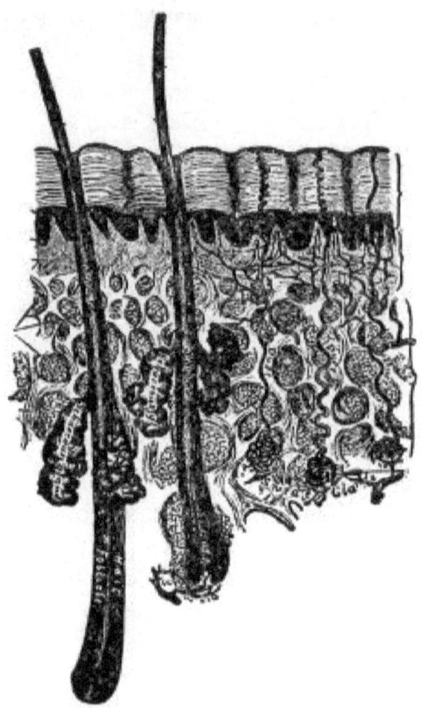

FIG. 2—A CROSS SECTION OF THE SKIN. (GRAY)

The skin is the seat of the organs of touch. The multitudes of sensory nerve endings convey the sensations of temperature, pressure and pain to the brain, thus informing the brain at all times, to keep the body from harm, and in a strong and healthful condition.

The skin is also the regulator of the body temperature, for connected with the skin are sweat glands, and sebaceous glands, each having important excretory functions.

The skin is also a protective coat, very elastic, and varies greatly in thickness. It is thinnest in the eyelids and thickest over the back of the neck, back of the shoulders, palms of the hands and the soles of the feet.

The color of the skin depends upon two things, first, on the pigment, which is found, one of the discriminating points between the races, named by the color of the skin as white, black, yellow, etc.; second, the color depends upon the amount of blood in circulation, the deepest hue being in the parts exposed to the air, light and the varied temperatures. Besides these the color of the skin varies with age, pinkest in the infant and becoming yellow with old age. It varies with exposure and with climate, the people living in the north having a much different complexion than those living in the south under the tropical sun. The color of the skin also varies with certain diseases, being extremely pale in anaemia, brown in Addison's disease, and yellow in jaundice.

The skin can be said to be moveable, although in places it is attached firmly to the underlying structures, especially on the scalp, the soles of the feet, and the palms of the hands.

Upon close examination the skin discloses a multitude of openings, creases, furrows, depressions, folds and hairs.

A dimple is a permanent pit or depression due to the adhesion of the surface to parts beneath.

Structure.—The skin consists of two intimately connected structures, the one is the *true skin, corium,* or *dermis* and is the deepest layer of the skin; and the other is the *false skin, cuticle,* or *epidermis,* and is the outermost layer of the skin.

The true skin, is composed mostly of connective tissues and elastic fibers. It is the real seat of the sense of touch, for it is here that the sensory nerves have their termination. In this layer we also have the termination of the minute capillaries of the skin.

The false skin, contains no blood vessels or nerves, and being without these it is practically dead tissue, and to illustrate this fact one can take a needle and run it through this outside layer without the least pain or the drawing of blood.

The false skin is the part which slips off in case of skin slip. In as much as the minute capillaries end at the termination of the true skin, when putrefaction and fermentation begin there is an oozing of water from the capillaries and the surrounding tissues, between the two layers of skin, causing a blister to form, and known as skin slip.

At the lowest part of the false skin is a layer of germinal cells, from which all the other cells are derived, and becoming more flattened and horny as they are pushed farther away from the blood supply; and also a layer of pigment cells, which give the discriminating color to the skin.

In the skin are seen numerous sebaceous and sweat glands.

The sweat glands are the organs by which a large portion of the aqueous and gaseous materials are excreted by the skin. Sweat glands are found in almost every portion of the skin, and are situated in small pits below the surface of the skin, surrounded by a quantity of adipose tissue or fat. They are small, round, reddish bodies, consisting of a single tubule, convoluted in form, which extends up through the skin and opens on the surface. The size of these glands, of course, vary, being especially large in those regions where the flow of perspiration is copious as in the axilla.

The sebaceous glands are small, sacculated, glandular organs, lodged in the substance of the skin. They are found in most parts of the skin and are usually connected with the hair follicles. Each gland consists of a single duct, more or less capacious, which terminates in a cluster of small secreting pouches or saccules. These glands secrete an oily fluid, which keeps the skin soft and also oils the shaft of the hair.

THE NAILS.

—The nails are a peculiar modification of the epidermis and have the same cellular structure as that of the epidermis. The nails are found on the dorsal surface of the fingers and toes and act as a protection, and enable one to pick up small objects, or to grasp more firmly any object. Were it not for the nails it would be impossible for one to pick up a needle from off the floor.

Each nail is convex on its outer surface, and its chief mass which is called *the body* lies upon the nail bed, or true skin; the free end projects out over the surface of the finger, and is that part which is not attached below, and since it is the continuation of the epidermis, it likewise will have no nerve or blood supply and therefore can be trimmed without pain to the individual.

The root is implanted in a groove in the skin and is composed of cells which have not become horny. The root is white in color and is the little half moon which you can see next to the skin.

The matrix is that part of the true skin beneath the body and the root of the nail, and is so called, because, it is that part from which the nail is produced and so long as the matrix at the root of the nail is uninjured, the nail will be reproduced after an accident.

After death the nail turns black, due to the infiltration of blood into the matrix.

Treatment by the Embalmer.—The blackened condition of the nail due to the infiltration of blood into the matrix can in many cases be overcome by carefully rubbing the nail at the time the body is being injected. After the discoloration is removed the fingers should be kept elevated so that the blood will not settle there again.

THE HAIR.

—The hair, like the nails, is a peculiar modification of the epidermis and consists of practically the same cellular structure as the epidermis. Hair is found on nearly every part of the body excepting the palms of the hands and the soles of the feet, the borders of the lips, etc. It varies much in length, thickness and in the different races of mankind. In the eyelids it is short, on the scalp it is of considerable length. In other parts as the eye-lashes, the hair of the pubis region, the whiskers and beard the thickness is remarkable.

A hair consists of the root and the shaft. The root of the hair or that part implanted in the skin presents at its extremity a bulbous enlargement, called the hair bulb. Into this bulb we find the small arterial capillary circulating and at its termination the beginning of the venous capillary. In this way the hair is nourished in life. We also find a small nerve going to the hair bulb. The shaft is the remaining part or that part coming out from the skin.

The hair grows from its roots and as it grows it pushes itself out from the skin and owes its growth to the small capillary circulation, carrying pure arterial blood to each and every hair, and for this reason you can understand for yourself the erroneous idea of what is termed the "post-mortem growth of hair." Only a few weeks ago one of the students declared that he had actually seen a subject shaved and the body at the time of the funeral was placed in a vault to await the arrival of a close relative who had to come from Europe.

Three weeks later the student, together with the undertaker and relatives, went to the vault to view the remains. The body was in a perfect state of preservation, only for a large growth of beard as the student supposed. This student had observed rightly, but he did not go far enough. He did not think of how the hair actually got its nourishment. The hair owes its life to the circulation of the blood, just as much as the heart or any other organ does, and will die and cease to grow just as soon as the body dies and the circulation is cut off. What this student saw was only an apparent growth, for after the body dies the tissues begin to shrink, squeezing the blood and fluid substances out of them, thus giving the hair cylinder a more projected appearance.

The student was very much surprised at his mistake, but after the explanation he saw that the hair owed its life to the circulation and that when this circulation was cut off, the hair must cease to grow.

The chief function of hair is that of protection from heat or cold and to help shield the brain from the effect of a blow upon the head.

The hair, next to the teeth and bones, is the least destructible part of the body.

THE FASCIA.

—The fascia (fascia, a bandage) is areolar or aponeurotic tissue of variable thickness and strength found in all regions of the body and invests or surrounds the softer and more delicate organs. From its situation in the body the fascia is divided into two groups, superficial and deep.

Superficial fascia is found immediately beneath the skin over almost the entire surface of the body. It connects the skin with the deep fascia and consists of areolar tissue.

The superficial fascia varies in thickness in different parts of the body and some places, especially in the groin is capable of being subdivided into several different layers. The first layer of the superficial fascia, which is just beneath the skin, usually contains a great amount of fat or adipose tissue. This, in most text books, has been termed the subcutaneous tissue. The second layer is comparatively devoid of adipose or fatty tissue and in this we find the trunks of the subcutaneous vessels and nerves, as for example, the radial and ulnar veins in the arms and the saphenous vein in the leg.

The superficial fascia facilitates the movement of the skin, serves as a soft medium for the passage of the vessels and nerves to the skin and retains the warmth of the body, since the fat contained in its meshes is a had conductor of heat.

Deep fascia or aponeurotic fascia is a dense inelastic, unyielding fibrous membrane, forming a sheath for the muscles and affording them broad surfaces for attachment. On removal of the superficial fascia, the deep fascia is usually exposed and can be seen as a dense, tough membrane, which not only binds down the muscles to each region, but gives to each a separate sheath as well as to the blood vessels and nerves.

Thus, on going down into the arm between the biceps and triceps muscles to raise the brachial artery, you would first cut through the skin, then the subcutaneous tissue, the superficial fascia and then you would come to a membrane investing the artery, vein and nerve. This membrane is the part of the deep fascia which covers the vessels, making a distinct sheath for them and you must go through this sheath before you can hope to raise the artery.

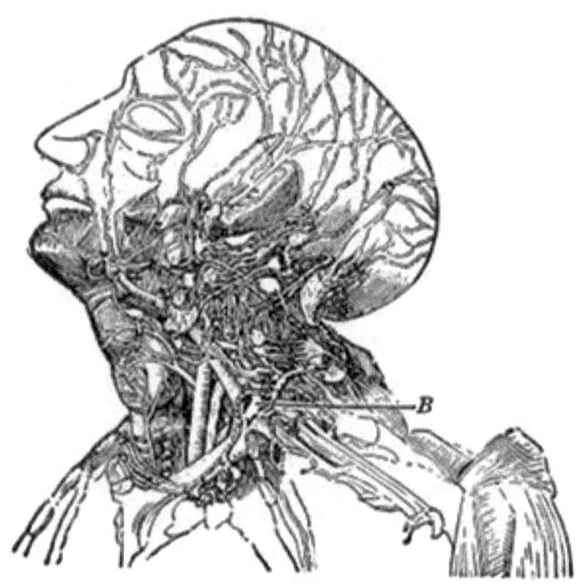

FIG. 3—LYMPHATICS OF THE HEAD AND NECK. B, THE THORACIC DUCT.

THE LYMPHATICS.

—The lymphatics occur in all parts of the body, and in many respects resemble the veins, one of the most striking similarities being that the lymphatics contain valves just the same as the venous system. The lymphatic capillaries are arranged in the form of a net work and resemble closely in structure the blood capillaries. These capillaries then unite to form the lymph vessels and these then convey the lymph to the subclavian veins. The lymph is a colorless fluid and contains numerous blood corpuscles known as lymphocytes. But in those lymphatic vessels, which have their origin in the walls of the small intestines, the lymph, especially during digestion, contains a great amount of fat, so that it has a milky appearance, and for this reason the lymphatics of this region, have been termed lacteals. There are two main lymphatic trunks, the one on the left side is called the thoracic duct. This duct extends from the lower border of the second lumbar vertebra, through the entire length of the thorax, and opens into the left subclavian vein, close to the point where it is joined to the left internal jugular. It receives the lymph from the lower limbs, the pelvic walls and viscera, the abdominal walls and viscera; the lower part of the right half and the whole of the left half of the thoracic viscera, the left side of the neck and head and the left arm.

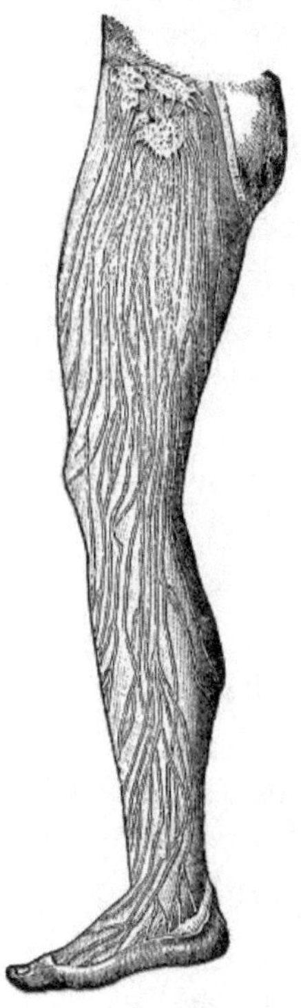

FIG. 4—LYMPHATICS OF THE LEG.

The other duct is called the right lymphatic duct and receives lymph from the upper part of the right side of the thoracic wall, part of the right side of the diaphragm and the right lobe of the liver, the whole of the right arm and neck and right side of the head. This trunk is very short and empties its supply of lymph into the right subclavian vein.

Receptaculum chyli is the expanded portion of the thoracic duct just at its beginning. Its function is to receive the lacteals which come from the villi of the intestines.

Lymph glands are the enlargements of the lymph vessels. They occur frequently in the lymphatic system, being most numerous in the axillary space, the cervical region (in the neck) and in Scarpa's triangle.

The lymphatic system aids greatly in warding off such diseases as blood poisoning, anthrax, etc.

The lacteals are the lymphatics which carry the chyme from the villi of the intestines and deposit it in the receptaculum chyli.

GLANDS.

—The glands of the human body are divided into three classes called tubular, alveolar and tubulo-alveolar glands.

Tubular Glands.—In these, the secreting portion consists of a long or short tubule, which may be relatively straight or variously twisted, one end of which ends blindly, while the other end opens on the free surface or into a duct.

Tubular glands may be simple, or having only a single tubule; they may be simple branched, having more than one tubule; or they may be compound branched, thus resembling the branching of a tree.

Some tubular glands would be the liver, kidneys, testes, lachrymal glands, serous glands of the mucous membranes, fundus glands of the stomach, uterine glands, the majority of the pyloric glands and the majority of the sweat glands.

Alveolar Glands.—In these, the secreting compartments have the form of variously shaped vesicles or saccules, known as alveoli which open on the free surface or into a duct.

Alveolar glands may be either simple, simple branched, or compound branched.

Some alveolar glands would be the sebaceous glands, pancreas, mammary gland, ovary and thyroid.

Tubulo-alveolar Glands.—In these, there is a combination of the tubular and the alveolar type. They may also be simple, simple branched or compound branched.

Some of this type would be certain of the pyloric glands, certain of the sweat glands, some mucous glands, the prostate and the lungs.

The most important glands will be discussed under the tissue or the organ in which they are situated.

CARTILAGE.

—Cartilage is a transition stage between connective tissue and bone; when it is boiled it yields condrin. It is found in various parts of the body, in the adults being found chiefly in the joints, in the sides of the thorax, and in various tubes which are not kept permanently open, such as the air passages, nostrils, ears, etc. In the foetus, the greater part of the framework is cartilaginous and as the foetus matures this cartilage is finally replaced by bone. Cartilage is divided into hyaline cartilage, elastic cartilage, and fibro cartilage.

Hyaline cartilage is found in the nose, larynx, trachea, and bronchi.

Elastic cartilage is found in the epiglottis and the cartilages of the larynx.

Fibro cartilage is found at the point of insertion of the ligaments, into the body of the bone, such as the cartilage which helps to hold the femur or long bone of the thigh into the hip.

BONES.

—Bone results from the calcification of cartilage or fibrous tissue. It is a highly specialized form of connective tissue. There are two varieties of bone; dense or compact bone and cancellous, loose, or spongy bone. Compact bone is dense, like ivory, and is always found on the exterior of bones.

Cancellous bone is found in the interior of bones, and has a lattice-work appearance.

Bone consists of one-third animal or organic matter and two-thirds earthy or inorganic matter. These proportions, however, vary with age. In youth it is nearly half and half, while in the adult the earthy is greatly in excess. It also varies with disease. With some defect of nutrition, the bone is deprived of its normal proportion of earthy matter, while the animal matter is of unhealthy quality, and we have as a result, a disease called rickets, so common in the children of the poor. The earthy or inorganic matter consists of phosphate, carbonate, fluoride of calcium, sodium chloride, and phosphate of magnesium. The animal matter consists of fat collagen, which when boiled with water is resolved into gelatin.

To illustrate the two substances, take a bone and place it in dilute hydrochloric acid. The acid will eat out all the mineral matter and we have left only the animal matter. After this operation one can take the bone and can bend it into any position whatever, which experiment shows that the animal matter gives elasticity to the bone.

The second experiment would be to put the bone on a bed of hot coals and burn it. Only the animal matter will burn and we will have the mineral matter remaining. After this operation one will find that the bone is very brittle and will easily break, which experiment shows that the mineral matter gives stability and support to the bone.

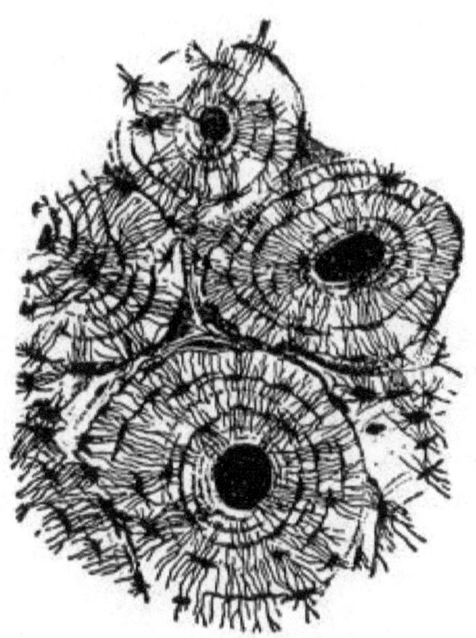

FIG. 5—CROSS SECTION OF BONE. (SHARPEY)

If a cross section is made of any long bone, such as the humerus, and this section placed under the low power of the microscope, the Haversian canal system can be discerned. The Haversian canal system consists of the numerous small openings or canals through which the blood vessels ramify in distributing the nourishment to the bone. Around each individual canal are seen smaller spaces arranged in a circle. These are known as the lacunae (small lakes). Going from the lacunae are smaller canals which take on the name canaliculae, and joining all the lacunae together, making the appearance of concentric circles, we have the lamellae. The outside covering of the bone is called the periosteum and the inside covering is called the endosteum. Most of the long bones and many of the smaller bones are supplied by a nutrient artery, which enters the bone near its center, enters the bone marrow, and divides into two branches, one going up and the other down in the marrow. The blood is then distributed through the Haversian canal system. Veins emerge from the long bones in three places: 1. One or two large veins accompany the nutrient artery. 2. Numerous veins emerge from the articular extremities. 3. Many small veins arise in and emerge from the compact substance.

Bones are divided, according to shape, into four classes: long, short, flat and irregular.

Long Bones. — These bones are usually used as a system of levers to confer the power of locomotion. A long bone consists of a shaft and two extremities. The shaft is a hollow cylinder within which is the medullary canal. The extremities are somewhat expanded for the purpose of articulation, and to afford a broad surface for the attachment of muscles. The long bones are as a rule curved in two directions to give greater strength to the bone. Some examples of this class of bone are the clavicle, radius, ulna, humerus, femur, tibia, fibula, metacarpal, metatarsal, and the phalanges.

Short Bones. — These bones are placed in that part of the skeleton where there is need for strength and compactness, and where the motion of the part is slight and limited. Some examples of this class of bone are the bones of the carpus and tarsus (in the hand and the foot).

Flat Bones. — Flat bones are found where the principle requirement is either extensive protection, or the need of a broad surface for the attachment of muscles. Some of the bones of this class are the occipital, parietal, frontal, nasal, lachrymal, vomer, scapula, sternum, and the ribs.

Irregular Bones. — These bones are such as from their peculiar shape and form can not be grouped under any of the preceding heads. Some of the bones of this class are the vertebrae, sacrum, coccyx, temporal, sphenoid, ethmoid, etc.

If the surface of a bone is examined, certain articular and non-articular eminences and depressions will be seen.

Articular Eminences. — Examples of this class are found in the heads of the humerus and the femur.

Articular Depressions. — Examples of this class are found in the glenoid cavity of the scapula and the acetabulum.

Non-articular Eminences. — These are designated according to their form.

A tuberosity is a broad, rough, and uneven elevation.

A tubercle is a small, rough prominence.

A spine is a sharp, slender, pointed eminence.

A ridge, line, or crest is a narrow, rough elevation, running some way along the surface.

Non-articular Depressions. — These are of variable form, and are described as notches, sulci, fossae, grooves, furrows, fissures, etc. These non-articular eminences and depressions may serve to increase the extent of surface for the attachment of ligaments and muscles or may receive blood vessels, nerves, tendons, ligaments, or portions of organs.

Canals or foramina are channels or openings in bone through which pass the nerves and blood vessels.

TEETH.

—In the human body we find two sets of teeth. One appearing in childhood, and are known as milk teeth, twenty in number, the permanent teeth replacing these about the sixth year.

There are thirty-two permanent teeth, divided into four incisors, two canines, four bicuspids and six molars.

Teeth are made up of three different substances, which are known as enamel, dentine and cement.

The enamel is a very hard substance, the hardest in the body, and may be compared to quartz. The enamel covers the entire tooth down as far as the gums.

The cement is a continuation of the enamel below the gums, and is closely adherent to the dentine. The cement consists of bone tissue, but the lamellae as a rule do not contain Haversian canals.

The dentine is, next to the enamel, the hardest tissue of the tooth, and composes the main body of the tooth. The pulp cavity is found within the center of the tooth, with the opening toward the jaw bone. The tooth is nourished by a nutrient artery and vein and nerve which pass into the pulp of the tooth.

NERVES.

—Nerves are divided into two general classes, called medullary and non-medullary nerves. The non-medullated type arise mostly from the sympathetic system, while the medullated type arise from the brain and cord. As a rule, the nerves of the body follow the course of the arteries, and are generally found in the same sheath with the artery and vein.

FIG. 6—SECTION OF A NERVE FIBRE. (KLEIN AND NOBLE SMITH)

They are easily distinguished from the arteries and veins by touch and by their color, being very inelastic and fibrous, hard to the touch, and unlike the artery or vein, since they have no central opening.

MUSCLES.

—Myology is that branch of anatomy which treats of the muscles. The muscles are formed of bundles of reddish fibres, endowed with the property of contractility. In the body we find two kinds of muscular tissue, called voluntary and involuntary muscle. The voluntary type is characterized by the striped appearance which it displays when seen under the microscope, and for this reason it is called striped or striated muscle. It is so named "voluntary" because it is capable of being put into action and controlled by the will. The involuntary muscles do not present any striped appearance, and consequently are called unstriped or non-striated, and are not under the control of the will. An example of voluntary muscle would be any muscle of the bony framework as for example, the biceps or triceps.

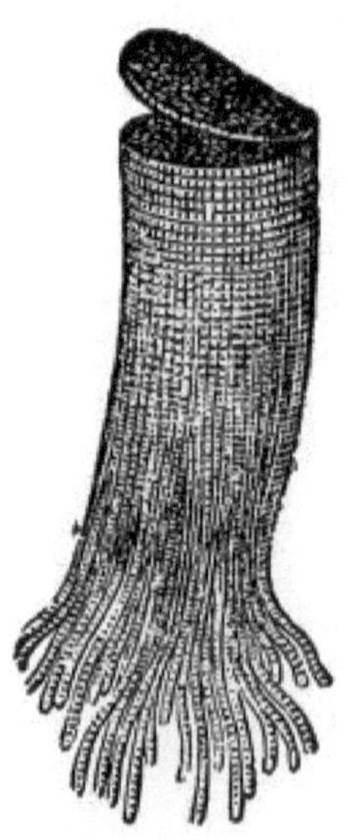

FIG. 7—VIEW OF MUSCLE FIBERS.

An example of involuntary muscle would be those of the intestines and stomach, the muscles of the bladder and uterus and the walls of the arteries and veins, etc.

When viewed under the microscope, the muscle is seen to be composed of many fibrils. The sheath covering each fibril is called the sarcolemma, and contains within its boundaries the muscle plasma, or protoplasm, and a nucleus. Many of the fibrils when grouped together constitute the entire muscle.

The muscles get their blood supply from the nutrient artery, which ramifies the tissues, the smallest capillaries coming in contact with each muscle cell.

TENDONS.

—Tendons are white, glistening, fibrous cords, varying in length and thickness, sometimes round, sometimes flattened, of considerable strength, and devoid of elasticity. It consists principally of a substance which yields gelatin.

Tendons do not have a direct blood supply.

APONEUROSES.

—Aponeuroses are flattened or ribbon-like tendons, of a pearly-white color, irridescent, glistening, and similar in structure to the tendons.

LIGAMENTS.

—Ligaments consist of bands of various forms, serving to connect the articular extremities of bones. They are strong bands of smooth, silverwhite fibrous tissue.

A ligament is pliable and flexible, so as to allow the most perfect freedom of movement, but at the same time it is tough and strong, so as not to yield readily under the severe applied force, and for this reason they serve as good connecting links for the binding of bones together.

Poupart's Ligament.—Poupart's ligament extends from the crest of the ilium to the top of the pubic bone. This ligament is of utmost importance to the embalmer, as it serves as a guide to locate the femoral artery. By placing the thumb on the crest of the ilium and the second finger on the top of the public bone, then letting the first finger drop midway between the two, which would be the center of Poupart's ligament, we have a point which marks the exit of the artery from the body and the beginning of the femoral artery.

Poupart's ligament also forms the base of Scarpa's triangle. The structure of this triangle will be taken up later.

FAT.

—Fat is a deposit of an oil in the cells of the tissues, just beneath the skin, giving roundness and plumpness to the body, and acting as an excellent non-conductor for the retention of heat.

So tiny are these cells, that there are over sixty-five million in a cubic inch of fat. As they are kept moist, the liquid does not ooze out; but, on drying, it comes to the surface, and thus a piece of fat feels oily when exposed to the air. The quantity of fat varies with the state of nutrition. In corpulent persons, the masses of fat beneath the skin, in the mesentery, on the surface of the heart and the great vessels, between the muscles, and in the neighborhood of the nerves, are considerably increased. Conversely, in the emaciated we sometimes find beneath the skin cells which contain only one oil drop. Many masses of fat which have an important relation to muscular actions—such as the fat of the orbit or the cheek, do not disappear in the most emaciated persons. Even in starvation, the fatty substance of the brain and spinal cord are retained.

Fat collects as pads in the hollows of the bones, around the joints and between the muscles, causing them to glide more easily upon each other. As marrow, it nourishes the skeleton, and also distributes the shock of any jar the limb may sustain.

Fat does not gather within the cranium, the lungs or the eyelids, where its accumulation would clog the organs.

MUCOUS MEMBRANES.

—Mucous membranes line all the open cavities of the body, or all those cavities which communicate with the outside.

At the edges of the openings into the body, the skin seems to stop and give place to a tissue which is redder, more sensitive, more liable to bleed, and is moistened by a fluid or mucous, as it is called. Really, however, the skin does not cease, but passes into a more delicate covering of the same general structure, and it is to this that the name mucous membrane is applied.

The entire alimentary canal, the entire respiratory tract, and the genito-urinary tract, are lined with a mucous membrane. Mucous membrane secretes a mucous fluid.

SEROUS MEMBRANES.

—Serous membranes line the closed cavities of the body. The pleurae, the pericardium and the peritoneum are examples of serous membranes. Serous membranes secrete a serous fluid.

SYNOVIAL MEMBRANES.

—Synovial membranes are serous in character, and consist of loose connective tissue, containing fat, vessels and nerves, its inner surface being usually lined with secreting cells. The fluid secreted is yellowish-white or slightly reddish, resembling very much the white of an egg. It contains fats, salts, albumen, extractives from the lymph, and a fluid known as synovia. The chief function of this fluid is to act as an oil to lubricate the joints and surfaces in which there is any friction.

Synovial membranes are divided into three classes, known as articular, bursal and vaginal.

Articular synovial membranes are found in every free movable joint.

Bursal synovial membranes are sacs interposed between the surfaces which move upon each other, producing friction, as in the gliding of a tendon or of the integument over projecting bony surfaces.

Vaginal synovial membranes serve to facilitate the gliding of a tendon in the bony canal through which it passes.

FIG. 8—SECTION OF ARTERY. (GRUNSTEIN)

ARTERIES.

—The arteries are cylindrical vessels which serve to convey the blood from both ventricles of the heart to every part of the body. They are called arteries from the Greek words which mean "to contain air," and they were supposed, by our ancients, to have this function until the time of Galen, when he refuted this opinion and showed that these vessels, though for the most part empty after death, actually contained blood. The distribution of the arteries may be compared to a tree, the common trunk of which corresponds to the aorta, and the smallest twigs corresponding to the minute capillaries. When one artery communicates with another it is said to anastomose, and this communication is very free between the larger as between the smaller branches. Anastomosis between trunks of equal size is found where great activity of the circulation is requisite, as at the base of the brain, where the two vertebrals unite to form the basilar artery.

In the limbs and arms the anastomoses are more numerous and of larger size around the joints. The branches of the artery above, unite with branches, from the vessels below. These anastomoses are called collateral circulations. The principal ones of interest to the embalmer are those of the deep brachial uniting with the recurrent radial and ulnar arteries, forming the collateral circulation in the arm; the deep femoral uniting with the recurrent posterior and anterior tibials, forming the collateral circulation in the leg; the superficial and deep mammary arteries, branches of the subclavian artery uniting with the superficial and deep epigastric arteries, branches of the external iliac, forming the collateral circulation over the abdomen and chest, and may be considered the longest collateral circulation in the body.

A terminal artery is one which forms no anastomoses; such vessels are found in the heart, brain, spleen, kidneys, lungs and mesentery.

Structure. — An artery consists of an internal, a middle and an external coat.

The inner coat consists of endothelial cells and elastic fibrous tissue, sometimes arranged longitudinally, but usually they form a distinct fenestrated membrane (similar to a doorscreen).

The middle coat consists mostly of elastic tissue and white fibrous tissue.

The external coat is called the fibrous coat. It contains fibrous connective tissue and elastic tissues.

Vasa-Vasorum. — Running in the outer wall of the artery, we find small capillary vessels, and their function is that of nourishing the outer wall, for the blood which passes through the artery does not nourish the artery from within, but depends on these small capillaries, called vasa-vasorum, for their nutrition.

The individual sheath, or arterial sheath, the covering for the artery, is composed of connective tissue, and at places may adhere very tightly to the artery.

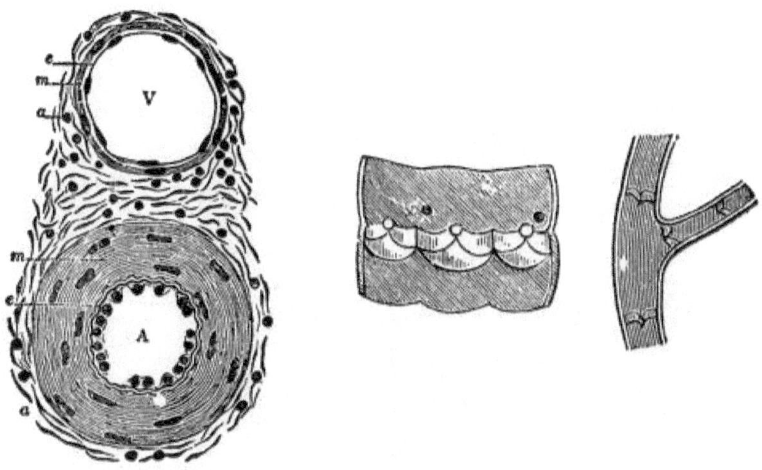

FIG. 9—VALVES OF THE VEINS.

**FIG. 10—CROSS SECTION THROUGH A SMALL ARTERY AND
VEIN. (KLEIN AND NOBLE SMITH)**

VEINS.

—The veins are the vessels which carry the blood from the capillaries back to the right auricle of the heart, and are found in nearly every tissue of the body. They commence as venous capillaries, uniting together into larger and larger veins, until we have the great ascending and descending venae cavae. In form the veins are perfectly cylindrical, like the arteries, but with this difference, that their walls collapse when empty and that they contain valves.

Structure.—The vein has about the same structure as the artery, only that the middle coat is much thinner and less elastic than the artery, and for this reason it easily collapses.

Veins are divided into superficial, deep and sinuses. Superficial veins are found between the layers of the superficial fascia, just underneath the skin.

Deep veins accompany the arteries, and are usually enclosed in the same common sheath with the artery.

Sinuses are venous channels, which in their structure and mode of distribution differ altogether from the veins. They are found only in the interior of the skull, and consist of channels formed by a separation of the two layers of the dura mater.

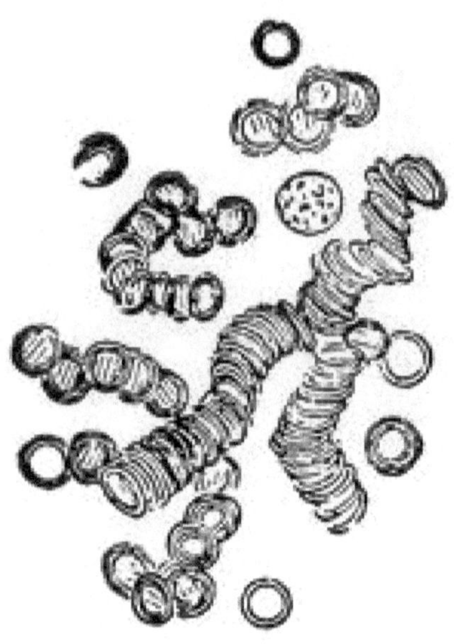

FIG. 11—HUMAN BLOOD.

BLOOD.

—The blood of the body is contained in a practically closed system of tubes, the blood vessels, within which it is kept circulating by force of the heart beat. It is usually spoken of as the nutritive liquid of the body, but the functions may be stated explicitly, although still in quite general terms, by saying that it carries to the tissues food stuffs after they have been properly prepared by the digestive organs; that it transports to the tissues oxygen, absorbed from the air by the lungs; that it carries from the tissues various waste products formed in the processes of dissimilation; that it is the medium for the transmission of the internal secretion of certain glands; that it aids in equalizing the temperature and water contents of the body.

The total quantity of blood in the body has been determined approximately for man as one-thirteenth of the body weight. The specific gravity of human blood in the adult may vary from 1.041 to 1.067, the average being about 1.055.

The blood is composed of a liquid part, the plasma, in which float a vast number of microscopical bodies, the blood corpuscles, known respectively as the red corpuscles, the white corpuscles or leucocytes, of which in turn there are a great many different kinds, and the blood plates.

Blood plasma, when obtained free from corpuscles, is perfectly colorless, in thin layers, for example, in microscopical preparation; when seen in large quantities it shows a slightly yellowish tint. The red color of the blood is not due, therefore, to coloration of the blood plasma, but is caused by the mass of red corpuscles held in suspension in the liquid. The proportion by bulk of plasma to corpuscles is usually given roughly as two to one. The blood plasma is composed of two substances, blood serum and blood fibrin. You have noticed that blood, after it has escaped from the vessels, usually clots or coagulates. The clot, as it forms, gradually shrinks and squeezes out a clear liquid, to which the name blood serum has been given. Serum resembles the plasma of normal blood in general appearance, but differs from it in composition. Here it is sufficient to say that blood serum is the liquid part of the blood after coagulation has taken place. You can prepare this experiment for yourself: If shed blood is whipped vigorously with a rod or some similar object while it is clotting, the essential part of the clot, namely the fibrin, forms differently from what it does when the blood is allowed to coagulate quietly. It is deposited in shreds on the whipper. Blood that has been treated in this way is known as defibrinated blood. It consists of blood serum plus the red and white corpuscles, and as far as appearances go it resembles exactly the normal blood; it has lost, however, its power of clotting.

Red blood corpuscles are bi-concave, circular disks, without nuclei; their average diameter is 7.7 microns (1 micron equals 1-25,000 of an inch); their number, which is usually reckoned as so many to a cu. millimeter, varies greatly under different conditions of health and disease. The average number is given as 5,600,000 per cubic millimeter for males and 4,500,000 per cubic millimeter for females.

The number of red corpuscles also varies in individuals with the constitution, nutrition and manner of life. It varies with age, being greatest in the fetus and in the new-born child. It varies with the time of the day, showing a distinct diminution after meals. In the female it varies somewhat with menstruation and pregnancy, being slightly increased in the former and diminished in the latter condition.

The red color of the corpuscles is due to the presence in them of a pigment, known as hemoglobin. Owing to the minute size of the corpuscles, their color when seen singly under the microscope is a faint yellowish red, but when seen in mass they exhibit the well-known blood-red color, which varies from a scarlet in arterial blood to a purplish red in venous blood, this variation in color being dependent upon the amount of oxygen contained in the blood in combination with the hemoglobin. The function of the red blood corpuscles is to carry oxygen from the lungs to the tissues. This function is entirely dependent upon the presence of hemoglobins, which have the power of combining easily with the oxygen gas.

White blood corpuscles or leucocytes contain no hemoglobin or coloring matter. They have a nucleus or center spot. Their size varies from 5 to 12 microns, and are less numerous than the red corpuscles, being in this proportion: one white corpuscle to 500 red corpuscles. The chief functions of the white corpuscles are: (1) That they protect the body from pathogenic or disease-producing bacteria. In explanation of this action it has been suggested that they may either ingest the bacteria and thus destroy them directly, or they may form certain substances, defensive proteids, that destroy the bacteria. White corpuscles that act by ingesting the bacteria are spoken of as phagocytes (meaning to eat the cell). (2) They aid in the absorption of fats from the intestines. (3) They aid in the absorption of peptones from the intestines. (4) They take part in the process of blood coagulation. (5) They help in maintaining the normal composition of the blood plasma in proteids.

Blood plates are small circular or elliptical bodies, nearly homogeneous in structure, variable in size, always much smaller than the red blood corpuscles. Less is known of their origin, fate and functions than in the case of the other blood corpuscles, but there is some considerable evidence to show that they take part in the process of coagulation or clotting.

Coagulation of the Blood. —One of the most striking properties of the blood is its power of clotting, or coagulating, shortly after it leaves the blood-vessels, or if any foreign elements come in contact with it. The general changes in the blood during this process are easily followed. At first perfectly fluid, in a few minutes it becomes viscous, and then sets into a soft jelly, which quickly becomes firmer, so that the vessel containing it can be inverted without spilling the blood. The clot continues to grow more impact, and gradually shrinks in volume, pressing out a greater or smaller amount of clear, faintly yellow liquid, to which the name blood serum is given. The essential part of the clot is the fibrin.

Fibrin is an insoluble proteid not found in normal blood. In shed blood, and under certain conditions while still in the blood-vessels, this fibrin is formed. In forming, it shows an exceedingly fine network of delicate threads that permeate the whole mass of the blood and gives the clot its jelly-like character. The shrinking of the threads causes the subsequent contraction of the clot. If the blood has not been disturbed during the act of clotting, the red corpuscles are caught in the fine fibrin mesh-work, and as the clot shrinks these corpuscles are held more firmly, only the clear liquid of the blood being squeezed out, so it is possible to get specimens of serum containing few or no red blood corpuscles. The white corpuscles or leucocytes, on the contrary, although they are also caught at first in the forming meshes of fibrin, in latter stages of the clotting they readily pass out into the serum, on account of their power of having movement. If the blood has been agitated during the process of clotting, the delicate net work will be broken in places, and the serum will be more or less bloody —that is, it will contain numerous red blood corpuscles. If during the time of clotting the blood is vigorously whipped with a bundle of fine rods, all the fibrin is deposited as a stringy mass on the whipper, and the remaining liquid part consists of serum plus red corpuscles. Blood that has been whipped in this way is known as defibrinated blood. It resembles normal blood in appearance, but is different in composition; it can not clot again. The way in which fibrin is normally deposited can be easily demonstrated by taking a drop of blood on a slide and covering it with a cover slip, allow it to stand several minutes until coagulation is complete, and view under a microscope. If the drop is examined, it is possible by careful focusing, to discover in the spaces between the masses of corpuscles many examples of delicate fibrin net work. The physiological value of the clotting of blood in life is that it stops hemorrhages by closing the openings of the wounded blood vessels, but the clotting of the blood after death, is to the embalmer one of the bugbears, and a real method of preventing it, or of dissolving the clot after it has once formed in the blood vessels is one of those difficult problems which remains as yet unsolved.

Since we have no real method of preventing coagulation in the blood vessels, let us search out the things which will hasten or retard this coagulation. Blood coagulates normally within a few minutes after it is liberated from the blood vessel, but this process may be hastened by increasing the amount of foreign substance with which it comes in contact. Thus the agitation of the liquid in quantity or the application of a sponge or handkerchief or the application of heat hastens the on-set of clotting.

Coagulation in drawn blood may be retarded or prevented altogether by a variety of means, of which the following are the most important:

(1) By cooling.

(2) By the action of neutral salts.

(3) By the action of oxalate solutions.

(4) By the action of sodium fluoride.

Summary.—To summarize then, the following statements may be made:

(1) The immediate factor necessary to the clotting of the blood is the fibrin.

(2) That blood does not clot normally in the blood vessels before death.

(3) That after death blood remains for a long time without clotting, provided some outside agent is not introduced to cause it.

Such an agent may be the blood coming in contact with the air, or the blood drainage tube. The one point then to be emphasized is that when a vein is cut, and the blood begins to flow, you know that the blood is not in a coagulated condition. Then work rapidly, put the blood drainage tube quickly into the vein and draw off as much blood as you can before it begins to clot at the end of the tube. The great trouble has been, that the embalmer does not work with precision. He first raises the vein, and exposes it on the surface of the incision. He then raises the artery. He places the drainage tube into the vein, but shuts it off till he is ready with the artery. Now, by the time he has placed the arterial tube in the artery, injected a few bulbs full to see that all is in working order, and has perhaps attended to a few other duties, he is amazed to find that the blood will not flow, that it has clotted. What is the reason? He gave it time to clot after the drainage tube was inserted.

A better procedure would be not to touch the vein until every other procedure has been attended to. Then raise the vein, insert the drainage tube and withdraw the blood quickly, and at the same time keep injecting slowly into the arterial sys-tem to keep up the needed pressure to keep the blood flowing.

(4) That when a clot is once formed in a blood vessel, it is not dissolved by the addition of fluid or any other solution.

(5) That sometimes when the blood has become clotted at the end of the drain-age tube, it can be loosened up or be slightly pushed away by attaching the pump to the drainage tube and injecting a few bulbs of fluid, which, when it runs out, will again start the flow of blood.

CHAPTER V.
OSTEOLOGY.

DEFINITION.

—Osteology is the science of the structure and functions of bones.

In regard to the treatment of this subject, it is not our aim to take up all the minute details concerning each bone, all we desire is to explain the form, uses and location of some of the principle bones and sets of bones of the body in so far as they may come to be used as landmarks for the embalmer.

THE SKELETON.

—The entire skeleton in the adult consists of 200 distinct bones.

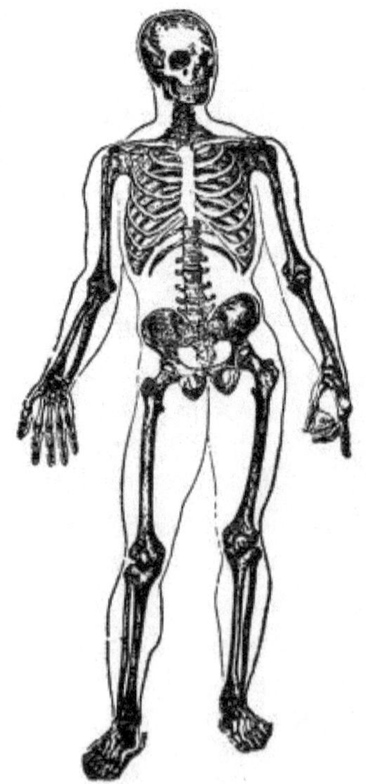

FIG. 12—THE SKELETON.

Spine—

Cervical	 7		
Dorsal	 12		
Lumbar	 5		
Coccygeal	 1		
Sacral	 1		
	26	26
Cranium	....		8
Face	....		14
Hyoid	....		1
Sternum	....		1

Ribs—

True	.... 7 Pair	
False	.... 3 "	
Floating	.... 2 "	
	12 "	24
Upper Extremities	....	64
Lower Extremities	....	62
		200

In the above outline the bones of the ear and the sesamoid bones are not considered. Different anatomists make different computations as to the number of bones in the skeleton. Some authorities add the bones of the ear, thus making 206 in all. If all the little sesamoid bones were added, the number could be greatly augmented.

THE VERTEBRAL OR SPINAL COLUMN. (THE SPINE).

—The spine is a flexuous and flexible column formed of a series of bones called vertebrae. There are twenty-six in number and may be divided as follows:

Cervical	7	bones
Dorsal	12	"
Lumbar	5	"
Sacral	1	"
Coccygeal	1	"

FIG. 13—THE SPINE.

The cervical vertebrae are smaller than those in any other region of the spine, and may be readily distinguished as they lie in the neck and extend from the base of the skull to the dorsal vertebrae, or the point of attachment of the first rib to the first dorsal.

The dorsal or thoracic vertebrae are the next in rotation down the spine and are intermediate in size between those in the cervical and those in the lumbar region, and increase in size from above downward.

The lumbar vertebrae, the next in rotation, are the largest of the vertebral column and can be distinguished as those lying in the lumbar region or the small of the back.

The sacrum, meaning sacred, so called, because it was the part selected in sacrifices. The sacrum is a large triangular bone, situated at the lower part of the vertebral column, and at the upper and back part of the pelvic cavity.

The coccyx, so called from having been compared to a cuckoo's beak. It is usually formed of four small segments of bones, and gradually diminish in size from above downward, and blend together so as to form a single bone.

The spinal column is situated in the median line, at the posterior part of the trunk. Its average length is about two feet, two or three inches. The female spine is about one inch shorter than the male.

The spinal canal in which runs the spinal cord, follows the different curves of the spine; the opening being the largest in those regions in which the spine enjoys the greatest freedom of movement, and the smallest where motion is more limited.

THE SKULL.

—The skull is the bony framework of the head. The cranium is the name applied when we do not consider the mandible (the lower jaw).

The skull is oval in shape, wider behind than in front, and is supported on the summit of the vertebral column.

The skull is composed of twenty-two bones and is divided as the following diagram will show:

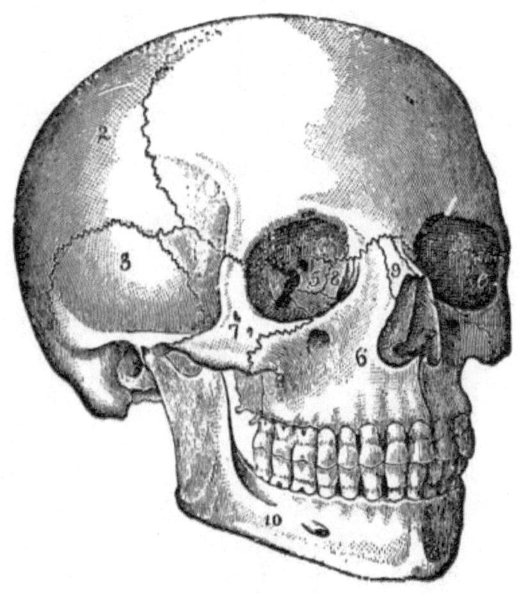

FIG. 14—THE SKULL.

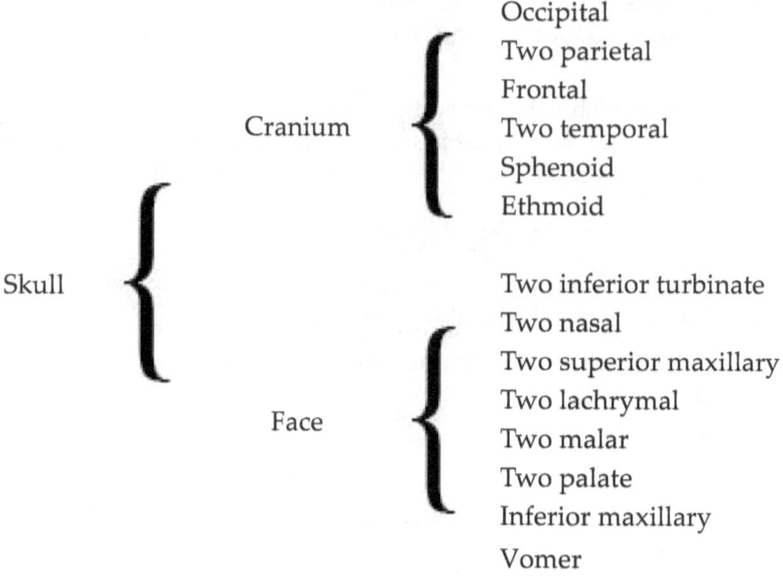

THE BONES OF THE CRANIUM.

—*Occipital Bone.*—The occipital bone is situated at the back part and base of the cranium.

Frontal Bone.—The frontal bone is situated at the anterior part of the cranium, and forms the forehead.

Parietal Bones.—The parietal bones, two in number, form, by their union, the sides and roof of the cranium. They are between the frontal and the occipital bones.

Temporal Bones.—The temporal bones, two in number, are situated at the sides and base of the skull.

Sphenoid Bone.—The sphenoid bone is situated at the anterior part of the base of the skull articulating with all the other cranial bones.

Ethmoid Bone.—The ethmoid is an exceedingly light, spongy bone, which is situated at the anterior part of the base of the cranium.

THE BONES OF THE FACE.

—*Nasal Bone.*—The nasal bones, two in number, are placed side by side at the middle and upper part of the face, forming, by their junction, "the bridge" of the nose.

Superior Maxillary Bones.—The superior maxillae, two in number, are the largest bones of the face, excepting the lower jaw, and form by their junction, the upper jaw.

Inferior Maxillary Bone.—The inferior maxillary bone is also called the mandible. This bone is the largest and strongest bone of the face. In a great many cases after death this bone drops down, and it becomes one of the first duties of the embalmer, to place this bone in the proper position, so that it will set with the gradual death stiffening. If the lower jaw has already set, in proper position, it is best not to break up the rigor, because, once broken up, it will be hard to set it in proper condition again without the use of stitches.

The upper and lower jaws are the fundamental bones for mastication.

Lachrymal Bones. — The lachrymal bones, two in number, are the smallest and most fragile bones of the face. They are situated at the front part of the inner wall of the orbit of the eye.

Malar Bones. — These are the cheek bones. There are two in number, situated at the upper and outer part of the face.

Palate Bones. — The palate bones, two in number are situated at the back part of the nasal fossae. Each bone assists in the formation of three cavities: the floor and the outer wall of the nose, the roof of the mouth, and the floor of the orbit.

Inferior Turbinated Bones. — The inferior turbinated bones are situated one on each side of the outer wall of the nasal fossae.

Vomer. — The vomer, a single bone, is situated vertically at the back part of the nasal fossae, forming part of the septum of the nose. It is thin and somewhat like a ploughshare in form.

THE HYOID BONE.

— *The hyoid bone* is named from its resemblance to the Greek letter U. It is also called the lingual bone, because it supports the tongue and gives attachment to its numerous muscles.

The omo-hyoid muscle, which crosses the carotid artery at its middle third, has its insertion with the hyoid bone.

THE BONES OF THE THORAX.

— *The Sternum* or *Breast Bone.* — The sternum is a flat, narrow bone, situated in the median line of the front of the chest. The lower end is called the ensiform process, to which the diaphragm has its anterior attachment.

The Ribs. — The ribs, which are curved arches of bone, form the chief part of the thoracic walls. There are twelve in number on each side, although this number may vary.

The ribs are divided into seven pairs of true ribs, three pairs of false ribs, and two pairs of floating ribs, as the following outline will show:

Ribs

7 true

3 false

2 floating

—

12 pairs in all.

The true ribs are connected behind to the spine and in front to the sternum.

The false ribs are connected behind to the spine, but are called false because they are not attached directly to the sternum, but indirectly, the cartilages attaching to the cartilage of the rib next above.

The floating ribs are so named because they are only attached at one place, which is the spine and are loose or float in front.

THE BONES OF THE UPPER EXTREMITIES.

—*The Shoulder girdle* consists of the *clavicle* and *scapula*.

The Clavicle.—The clavicle or key bone, so-called because of its supposed resemblance to the key used by the Romans, forms the anterior portion of the shoulder girdle. It is often commonly called the collar bone.

The Scapula.—The scapula comes from a Greek word meaning "a spade." It forms the back part of the shoulder girdle.

The arm is that portion of the upper extremity which is situated between the shoulder and the elbow.

The Humerus.—This is the largest and strongest bone of the upper extremity and is found in the arm between the shoulder and the elbow. It is the only bone in the arm.

The fore arm is that portion of the upper extremity which is situated between the elbow and the wrist. The fore arm has two bones, the *ulna* and the *radius*.

The Ulna.—A long thin bone, but larger than the radius, and situated on the inside of the fore arm.

The Radius.—So-called because it is the rotary bone of the fore arm. It is situated on the outside of the fore arm and parallel with the ulna.

The hand is subdivided into the wrist or *carpus* bones, the *metacarpus* or the bones of the palm, and the *phalanges* or the bones of the digits. There are twenty-seven bones in each hand.

THE BONES OF THE LOWER EXTREMITIES.

—The bones of the lower extremities consist of *the pelvic girdle, the thigh, the leg* and *the foot*.

The pelvic girdle consists of three portions, the *ilium*, the *pubis*, and the *ischium*.

The Ilium.—The ilium is the superior, broad and expanded portion and forms the prominence of the hip. The top part is called *the crest*.

The Ischium.—The ischium is the lowest portion of the girdle, and is the portion which supports the body when in a sitting position.

The Pubis. — This bone forms the front of the pelvis, and supports the external organs of generation.

The thigh is that portion of the lower extremity which is situated between the pelvis and the knee. It consists of a single bone called the femur.

The Femur. — The femur is the largest, longest and strongest bone in the skeleton. It is almost perfectly cylindrical. It extends from the hip to the knee.

The bones of the leg are three in number and are as follows: patella, tibia, and fibula.

The Patella. — This bone is often called the knee cap or the knee pan. It is a flat triangular bone, situated at the anterior part of the knee joint.

The Tibia. — The tibia is situated at the front and inner side of the leg, and is next to the femur in strength and size. It is sometimes called the shin bone.

The Fibula. — The fibula is sometimes called the calf bone. It is situated at the outer side of the leg, and is a quite slender bone.

The foot is divided into the *tarsus, metatarsus,* and the *phalanges*. There are seven tarsus bones, five metatarsus bones, and fourteen phalanges bones, making a total of twenty-six bones for each foot.

CHAPTER VI.
ORGANOLOGY.

The body itself is divided into the upper and the lower extremities and the trunk. The upper extremities consist of the head and arms. The lower extremities consist of the legs. The trunk is that part of the body remaining after the head, arms, and legs have been severed from the body.

THE CAVITIES.

—The body has three principal cavities: namely, the cerebro-spinal, the thoracic, and the abdominal.

THE CEREBRO-SPINAL CAVITY.

—The cerebro-spinal cavity is formed by the cranial bones, and the vertebral column. The cerebro-spinal cavity is divided into the sub-cavities, called the cranial cavity and the spinal cavity.

In the cranial cavity we find the brain. The brain is the seat of the mind, and the functions which the brain performs distinguishes man from the other animals, as man becomes a conscious, intelligent, responsible being through the action of the brain. The brain is egg-shaped, soft and yielding, closely fitting the cranial cavity. The front and top of the brain is called the cerebrum, which is the center for intelligence, reason, and will. This part of the brain is convoluted, and the depth of the convolutions to a great extent indicates the amount of intelligence.

Below the cerebrum and lying in front of the occipital bone, we find the cerebellum, which is the seat of memory and the center for the co-ordination of muscle movements. By co-ordination of muscle movement is meant that the muscles will do just what we want them to do, that they will act harmoniously, the one with the other. The condition of Saint Vitus' Dance would be an example showing a lack of co-ordination. This part of the brain is also convoluted.

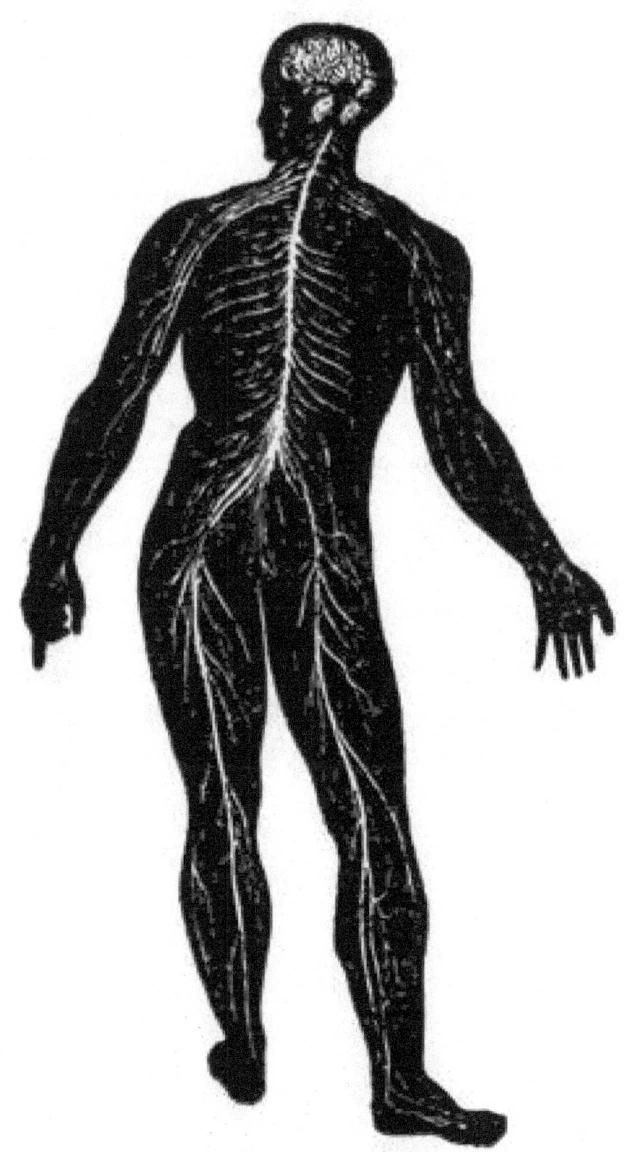

FIG. 15—BRAIN AND SPINAL CORD.

Between the cerebrum and the cerebellum, and connecting the two, is found the pons Varolii. The word pons means bridge, and the word Varolii means to cross over. It is in this part of the brain, then, that the nerve fibers cross over to the opposite side. A person having a paralytic stroke on the right side of the body would indicate that the left side of the brain had become affected.

Joined to this is the medulla oblongata. This is the lowest part of the brain and is the connecting link between the brain and the spinal cord. The medulla controls the circulation, respiration, and deglutition (swallowing).

Closely adhering to the brain, is a delicate membrane, sinking into the convolutions, and following the surface of the brain valleys throughout. This membrane is called the pia mater. In it is found the capillaries, which supply the brain with its nutritive blood in life and with embalming fluid after death. These capillaries do not penetrate the substance of the brain, but the process is one of osmosis, absorption or transfusion. Covering the outer most part of the brain, and closely adhering to the cranial bones is a dense, tough, glistening, membrane, called the dura mater. In the dura mater is found the sinuses of the brain.

In between the pia mater and the dura mater is a delicate double membrane forming a closed sack, called the arachnoid membrane. This sac contains a serous fluid, which offers great protection to the brain. These same three membranes also cover the spinal cord, and are called all together the meninges of the brain and cord.

The brain is composed of white and gray matter. The gray matter is on the outside, and the white matter is on the inside.

The spinal cavity is formed by the bones of the vertebral column. In this spinal cavity is found the spinal cord. It is cylindrical and usually about seventeen inches in length, and extends from the medulla oblongata, to the lower border of the first lumbar vertebra, where it terminates in a slender filament of gray substance.

There originate from the under surface of the brain twelve pairs of nerves, as follows:

1. Olfactory

2. Optic

3. Motor Oculi

4. Trochlear

5. Trigeminal

6. Abducens

7. Facial

8. Auditory

9. Glosso-pharyngeal

10. Pneumogastric

11. Spinal accessory

12. Hypoglossal

There originate from the cord thirty-one pairs of nerves, as follows:

Cervical region   8   pairs.

Thoracic region	12	"
Lumbar region	5	"
Sacral region	5	"
Coccygeal region	1	"
	—	
	31	"

The circulation of the blood through the brain will be taken up later.

CHAPTER VII.

ORGANOLOGY.—CONTINUED.

THE THORACIC CAVITY.

—The thorax, or chest is a bony, cartilaginous cage. It contains and protects the principle organs of respiration and circulation.

The thorax is bounded in front by the sternum and costal cartilages, behind by the twelve dorsal vertebrae and the posterior parts of the ribs, on the sides by the ribs, above by the root of the neck and below by the diaphragm.

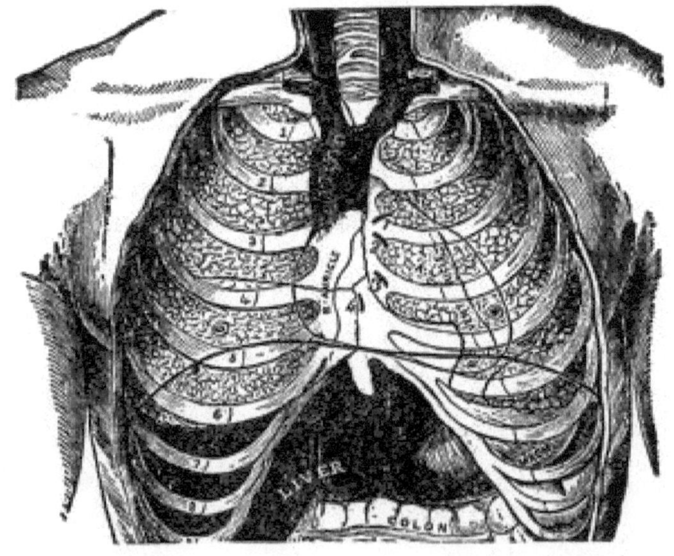

FIG. 16—FRONT VIEW OF THE THORAX. (GRAY)

In the female the thorax differs as follows from the male: Its general capacity is less, the sternum is shorter, and the upper ribs are more movable and so allow a greater enlargement of the upper part of the thorax than the male.

The capacity of the cavity of the thorax does not correspond with its apparent size externally, because, (1) the space enclosed by the lower ribs is occupied by some of the abdominal viscera; and (2) the cavity extends above the first rib into the neck. The size of the cavity of the thorax is constantly varying during life, with the movements of the ribs and diaphragm, and with the degree of distention of the abdominal viscera.

From the collapsed state of the lungs, as seen when the thorax is opened, in the dead body, it would appear as if the viscera only partly filled the cavity of the thorax, but during life there is no vacant space, that which is seen after death being filled up during life by the expanded lungs.

LARYNX.

—The larynx is the organ of voice, placed at the upper part of the air passage. It is situated between the trachea and the base of the tongue, at the upper and fore-part of the neck, where it forms a considerable projection in the middle line. It is for this reason that it is of considerable importance to embalmers, for it is just opposite this projection, on either side of the neck, that the common carotid divides into the internal and the external carotid.

On either side of it lie the great blood vessels of the neck, behind it forms a part of the boundary of the pharynx, and is covered by the mucous membrane lining that cavity.

Its vertical extent corresponds to the fourth, fifth, and sixth cervical vertebrae. It is placed somewhat higher in the female than in the male.

The movements of the head affect the position of the larynx. When the head is drawn back, the larynx is lifted, and when the chin approaches the chest the larynx is depressed. During swallowing the larynx moves distinctly; during singing it moves slightly.

Until puberty there is no marked difference between the larynx of the male and that of the female. In the male after puberty all the cartilages increase in size, and the larynx becomes prominent as the Adam's apple in the middle line of the neck. In the female after puberty the increase of size is only slight.

The larynx is broad above, where it presents a triangular appearance, flattened behind and at the sides. Below it is narrow and cylindrical.

It is composed of cartilages which are connected together by ligaments and moved by numerous muscles. It is lined by a mucous membrane which is continuous above with the lining of the pharynx and below with that of the trachea.

The arteries that supply the larynx are the laryngeal arteries, branches of the superior and inferior thyroid arteries.

The superior laryngeal vein runs into the superior thyroid vein and then into the internal jugular vein, while the inferior laryngeal vein runs into the inferior thyroid vein and then into the innominate vein.

THE TRACHEA.

—The trachea or windpipe is a cartilaginous elastic, cylindrical tube, flattened posteriorly. It extends from the lower part of the larynx, on a level with the sixth cervical vertebra to opposite the body of the fourth dorsal, where it divides into two bronchi, one for each lung.

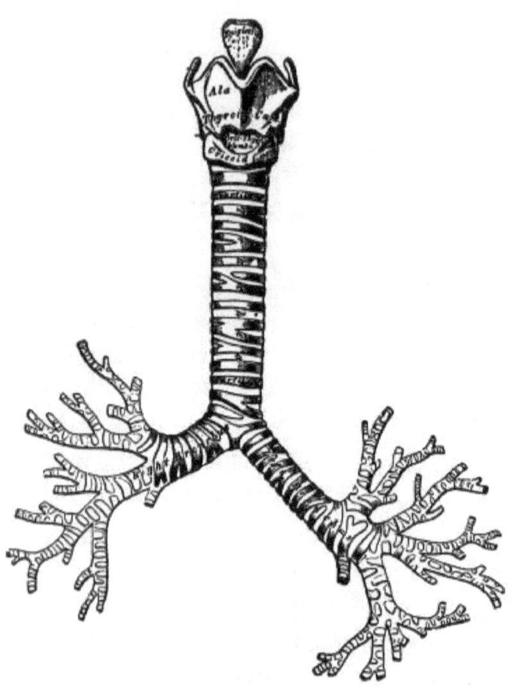

**FIG. 17—THE CARTILAGES OF THE LARYNX; THE TRACHEA
AND BRONCHI. (GRAY)**

The trachea is in the median line of the body. It measures about four and one-half inches in length. The diameter is from three quarters to one inch, being always greater in the male than in the female.

The trachea is composed of imperfect cartilage rings, not coming quite together in the back.

The artery that supplies the trachea is the inferior thyroid artery.

The vein that withdraws the blood is the inferior thyroid vein.

The Right Bronchus.—The right bronchus is shorter, and wider than the left bronchus. It is about one inch in length. It enters the lung opposite the fifth dorsal vertebra.

The Left Bronchus.—The left bronchus is smaller and longer than the right. It is two inches in length and enters the lung at a point opposite the body of the sixth dorsal vertebra.

Each bronchus divides into smaller divisions called bronchial tubes.

Each bronchial tube divides into still smaller divisions called bronchioles.

Each bronchiole ends in the air cell.

THE PLEURAE.

—Each lung is invested upon its external surface by an exceedingly delicate serous membrane, the pleura. This encloses the organ as far as its root, and is then reflected upon the inner surface of the thorax.

The *pulmonary pleura* is the portion investing the surface of the lung, and dipping into the fissures between its lobes.

The *parietal pleura* is that which lines the inner surface of the chest.

The space between these two layers is called the cavity of the pleurae, (the pleural cavity); and contains nothing but a very little clear fluid.

In the healthy condition the two layers are in contact and there is no real cavity, but after death the lungs become collapsed and separate from the walls of the chest. Each pleura is therefore a shut sac, one occupying the right, and the other the left half of the thorax, and they are perfectly separated from one another. The two pleurae do not meet in the middle line of the chest, excepting for a short distance between the second and third pieces of the sternum—a space being left between them, which contains all the viscera of the thorax excepting the lungs; this is called the mediastinum.

The mediastinum then, is the space between the right and left pleural sacs.

The arteries of the pleura are derived from the intercostal, internal mammary, musculo-phrenic, thymic, pericardiac, bronchial.

The veins correspond to the arteries.

THE LUNGS.

—The lungs are the essential organs of respiration. They are two in number, placed one on each side of the chest, separated from each other by the heart and the contents of the mediastinum. A healthy lung hangs free within the pulmonary space. The lung is suspended by the root. The root of the lung is formed by the bronchial tubes, pulmonary artery, pulmonary veins, bronchial arteries, bronchial veins, etc., all of which are enclosed by the reflections of the pleurae.

The *root of the lung* may be described as being that part where all the great blood vessels and the bronchial tubes, enter the lungs.

In many cases the lung does not hang free, but as a result of former pleurisy, the area of the pulmonary pleura is adherent to the parietal pleura.

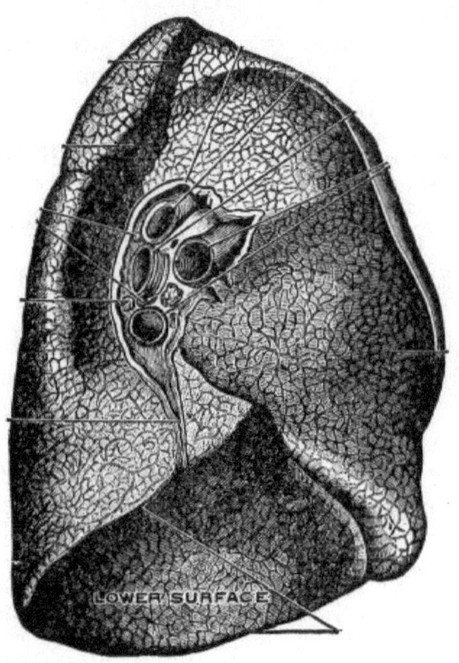

FIG. 18—THE ROOT OF THE LEFT LUNG. (TOLDT)

Each lung is conical in shape, and presents for examination, an apex, a base, and two surfaces.

The Apex forms a tapering cone which extends into the root of the neck about an inch and a half to two inches above the level of the top of the first rib.

The Base is broad and concave and rests upon the convex surface of the diaphragm, which separates the right lung from the upper surface of the right lobe of the liver and the left lung from the upper surface of the left lobe of the liver, the stomach, and spleen.

Surfaces.—There are two in number. The external, costal or thoracic surface is smooth, convex and corresponds to the form of the cavity of the chest. The inner or mediastinal surface is concave, and the middle portion, where all the vessels enter and leave the lung is called the root.

Lobes.—Each lung is divided up into lobes. The right lung has three lobes, and the left lung has two lobes.

Weight.—The weight of both lungs together is about 42 ounces, the right lung being a little heavier than the left. The lungs are heavier in the male than in the female. The male lungs weigh from 42 to 45 ounces, and the female lungs weigh from 32 to 35 ounces.

Color.—The color of the lungs at birth is a pinkish white, in adult life a dark slate color, mottled in patches and as age advances this mottling assumes a black color.

Substance.—The substance of the lung is of a light porous, spongy texture. It floats in water, if it has once been filled with air. It is elastic and for this reason we always find the lung collapsed after death.

The structure of the lung is such that the blood brought by the pulmonary artery comes into close relation with the air in the air-cells which enters from the bronchioles. The blood gives off carbon dioxide to the air-cells and the air in the cells furnishes oxygen for the blood. The process of respiration causes the dark blood brought from the heart by the pulmonary arteries to return to the heart as red blood in the pulmonary veins.

Arteries.—The bronchial arteries supply the lungs with nutrition.

The pulmonary arteries convey venous blood from the heart to the lungs to be purified.

Veins.—The bronchial veins carry off the impure blood from the lungs.

The pulmonary veins convey the blood which has been purified by the lungs, back to the heart.

THE MEDIASTINUM.

—The mediastinum is the space left in the middle portion of the chest by the non-approximation of the two pleurae. It extends from the sternum in front to the spine behind.

Within it are the contents of the thorax, excepting the lungs. The mediastinum may be divided into two parts.

The superior mediastinum is that portion of the interpleural space which lies above the level of the pericardium. This space contains the arch of the aorta, innominate, part of the left carotid artery, part of the left subclavian artery, the upper half of the superior vena cava, the upper half of the innominate vein, the left superior intercostal vein, trachea, esophagus, thoracic duct, remains of the thymus gland, etc.

The inferior mediastinum is divided into three portions:

The anterior mediastinum is that portion in front of the pericardium. It contains nothing but some loose areolar tissue.

The posterior mediastinum is that portion back of the pericardium. It contains the descending thoracic aorta, the greater and lesser azygos veins, the esophagus, the thoracic duct, etc.

The middle mediastinum is that part within the pericardium or heart sac. It is the largest space of all the mediastinal spaces. It contains the heart, the ascending aorta, the lower half of the superior vena cava, the vena azygos, the bifurcation of the trachea, the pulmonary artery, etc.

The middle mediastinum is sometimes called the cardiac cavity, because it contains the heart.

THE PERICARDIUM (HEART SAC).

—The pericardium is a serous sac in which is located the heart and the commencement of the great blood vessels.

Behind we find the bronchi, esophagus and descending thoracic aorta. To the sides we find the pleura, the phrenic nerve and the accompanying vessels. In front we find the sternum and the remains of the thymus gland. It is attached above to the great blood vessels and below to the diaphragm.

THE HEART.

—The heart is a hollow, muscular organ of a conical (cone shaped) form, placed between the lungs and enclosed in the pericardium.

The heart is placed obliquely in the chest. The base is directed upward, backward and to the right, and corresponds to the dorsal vertebrae from the fifth to the eighth inclusive.

The apex is directed downward, forward and to the left and corresponds to the space between the cartilages between the fifth and sixth ribs.

The exact location of the apex of the heart would be ¾-inch to the inner side, and an inch and one-half below the left nipple, or about three and one-half inches from the middle line of the sternum or breast bone.

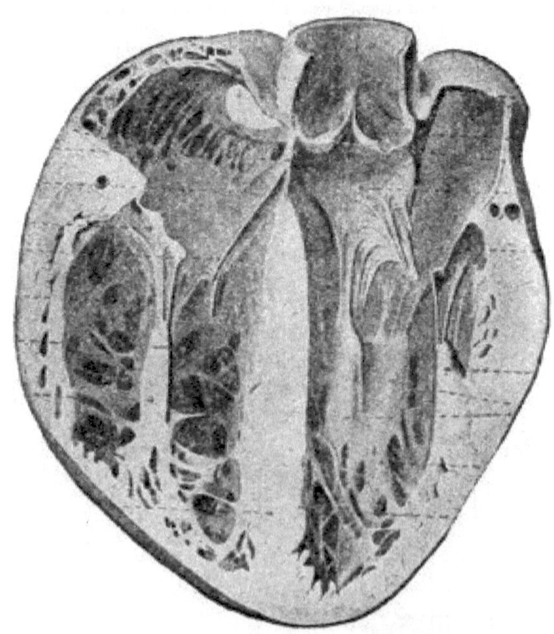

FIG. 19—A CROSS SECTION OF THE HEART SHOWING VALVES. (SPALTEHOLZ)

The heart is placed behind the sternum, and extends about three inches to the left of the median line, and about one and one-half inches to the right, or in other words, about one-third of the heart lies to the right of the median line, and two-thirds lies to the left of the median line.

The heart in the adult measures five inches in length, three and one-half inches in breadth in its broadest part, and two and one-half inches in thickness. The weight of the male heart varies from ten to twelve ounces, and that of the female from eight to ten ounces.

The capacity of the ventricles of the heart averages about three and one-half ounces of blood to each ventricle, and the auricle a little less than four ounces, making the total capacity of the heart average about fifteen ounces.

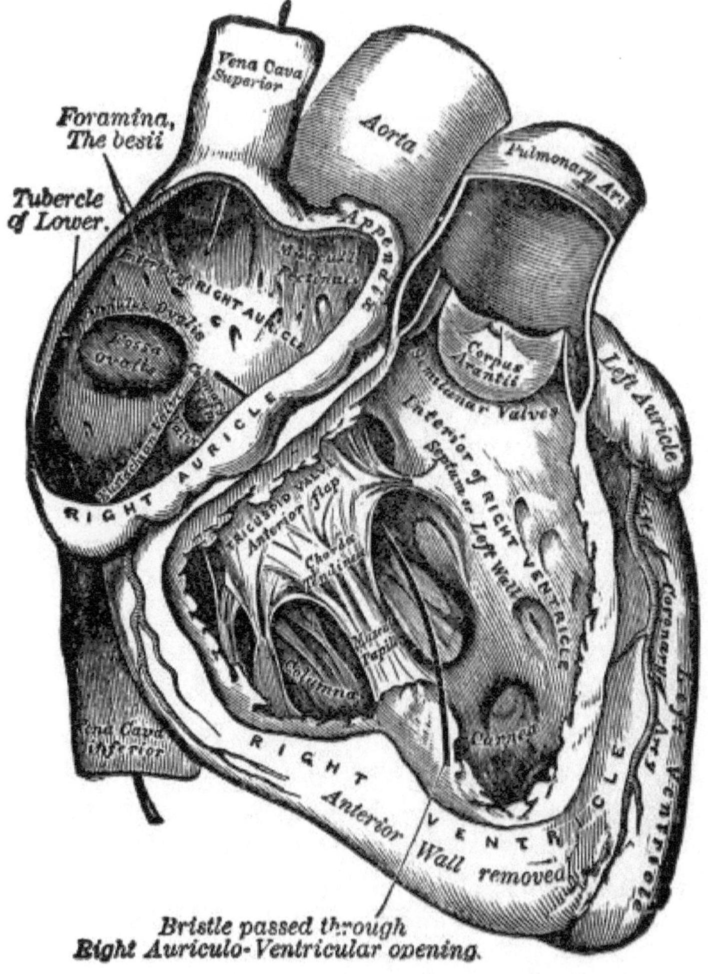

FIG. 20—THE RIGHT AURICLE AND VENTRICLE LAID OPEN.
(GRAY)

The heart is divided by a muscular septum (separation wall) into two lateral halves, which are named respectively the right or venous side and the left or arterial side. The septum is called the longitudinal septum. Each side of the heart is further sub-divided into an upper and lower compartment, the upper on each side is called the auricle and the lower the ventricle. The upper and lower compartments of the heart (auricles and ventricles) are separated by the auricular-ventricular septums (meaning a separation between the auricle and ventricle).

The superior and inferior venae cavae empty into the right auricle of the heart, also the blood from the coronary sinus.

In fact, this compartment receives all the venous or impure blood from all parts of the body, and sends it through what is known as the tricuspid valve into the right ventricle or lower compartment. After getting into the right ventricle, the blood is sent forth into the lungs by first passing through the pulmonary semi-lunar valve into the pulmonary artery, which enters the lungs at the root of the same.

This would then finish the circulation through the right side of the heart, and after the purification has been accomplished by the lungs, we find the blood being returned to the left side of the heart through the four pulmonary veins. The pulmonary veins extend from the lungs (two on each side) to the left auricle (upper compartment of the heart) and deliver the purified blood to the left or arterial side. The course of the blood from the left auricle is downward into the left ventricle (or lower compartment) through what is known as the bicuspid or mitral valve.

The blood is then sent out into the body to nourish all the tissues, by being forced through the aortic semi-lunar valve into the great aorta artery. The circulation is then completed by the blood running into the branch arteries and from them into the smaller branches and into the capillaries from which the course of the blood is into the smaller veins and into the larger veins, finally terminating into the two large trunk veins, the ascending (or inferior) and descending (or superior) venae cavae. Of these two large trunk veins the ascending vena cava is the only one to have a valve at its termination (eustachian). The functions of this valve are to prevent a backward flow of blood into the vein from the auricle.

The heart has three walls, the inner wall is called the endocardium, the middle wall is called the myocardium, and the outer wall is called the epicardium.

The heart is surrounded by a serous sac called the pericardium.

The heart receives its blood supply from the coronary arteries, which are branches of the ascending aorta, just after it leaves the aortic semi-lunar valve.

The coronary veins bring the venous blood back from the tissues of the heart and empty into the coronary sinus, back of the right auricle of the heart.

The veins which originate about the region of the right auricle, empty directly into the right auricle of the heart through the valves of Thebesii.

THE ALIMENTARY CANAL.

—The alimentary canal is a muscular membranous tube. It is about thirty feet in length, and extends from the mouth to the anus. It is lined throughout by a mucous membrane.

The following outline will show the parts of the alimentary canal:

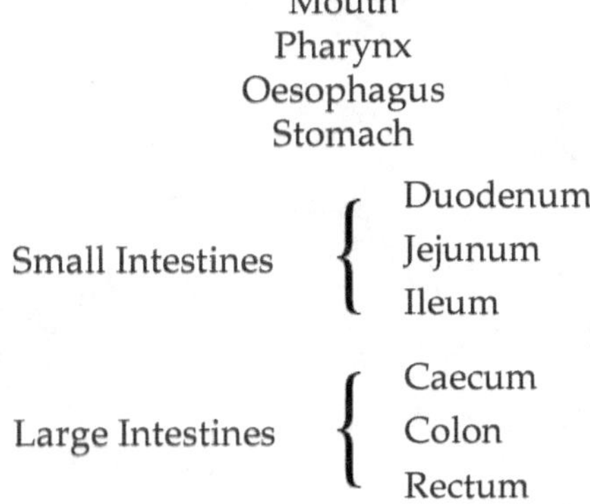

The accessory organs to the alimentary canal are the following:

Teeth, Salivary glands, Liver, Spleen, Pancreas.

THE MOUTH.

—The mouth is placed at the commencement of the alimentary canal. It is a nearly oval shaped cavity.

In this cavity the mastication of the food and the insalivation of the food takes place.

THE TEETH.

—The structure of the teeth has been considered under the head of tissues.

THE PALATE.

—The palate forms the roof of the mouth. It consists of two portions: The hard palate is in front and the soft palate is in the back.

THE SALIVARY GLANDS.

—By the term salivary glands is usually understood the three chief glands on each side of the face.

The parotid gland is placed near the ear. The submaxillary gland is placed below the jaw. The sublingual gland is placed below the tongue.

These glands secrete the salival juices which are brought into the mouth by three small ducts, where it aids in the digestion of the food. The digestive action of the saliva is limited to the starchy foods. Its action is to change starches into sugars.

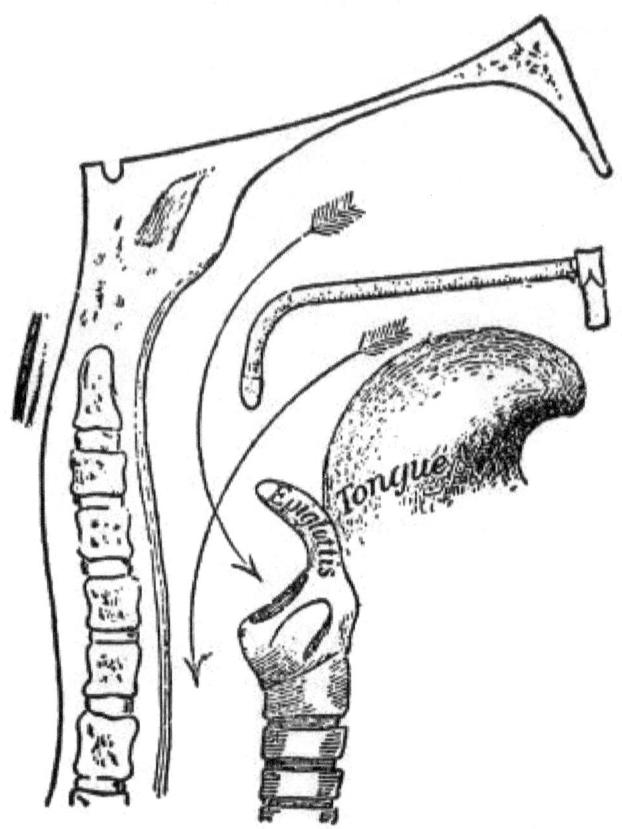

FIG. 21—PASSAGE INTO TRACHEA AND ESOPHAGUS; PHAR-
YNX.

It also fulfills other important functions. By moistening the food it enables us to reduce the material to a consistency suitable for swallowing and for manipulation by the tongue and other muscles. The saliva also serves as a kind of lubricator that insures the smooth passage along oesophageal canal.

THE PHARYNX.

—The pharynx is that part of the alimentary canal, which is placed behind, and communicates with the nose, mouth and larynx. It is a muscular, membranous tube which extends from the back of the mouth and under surface of the skull to the level of the cricoid cartilage or to a point between the fifth and sixth cervical vertebrae.

The pharynx is about four and one-half inches in length.

Seven openings communicate with it, as follows:

Two posterior nares, two eustachian tubes, mouth, larynx, esophagus.

THE ESOPHAGUS.

—The esophagus or gullet is a muscular canal about nine or ten inches in length, extending from the pharynx to the stomach.

It begins at a point between the fifth and sixth cervical vertebrae and descends along in front of the spine through the posterior mediastinal space, passes through the diaphragm, and entering the abdomen, terminates in the stomach wall at a point opposite the tenth dorsal vertebra.

At its commencement it is placed in the median line and gradually inclines to the left as it passes forward to the esophageal opening to the diaphragm.

The esophagus is from one-half to an inch in diameter.

Arteries.—The arteries which supply the esophagus are the esophageal, which are branches from the aorta.

Veins.—The esophageal veins empty into the ascending vena cava.

THE DIAPHRAGM.

—The diaphragm (a partition wall) is a dense, muscular, fibrous septum, placed obliquely across the trunk. It separates the thoracic from the abdominal cavity, forming the floor of the thoracic and the roof of the abdominal cavity.

It is attached in front to the ensiform process of the sternum, on the sides to the inner surface of the cartilages and bony portions of six or seven inferior ribs, and behind it is attached to the lumbar vertebrae.

The diaphragm has three openings, as follows: opening for the esophagus, opening for the aorta, opening for the ascending vena cava.

The diaphragm is the principal muscle of respiration.

The arteries which supply the diaphragm are the phrenic arteries.

The phrenic veins receive the blood from the diaphragm.

CHAPTER VIII.

ORGANOLOGY.—CONTINUED.

THE ABDOMEN.

—The abdomen is the largest cavity in the body. It is oval in form, the extremities of the oval being directed upward and downward.

To facilitate description, the abdomen is artificially divided into two parts:

An upper and larger part, the abdomen proper.

A lower and smaller part, the pelvis.

These two cavities are not separated from each other, but the limit between them is a line drawn around the brim of the true pelvis.

The abdomen proper differs from the other great cavities of the body, in being bounded for the most part by muscles and fascia.

It varies in capacity and shape according to the condition of the viscera which it contains and in addition, it varies in form and extent with age and sex.

Boundaries.—The diaphragm forms the dome over the abdomen, the cavity of the abdomen extending high into the bony thorax.

The lower end of the abdomen is limited by the bones of the pelvis.

In front and at the sides it is bounded by the lower ribs and abdominal muscles.

Behind by the vertebral column and muscles.

Regions.—For convenience of description of the viscera, the abdomen is artificially divided into nine regions. Thus if two circular lines are drawn around the body, the one at the extremities of the ninth ribs where they join the costal cartilages, and the other around the crest of the ileum, the abdominal cavity is divided into three zones.

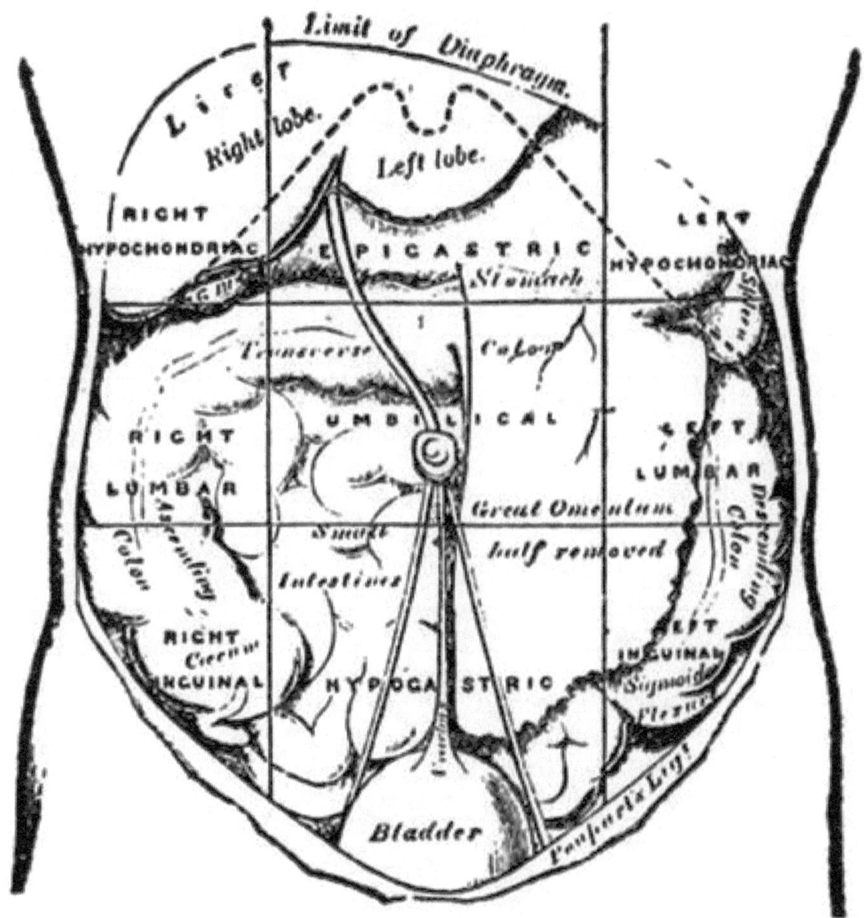

FIG. 22—THE REGIONS OF THE ABDOMEN AND THEIR CONTENTS. (GRAY)

If two parallel lines are now drawn perpendicular upward from the center of Poupart's ligament, each of these zones is subdivided into three parts.

The middle region of the upper zone is called the epigastric; and the two lateral regions, the right and left hypochondriac. The central region of the middle zone is called the umbilical; and the two lateral regions, the right and left lumbar regions. The middle region of the lower zone is called the hypogastric; and the two lateral regions are called the right and the left inguinal regions.

The viscera contained in each of these are as follows:

Right Hypochondriac	Epigastric Region	Left Hypochondriac
The greater part of the right lobe of the liver, the hepatic flexure of the colon and part of the right kidney.	The greater part of the stomach including both cardiac and pyloric orifices, the left lobe and part of the right lobe of the liver and the gall-bladder, the pancreas, the duodenum, the suprarenal capsules and parts of the kidneys.	The fundus of the stomach, the spleen, the extremity of the pancreas, the splenic flexure of the colon and part of the left kidney and small portion of the left lobe of the liver.
Right Lumbar	**Umbilical Region**	**Left Lumbar**
Ascending colon, part of the right kidney and some convolutions of the small intestines.	The transverse colon, part of the great omentum and mesentery, transverse part of the duodenum and some convolutions of the jejunum and ileum and part of both kidneys.	Descending colon, part of the omentum, part of the left kidney and some convolutions of the small intestines.
Right Inguinal or Iliac	**Hypogastric Region**	**Left Inguinal or Iliac**
The caecum and vermiform appendix and a portion of the ascending colon.	Convolutions of the small intestines, the bladder in children and in adults if distended, and the uterus during pregnancy.	Sigmoid flexure of the colon and a portion of the descending colon.

THE STOMACH.

—The stomach is the principal organ of digestion. It is the most dilated part of the alimentary canal, and is situated between the termination of the esophagus and the commencement of the small intestines. It is placed in part immediately behind the anterior wall of the abdomen and beneath the diaphragm.

The lesser curvature of the stomach extends between the cardiac and the pyloric orifices along the right border of the organ.

The greater curvature of the stomach is directed to the left, and is four or five times as long as the lesser curvature.

The cardia is the point at which the esophagus enters the stomach wall.

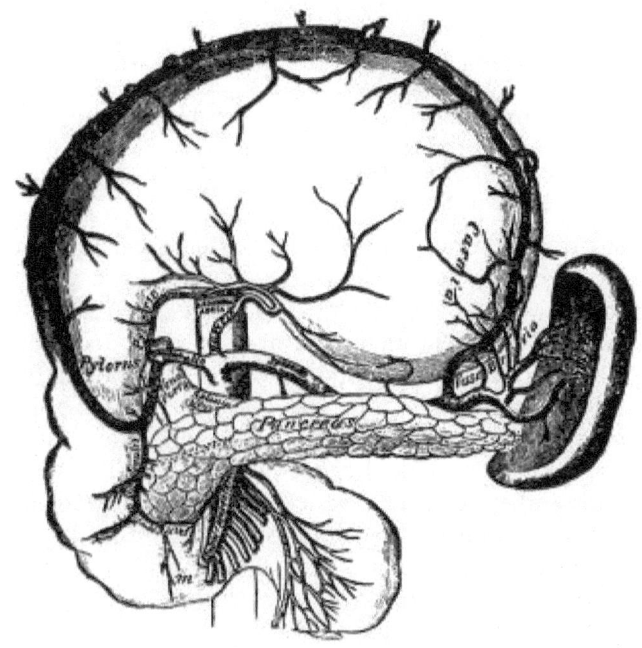

FIG. 23—THE COELIAC AXIS AND ITS BRANCHES. (GRAY)

The cardiac orifice is the opening by which the esophagus communicates with the stomach. It is sometimes called the esophageal opening. It is situated on a level with the body of the tenth and eleventh dorsal vertebrae. It is to the left of and in front of the aorta. On the anterior surface of the body the cardiac orifice corresponds to the articulation of the seventh left costal cartilage to the sternum.

The pylorus is the point at which the stomach passes into the duodenum.

The pyloric orifice is the opening by means of which the stomach communicates with the duodenum.

This orifice is guarded by the *pyloric valve*. When the stomach is empty the pylorus is situated just to the right of the median line of the body on a level with the upper border of the first lumbar vertebra. On the anterior surface of the body its position would be indicated by a point one inch below the tip of the ensiform process and a little to the right.

The size of the stomach varies considerable in different subjects. The distance between the two orifices is from three to six inches. The weight of the stomach is about four and one-half ounces.

The capacity of the adult male stomach is from five to eight pints. The stomach of a new born child holds about one ounce.

The stomach is held in place by the attachment of the esophagus to the diaphragm and the fixation of the duodenum to the front of the vertebral column.

The wall of the stomach consists of four coats: serous, muscular, areolar, and mucous.

The glands of the stomach are of three kinds: gastric, pyloric, and cardiac. These glands furnish the digestive enzymes of the stomach, namely: pepsin, renin, and hydrochloric acid.

Arteries.—The arteries that supply the stomach are the gastric, and branches from the splenic and the hepatic.

It must be remembered that when a body is arterially injected after death, that the fluid only goes to the stomach walls and there ends in the capillary system. No doubt a little of this fluid will soak through into the inside of the stomach, and tend to preserve the contents of the stomach, but it must be added that if the stomach contains a considerable quantity of food and water, that there will not be enough fluid soak through the stomach wall to preserve the contents of the stomach and as a result gases arise which cause distention of the abdomen and perhaps purging from the mouth and nose. As a rule then it is safe to say that when we have purging from the mouth and nose, with a visible distention of the abdominal cavity, indicating gases in the stomach and the intestines that fluid has not reached the contents of the stomach and the fecal matter of the intestines, and therefore it will be necessary to introduce fluid to these parts, in order to preserve the contents, and prevent further formation of gases. The method for doing this will be given under cavity embalming.

THE SMALL INTESTINES.

—The small intestine is a convoluted tube, extending from the pyloric end of the stomach to the ileo-caecal valve where it terminates in the large intestines. It fills up the greater part of the abdominal and the pelvic cavity. It is about twenty feet in length and gradually diminishes in size from the commencement to the termination.

The small intestines are surrounded at the top and at the sides by the large intestines. The small intestines are held in place by the mesentery, a part of the peritoneum, which connects or fastens to the spine.

The small intestines are divisible into three portions: Duodenum, Jejunum, and the Ileum.

Arteries.—The main arterial supply to the small intestines is through the superior mesenteric artery.

The superior mesenteric vein withdraws the main part of the blood from the small intestines.

DUODENUM.

—The duodenum has received its name from being about equal in length to the breadth of twelve fingers (ten inches).

It is the shortest, widest and the most fixed part of the small intestines, being closely and firmly attached to the posterior abdominal wall. It is not covered by the mesentery. The upper half of the duodenum is in the epigastric region and the lower half is in the umbilical region. It is practically in the median line of the body.

The duodenum is shaped like a horseshoe, the opening being directed toward the left. The arteries supplying the duodenum are the pyloric and the pancreatic duodenal branch of the superior mesenteric. The veins correspond to the arteries.

The pancreatic duct and the bile duct empty into the duodenum at its middle portion.

JEJUNUM.

—The jejunum is the second portion of the small intestines, it derives its name from the latin word "jejunas," meaning empty, because it was formerly supposed to be empty after death.

It is wider, thicker, more vascular and of a deeper color than the ileum. The jejunum is about eight feet in length or two-fifths of the length of the small intestines.

The arteries which supply the jejunum are the branches of the superior mesenteric artery. The veins are of the same name.

The jejunum is fastened to the posterior wall of the abdomen by an extensive fold of the mesentery.

ILEUM.

—The ileum is derived from a Greek word meaning to twist, and is so named on account of its numerous coils and convolutions. It is the third portion of the small intestines and is placed below the jejunum. It is much narrower and thinner than the jejunum, about twelve feet in length or three-fifths of the length of the small intestines. It is also attached to the posterior abdominal wall by means of the mesentery. The arteries which supply the ileum are the branches of the superior mesenteric artery. The veins are of the same name.

The villi are minute projections on the mucous membrane of the small intestines. They are largest and most numerous in the duodenum and jejunum, and become fewer and smaller in the ileum. It is in the villi of the intestines that we find the termination of the mesenteric arteries, the beginning of the mesenteric veins and the commencement of the lacteals.

As the food passes down the intestines, having been previously prepared in the stomach and intestines for absorption, it comes in very close contact with the villi of the intestines and it is here that the nutrition from the food is absorbed through the villi wall into the lacteals, and hence carried to the receptaculum chylii.

THE LARGE INTESTINES.

—The large intestine extends from the termination of the ileum to the anus. It is about five or more feet in length or about one fifth of the whole extent of the intestinal canal. It is largest at its commencement at the caecum, and gradually diminishes in size as far as the rectum, where there is a dilatation of considerable size just above the anus.

The large intestine differs from the small intestine in its greater size, its more fixed position, its sacculated form.

The large intestine in its course describes an arch, which surrounds the convolutions of the small intestines. It commences in the right inguinal region, in a dilated part of the caecum. It ascends through the right lumbar and the right hypochondriac regions to the under surface of the liver, it here takes a bend to the left, the hepatic flexure, and passes transversely across the abdomen on the confines of the epigastric and umbilical regions, to the left hypochondriac region; it then bends again, the splenic flexure, and descends through the left lumbar region to the left inguinal region, where it becomes convoluted and forms the sigmoid flexure; finally it enters the pelvic cavity and descends along the posterior wall to the anus.

The large intestine is supplied by the branches of the inferior mesenteric artery, and the veins are of the same name.

The large intestines are divided into the caecum, colon and rectum.

CAECUM.

—The caecum is the commencement of the large intestines, it is a large blind pouch situated below the ileo caecal valve. *The ileo caecal valve* is the valve between the exit of the small intestines and the commencement of the large intestines. The caecum is held mostly in place by the folds of the peritoneum.

The Vermiform Appendix.—The appendix is found only in the human, the higher apes, and the wombat, although in certain rodents a somewhat similar arrangement exists. The appendix is a long, narrow, worm shaped, musculo-membranous tube, which starts from the inner side of the posterior wall of the caecum, below and behind the termination of the ileum. It is the seat for a very common disease called appendicitis. It varies from one half to nine inches in length, its average being about three inches. Its diameter is from one eighth to one quarter of an inch.

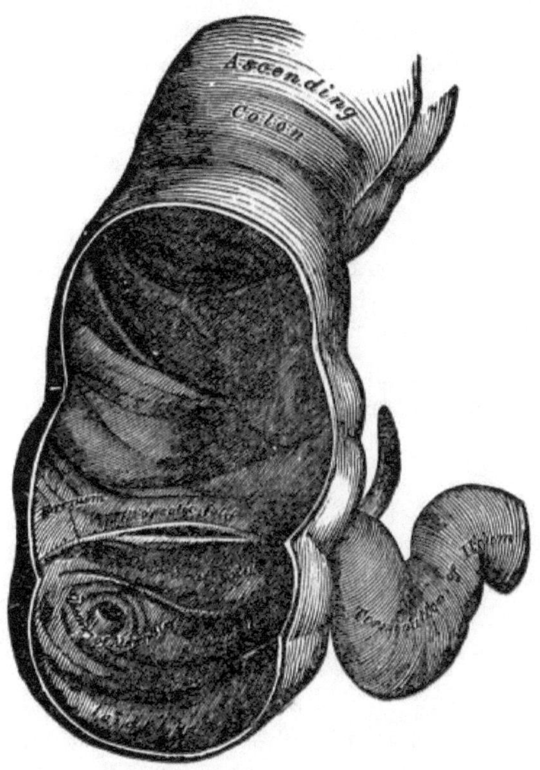

FIG. 24—THE CAECUM AND COLON LAID OPEN TO SHOW THE ILEO-CAECAL VALVE. (GRAY)

THE COLON.

—The colon is divided into three parts, the ascending, transverse and the descending colon.

The ascending colon is smaller than the caecum, with which it is continuous. It passes upward from its commencement at a point corresponding to the ileo-caecal valve, to the under surface of the right lobe of the liver, on the right of the gall bladder, where it is lodged in a shallow depression on the liver; here it bends abruptly inward to the left, forming the hepatic flexure. It is held to the posterior wall of the abdomen by folds of the peritoneum.

The transverse colon is the longest part of the small intestines, passes transversely from the right to the left across the abdomen, opposite the confines of the epigastric and umbilical regions, where it curves downward beneath the lower end of the spleen, forming the splenic flexure. In its course the transverse colon describes an arch, the concavity of which is directed backward toward the vertebral column and a little upward.

This is the most movable part of the colon, only covered by peritoneum and held to the back wall by the folds of the peritoneum. The transverse colon is in relation, by its upper surface with the liver and gall bladder the great curvature of the stomach, and the lower end of the spleen; by its under surface with the small intestines; by its anterior surface with the anterior layers of the great omentum and the abdominal wall; its posterior surface on the right is in relation with the duodenum and on the left it is in contact with the convolutions of the jejunum and ileum.

The descending colon passes downward through the left hypochondriac region and lumbar region along the outer border of the left kidney. At the lower end of the left kidney it turns inward where it terminates in the formation of the sigmoid flexure. The descending colon is held to the back wall by folds of the peritoneum.

The sigmoid flexure, the narrowest part of the colon, is situated in the left inguinal region and communicates with the rectum.

THE RECTUM.

—The rectum is the terminal part of the large intestines, and extends from the termination of the sigmoid flexure to the anus. The adult rectum in male is from four to six inches in length, and in the female is from three to five inches in length.

The anus is the terminal opening of the alimentary canal.

LIVER.

—The liver is the largest gland in the body, and is situated in the upper and right part of the abdominal cavity, occupying almost the whole of the right hypochondriac, the greater part of the epigastric, and extending almost to the middle of the left hypochondriac region.

In the male it weighs from fifty to sixty ounces, and in the female, from forty to fifty.

It is relatively much larger in the foetus, being about one-eighteenth of the body weight in the foetus, and in the adult, about one-thirty-sixth of the body weight.

Its greatest width is from seven to eight inches, is about twelve inches long, and in its greatest thickness about three inches.

The liver is very soft and is easily lacerated and friable; its color is a dark reddish brown. To obtain a correct idea of its shape, you might compare it to a wedge, the base of which is directed to the right, and thin edge toward the left.

The liver has five surfaces, superior, inferior, anterior, posterior and right lateral.

The liver has five lobes, right and left, caudate, quadrate, and lobus spigelii. It has five ligaments, right and left lateral or triangular, falciform, coronary and round. The liver has five fissures, the umbilical, the fissure of the ductus venosus, the transverse fissure, the fissure for the gall bladder, the fissure for the vena cava. These fissures can be represented by the letter H.

L E F T	Fissure of Ductus venosus	BACK Transverse	Fissure inferior vena cava	R I G H T
	Umbilical fissure	FRONT	Fissure for gall bladder	

The liver is movable within certain narrow limits. It moves with respiration. On inspiration, it moves down with the diaphragm to a little below the right nipple line. The ligaments do not give the liver much support because they lie relaxed, but it does get its main support from the connective tissue which unites the liver to the diaphragm, the hepatic veins which join the vena cava and also by the intra-abdominal pressure resulting from the tonic contraction of the abdominal muscles.

Also when the abdominal tension is normal, the intestines are driven up, and become a bed for the liver.

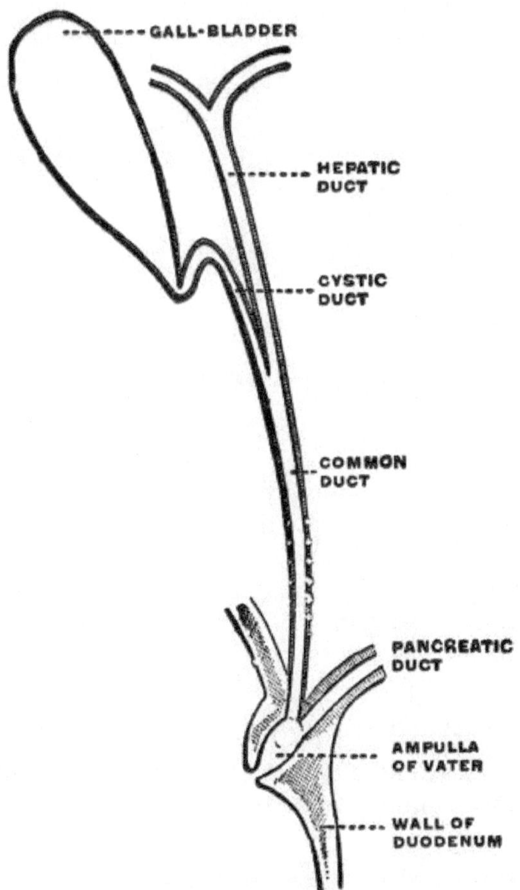

FIG. 25—EXCRETORY APPARATUS OF THE LIVER. (POIRIER AND

CHARPY)

The most important function is the secretion of the bile; it is also the excretor of deleterious matter and impurities. It also effects important changes of the blood in its passage through it, for the portal circulation.

The excretory apparatus of the liver consists (a) of the hepatic duct, (b) the gall bladder, (c) cystic duct, (d) the common bile duct.

The hepatic duct is formed by two main trunks nearly of equal size which issue from the liver, one from the right and one from the left lobe. The hepatic duct passes downward and to the right from one to two inches where it is joined at an acute angle with the cystic duct.

THE GALL BLADDER.

—The bladder is a reservoir for the bile. It is a conical or pear-shaped sack, lying on the under surface of the right lobe of the liver. It is about four inches in length, one inch in depth and holds from eight to ten drams.

The cystic duct is about an inch and a half in length, and passes obliquely downward to the left from the neck of the gall bladder, and joins the hepatic duct.

The common bile duct (ductus communis choledochous) is the common excretory duct of the liver and the gall bladder, and is formed by the union of the cystic and hepatic ducts. It descends to the middle portion of the duodenum, where it unites with the pancreatic duct, the two passing obliquely through the wall of the descending portion of the duodenum. The tissues of the liver are nourished by the blood from the hepatic arteries.

THE PANCREAS.

—The pancreas (the sweet bread) is a gland similar in structure to the salivary glands; is about seven inches long, of a grayish white color; its weight varies from two to six ounces. It is situated behind the stomach, and it secretes the pancreatic juice. It extends to the right in a part of the epigastric space. The tail lies above the left kidney, and is in contact with the lower end of the spleen and in the left hypochondriac region; the body lies behind the stomach and transverse colon and in front of the great aorta, portal vein and inferior vena cava. The arteries nourishing it are the large and small pancreatic, which are branches of the splenic artery.

The pancreatic duct is the principal excretory duct of the pancreas. It extends transversely from the left to the right through the substance of the pancreas.

After leaving the body of the pancreas, it unites with the common bile duct of the liver where it empties into the duodenum (first section of the small intestines after leaving the stomach).

The pancreatic duct carries pancreatic juice (a digestive fluid) from the pancreas to the duodenum.

THE SPLEEN.

—The spleen belongs to that class of bodies known as ductless glands and has no excretory duct; is oblong, flattened, soft, very brittle, very vascular, of a very dark bluish red color; is situated in the left hypochondriac region behind and to the left of the stomach; is five inches long, three inches wide and two inches thick and weighs about seven ounces. The vessels which nourish it are the splenic artery and splenic vein. Function. It is supposed to furnish blood corpuscles.

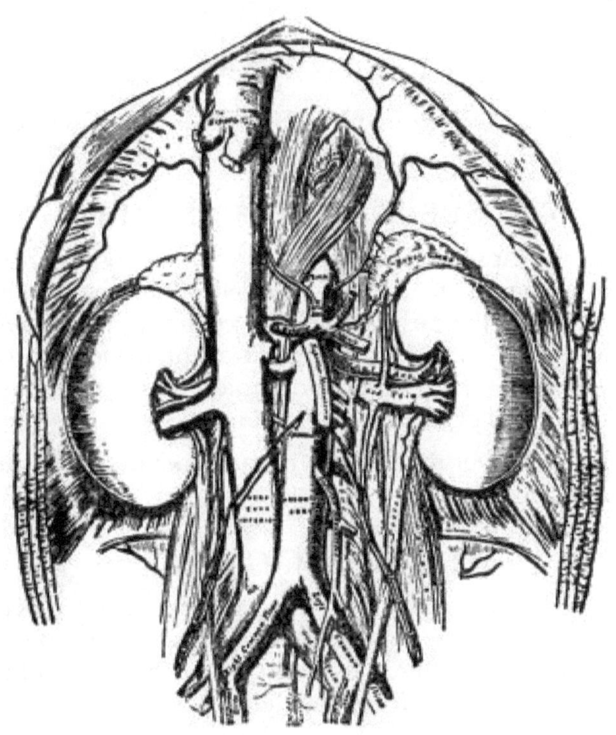

FIG. 26—THE ABDOMINAL AORTA AND ITS BRANCHES. (GRAY)

THE KIDNEYS.

—The kidneys are large glands, two in number and are situated from five to six inches apart or about three inches on either side of the median line in the right and left lumbar regions.

The upper extremity of the kidneys lies on the level of the twelfth dorsal vertebra and the lower extremity on the level of the third lumbar vertebra. Each kidney is four and one-half inches in length, two to two and one-half inches in breadth, a little more than one inch in thickness.

The weight of the kidney in the adult male is from four and one-half to six ounces each. In the adult female the weight would be from four to five and one-half ounces.

Their function is to separate from the blood certain waste products and an excess of water, the combination of which we know as urine. The principal products excreted by the kidneys from the blood along with water are ammonia and urea. The blood is taken to the kidneys by the renal arteries and the renal veins carry it back to the blood circulation.

The urine is then taken from the kidneys by the ureters and conveyed to the urinary bladder.

THE URETERS.

—The ureters are cylindrical tubes about sixteen inches in length and of diameter of a goose-quill.

THE SUPRARENAL CAPSULES.

—The suprarenal capsules belong to that class of bodies known as ductless glands and are two small flattened bodies of yellowish color, situated at the back of the abdomen, behind the peritoneum (the covering for all of the abdominal organs), and immediately above and in front of the upper end of each kidney. The name is derived from the position it occupies in relation to the kidney, supra meaning above, and renal pertaining to the kidneys.

The functions are as yet unknown. The suprarenal arteries furnish nourishment for the suprarenal capsules.

THE PELVIC CAVITY.

—The pelvic cavity is that portion of the abdomen situated between the ilium and pubic bones, or in other words the extreme lowest portion of the abdominal cavity. The organs located within this cavity are the bladder in the male and the bladder and the uterus (womb) in the female.

THE BLADDER.

—The urinary bladder is a reservoir for the urine, situated in the pelvic cavity behind the pubic bone. In life it is supplied with blood by the anterior branches of the internal iliac arteries accompanied by the internal iliac veins.

THE UTERUS.

—The uterus is the organ of gestation, receiving the fecundated ovum into its cavity, retaining it, and supporting it during the development of the foetus, and becoming the principal agent in its expulsion at the time of parturition (delivery). It is nourished in life by branches of the internal iliac artery, which is accompanied by the iliac vein.

The uterus is situated in the pelvic cavity between the rectum and the bladder, and is held in position by the lateral and round ligaments on each side. The uterus is about 3 inches in length, 2 inches in breadth and weighs from one to two ounces. It is composed of three coats, external serous, middle muscular, and internal mucous.

The serous coat, derived from the peritoneum, is thin and vascular.

The muscular coat is the chief coat, it is dense, firm, of a grayish color and cuts like cartilage.

The mucous coat is thin, smooth and closely adherent to the muscular coat. It is highly vascular.

The blood supply to the uterus is the uterine arteries which are the posterior branches of the internal iliac arteries, and the ovarian arteries which are branches of the aorta. These break up in capillaries and form a fine network plexus in the coats of the uterus.

The veins are of large size and are the uterine which empty into the internal iliac veins and the ovarian veins. On the right side the ovarian vein empties into the ascending vena cava, and on the left side into the renal vein.

PROSTATE.

—The prostate gland is a pale, firm glandular body, which surrounds the neck of the bladder in the male. Its shape and size resembles a horse chestnut. It weighs from one-half to one ounce and measures one and one-half inches across and three quarters of an inch deep. Its structure is inclosed by a firm thin fibrous capsule. Its substance is of a pale reddish grey color and is composed of glandular substance and muscular tissue.

The arteries that supply the prostate are derived from the internal pubic, a branch of the internal iliac.

The veins form a plexus around the gland and communicate with veins which empty into the internal iliac veins. Its function is to secrete an opaque fluid.

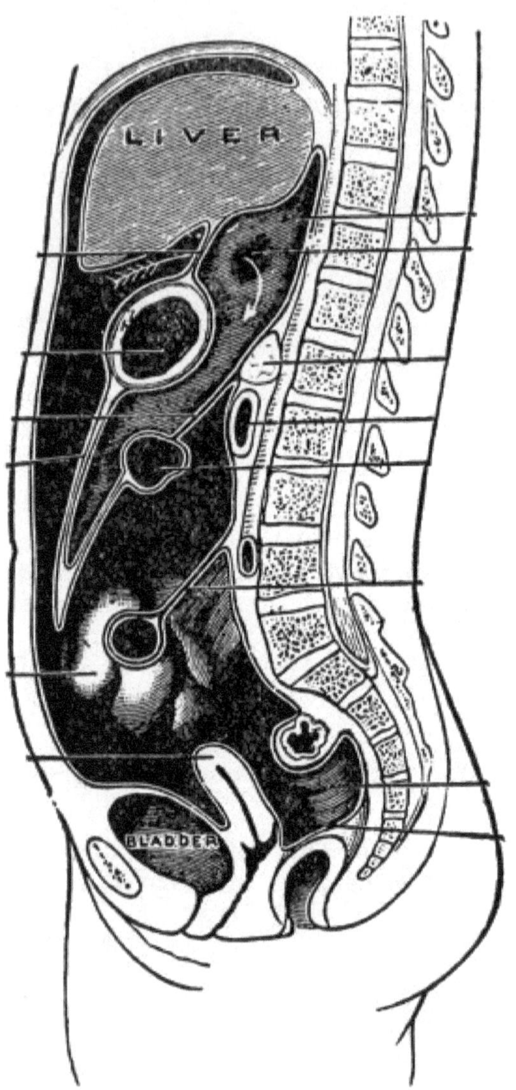

FIG. 27—THE PERITONEUM. (GRAY)

THE PERITONEUM.

—During life and in the uncut corpse the peritoneal cavity is air-tight. It is not a real cavity, as muscular tension and atmospheric pressure permit no vacant space to form. When the surgeon or embalmer opens the abdomen, the peritoneal cavity is at that moment produced.

The peritoneum is the largest serous membrane in the body. In the male it is a closed sac, a part of which is applied against the abdominal sides, while the remainder is reflected over the contained viscera. In the female it is not a closed sac, since the free extremities of the fallopian tubes open directly into the peritoneal cavity.

The parietal peritoneum is that portion applied against the abdominal sides.

The visceral peritoneum is that portion reflected over the viscera.

The peritoneum consists of two sacs.

The greater sac lines the greater part of the abdominal cavity as almost all of the viscera are covered by it.

The lesser sac is placed behind the stomach. These two sacs communicate with each other by a narrow orifice called the *Foramen of Winslow.*

The peritoneum, as it covers different organs or sets of organs, receives special names.

The lesser omentum consists of two layers, these split to envelope the stomach.

The greater omentum consists of four layers. Two of these layers extend from the stomach and together with two other layers of the same structure which envelope the transverse colon, form an apron for the intestines.

The mesentery consists of two layers which invests the small intestines. Between the two layers of the mesentery we find the blood vessels, nerves, lacteals, and glands, leading to and from the intestines. The mesentery is fan shaped, and is attached to the second lumbar vertebra. The length of the mesentery fan is about eight inches from commencement to termination at intestine. It extends the whole length of the intestines, which is about twenty feet.

CHAPTER IX.
THE VASCULAR SYSTEM.

THE VASCULAR SYSTEM.

—The vascular system is composed of the organs immediately concerned in the circulation throughout the body of the fluids which convey to the tissues the nutritive substances and oxygen necessary for their metabolism and carry from them to the excretory organs the waste products formed during metabolism.

The system is usually regarded as being composed of two portions, the one consists of organs in which circulate the red fluid which we term blood, and called the *blood vascular system,* while the organs of the other contain a colorless or white fluid known as lymph or chyle, and is known as the lymphatic circulation.

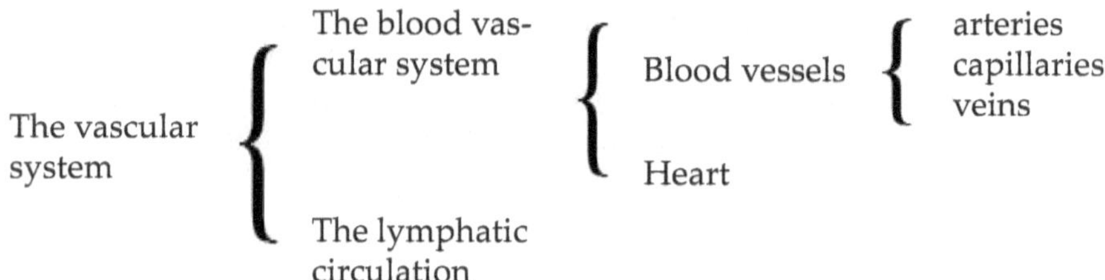

THE BLOOD VASCULAR SYSTEM.

—A knowledge of the general features of the circulatory system are essential to the undertaker and the embalmer as a means of enabling him not only to perform the ordinary operations and duties of his profession intelligently, but to equip him with the knowledge necessary to meet the exceptional conditions which sometimes arise.

There is a growing appreciation of the fact, also, that thoroughness in the practice of embalming is worth striving after. Many cases of embalming, no doubt, require a minimum amount of attention, particularly where the body is to be kept but a short time. Where preservation for longer periods is required, as for transportation, or where disease and accident have interfered seriously with the circulation, a more exact knowledge is evidently desirable.

The blood vascular system comprises the heart, which is the central organ of the whole system, and all the blood vessels. This system, with its arteries and veins, permeates the whole body and becomes divided and subdivided at its outer portion into vessels constantly decreasing in size, until those extremely minute vessels, the capillaries, are reached. All the tissues of the body are very rich in these, so that all portions of the body are supplied with blood, which is essential for the nourishment and rebuilding of the tissues. The large vessels which convey blood from the heart are termed arteries, while the vessels which convey the blood back to the heart are termed veins.

For one to properly embalm the human body, it is necessary to understand the way the fluid will circulate through the body, and the only way we can do this is to study the circulation of the blood as it would occur in life.

To facilitate the description of the blood vascular system, it has been divided into six subdivisions as follows:

(1) Systemic.

(2) Pulmonary.

(3) Coronary.

(4) Portal.

(5) Foetal.

(6) Collateral.

THE SYSTEMIC CIRCULATION.

—The systemic circulation is called the greater circulation of the body. The course of the blood is from the left ventricle of the heart through the aortic semi-lunar valve to the great aorta and its branches which end in capillaries in the tissues of the body then through the veins the terminal trunks of which end in the right auricle of the heart. So the systemic circulation is the circulation of the blood from the left ventricle of the heart to the right auricle of the heart and this circulation has the important function of carrying oxygen to the tissues to nourish them, and of carrying carbonic acid gas back to the heart which is a waste product of the tissues.

The systemic circulation is divided for the sake of convenience into the following:

(1) The arterial system.

(2) Capillary.

(3) The venous system.

FIG. 28—THE ARCH OF THE AORTA AND ITS BRANCHES. (GRAY)

THE ARTERIAL SYSTEM.

—The blood leaving the heart passes from the left ventricle through the aortic semi-lunar valve, into the ascending aorta. Here the two coronary arteries come off which go to supply the muscular tissues of the heart. The ascending aorta passes into the arch of the aorta. Here are given off the innominate artery to the right and the common carotid and the subclavian to the left. The innominate is only about an inch or two in length, and divides into the right common carotid and the right subclavian arteries. On each side the subclavian passes down beneath the clavical bone and enters the axillary space where it is known as the axillary artery. After leaving the axillary space, the artery passes down the arm and is known as the brachial artery. About one inch below the bend of the elbow the artery divides into two branches, known as the radial and ulnar. The radial goes to the thumb side of the hand, and the ulnar to the little finger side of the hand. The ulnar artery and a branch of the radial form the palmar arch, which gives off the branches to the fingers. Coming off the brachial are the deep brachial arteries and the anastomotica magna arteries which anastomose and give collateral circulation to the forearm, by means of the recurrent radial and ulnar arteries.

The common carotid arteries pass up each side of the neck to a point opposite the Adam's apple, where they, divide into the external carotid, which supplies the muscular tissue of the face, and the internal carotid artery, which goes up through the skull and helps to form the circle of Willis.

The vertebral arteries come off the subclavian arteries on either side and pass upward, winding through the foramen of the vertebrae, until finally arriving inside the cranial cavity, unite to form one artery called the basilar, which helps to form the circle of Willis.

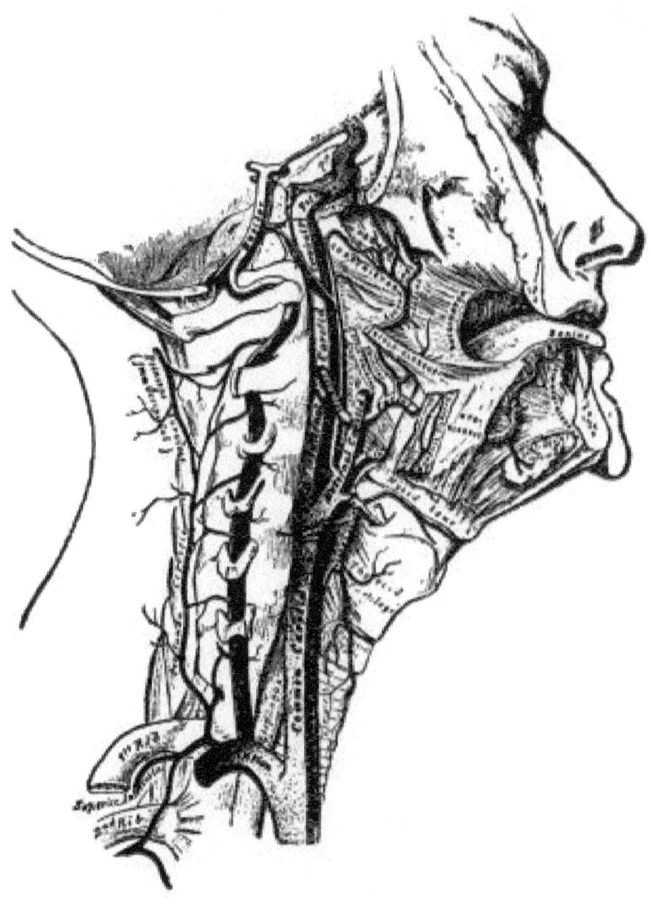

**FIG. 29—THE INTERNAL CAROTID AND VERTEBRAL ARTERIES.
(GRAY)**

The circle of Willis is situated at the base of the brain and gives off to the front the two anterior cerebral arteries, to the sides the two middle cerebral arteries, and to the back the two posterior cerebral arteries. The two anterior cerebral arteries are connected by the anterior communicating branch, and the middle cerebral artery and the posterior cerebral arteries on each side are connected by the posterior communicating branches. The cerebral arteries terminate in the piamater as a dense capillary network, and from there supply the substance of the brain with nutrition.

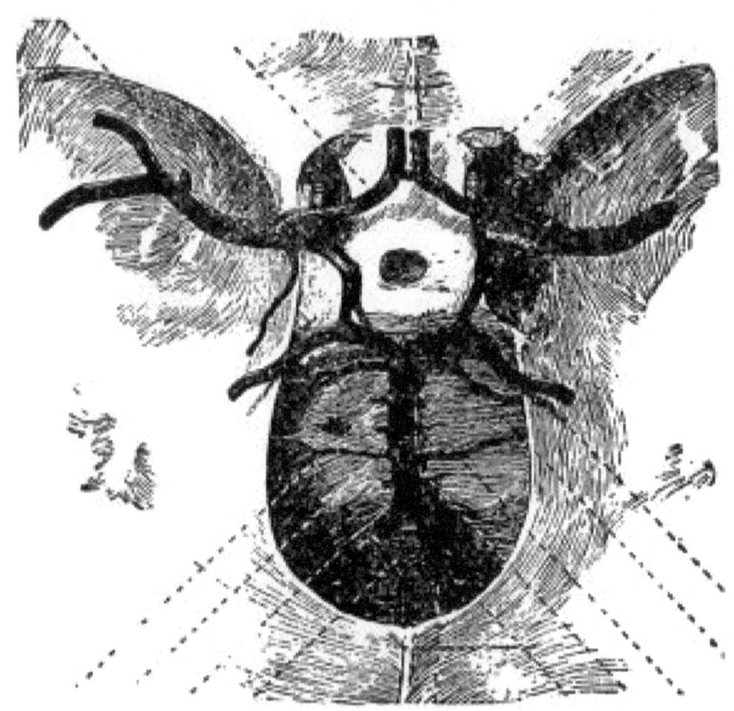

FIG. 30—THE CIRCLE OF WILLIS. (SPALTEHOLZ)

The external carotid artery supplies the muscular tissues of the face. The external carotid artery arises from the common carotid artery at about the level of the upper border of the thyroid cartilage—a level which corresponds with the body of the fourth cervicle vertebra. Thence it is directed upward and slightly backward towards the angle of the jaw, where it enters the substance of the parotid gland and continues upward in that structure to just below the root of the zygoma. Here it gives rise to a large branch, the internal maxillary, and is then continued upward over the root of the zygoma upon the side of the skull, this terminal portion of it being termed the superficial temporal artery. The branches of the external carotid artery from below upward are (1) the ascending pharyngeal, (2) the superior thyroid, (3) the lingual, (4) the occipital, (5) the facial or external maxillary, (6) the posterior auricular, (7) the internal maxillary, (8) the superficial temporal.

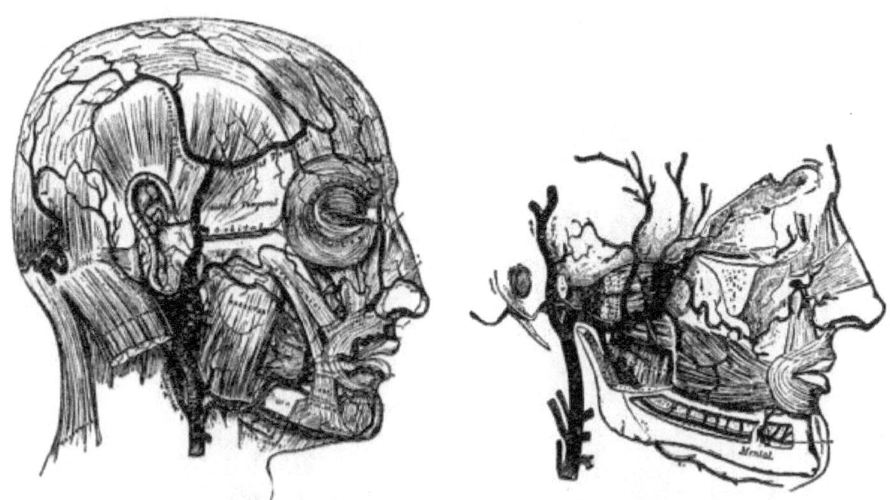

FIG. 31—THE ARTERIES OF THE FACE AND SCALP. (GRAY)FIG

FIG 32—THE EXTERNAL CAROTID AND ITS BRANCHES. (GRAY)

The arch of the aorta now continues into the thoracic aorta, so called while it is in the thoracic cavity, and after it has passed through the diaphragm becomes the abdominal aorta. At a point opposite the umbilicus or navel the abdominal aorta divides into the two common iliac arteries. Each common iliac artery divides into an internal iliac artery, which supplies the organs of the pelvic cavity, and an external iliac artery, which passes beneath Poupart's ligament. As the artery passes down the leg it is known as the femoral artery, until it passes into the popliteal space, where it is called the popliteal artery. About one inch below the popliteal space the artery divides into the anterior tibial artery, which runs on a straight line down the front and outside of the leg to a point between the big toe and the one next to it, and the posterior tibial artery which passes down the back part of the foreleg between the inside ankle and the heel. The peroneal, a branch of the posterior tibial, passes down the foreleg between the outside ankle and the heel. The anterior tibial artery, as it passes through the instep is known as the large dorsal artery and further on is known as the small dorsal artery. In the foot is the plantar arch, formed by branches of the posterior and anterior tibial arteries, which send out branches to each toe.

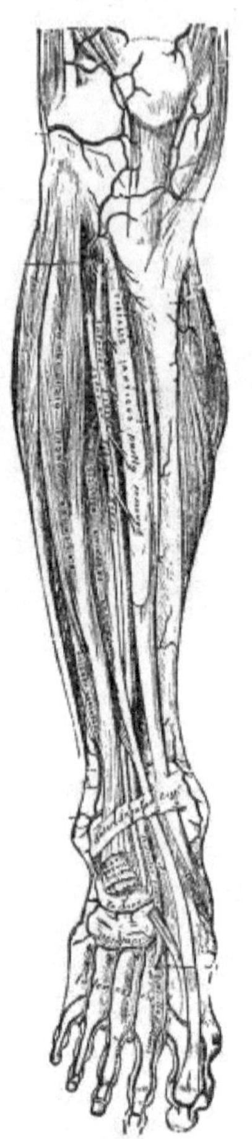

FIG. 33—THE ANTERIOR TIBIAL ARTERY. (GRAY)

FIG. 34—THE POPLITEAL, POSTERIOR TIBIAL, AND PERONEAL ARTERIES. (GRAY)

Coming off the femoral are the deep femoral and the anastomotica magna arteries, which anastomose and form collateral circulation to the foreleg by means of the recurrent anterior and posterior tibial arteries.

Coming off the subclavian arteries are the superior and inferior mammary arteries, which pass down over the chest wall, anastomose and give collateral circulation to the lower extremities by means of the superior and inferior epigastric arteries, branches of the external iliac and femoral arteries.

The thoracic aorta gives off the intercostal arteries, which supply the ribs, the bronchials which supply the lungs, the esophageal which supplies the esophagus, and the pericardiac which supplies the pericardium.

The abdominal aorta gives off in rotation the coeliac axis, which as a hub in a wheel gives off three spokes, the gastric artery to the stomach, the hepatic to the liver, and the splenic artery to the spleen. The next branch is the phrenic, which supplies the diaphragm, then the suprarenal artery, two or more in number coming off of both the aorta and the renal arteries. The suprarenal arteries supply the suprarenal capsules. The next branch is the superior mesenteric artery, which supplies the small intestines; the next branch is the renal arteries, which supply the kidneys; the next branch is the spermatic or the ovarian arteries, which supply the testes in the male or the ovaries in the female; the inferior mesenteric artery, which supplies the large intestines. Also coming off the aorta at regular intervals are the lumbar arteries, which supply the side walls.

THE CAPILLARY CIRCULATION.

—The capillaries are very minute blood vessels, forming a network between the terminating arteries and the commencing veins.

They derive their name from the word capillus (hair). They vary in size from 1-3500 to 1-3000 of an inch, the largest capillaries being those of the skin. These little vessels are so thickly distributed throughout most of the tissues of the body as to make it impossible to insert a cambric needle in the flesh without pricking scores of them.

When we embalm a body the object should be to introduce a sufficient amount of fluid through the arterial system so that these tiny capillaries will be filled. These little vessels are so minute and the walls are so thin that the fluid is immediately taken up into the tissues. If every tissue of the body can be supplied with fluid by means of the capillaries, we would have the ideal, the body would be perfectly embalmed. Let us then not only be arterial embalmers, but, better still, let us be capillary and tissue embalmers.

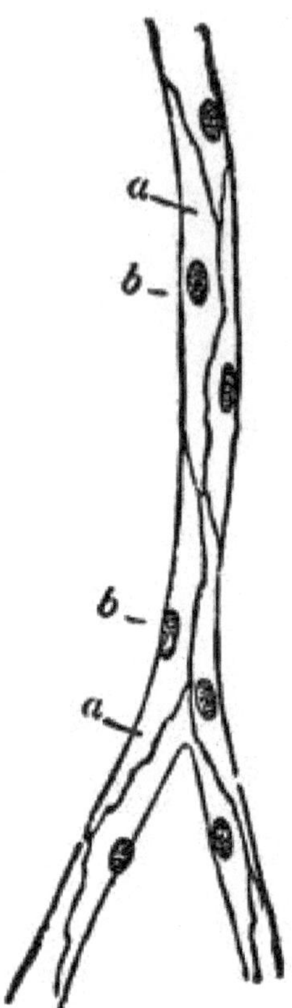

FIG. 35—CAPILLARIES A, CELLS; B, NUCLEI. (GRAY)

Capillaries have one wall, which is the continuation of the inner wall of the artery, thus making the capillary so thin that fluid finds its way easily through it into the surrounding tissues.

Some parts of the body are more vascular than others and some tissues of the body, such as the cornea of the eye, the epidermis, cartilage, the substance of the brain, etc., are entirely destitute of capillaries.

The combined area of all the capillaries of the body is many times greater than the combined area of the trunk vessels. If this were not so, the high pressure on the arterial system would break the thin capillary walls and also the greater area allows the blood to circulate more slowly which gives time for the liberation of oxygen to the tissues and for the absorption of carbon dioxide.

THE VENOUS SYSTEM.

—The veins, like the arteries, are tubular vessels, their function being to receive the blood from the capillaries and convey it to the auricles of the heart. There are two classes of veins, **systemic** and **pulmonic**.

The systemic veins receive the impure or carbonized blood from the capillaries and convey it to the right auricle of the heart.

The pulmonic veins receive the pure oxygenized blood from the lungs and convey it to the left auricle of the heart. The pulmonic veins will be taken up and discussed later under the pulmonary circulation.

Systemic veins are divided into superficial and deep veins and sinuses.

The superficial veins are found between the layers of the superficial fascia, just beneath the skin, and communicate with the deep veins by branches which pierce the fascia.

The deep veins are found deeper down, between the muscles, and are surrounded by the deep fascia.

The smaller arteries, such as the radial, brachial, posterior and anterior tibial, and the peroneal arteries, are each accompanied by two veins, one on each side of the artery, which are called venae comites (accompanying veins). The larger arteries, such as the common carotid, the femoral and the iliac, are accompanied by only one vein.

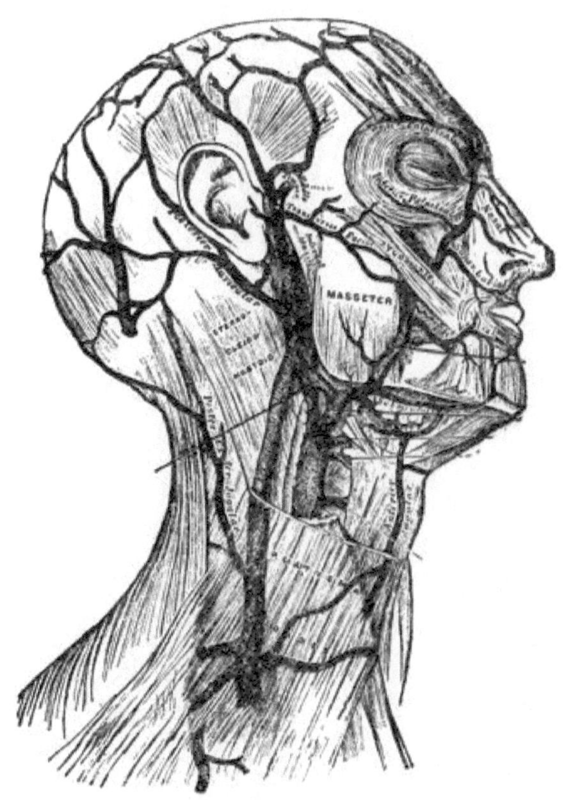

FIG. 36—SUPERFICIAL VEINS OF THE HEAD AND NECK. (GRAY)

Veins arise from the capillaries, or, rather, from the minute capillary plexus, formed by a massing or blending of the tiny venules. These small vessels unite to form larger trunks, and as they continue toward the heart increase in size until they finally unite to form the ascending and descending venae cavae.

The Sinuses.—The cerebral veins are small vessels that arise from the capillaries of the brain, and terminate in the sinuses of the dura mater. There are many sinuses in the cranial cavity, and differ from the vein, in that the walls are thinner, having only two walls while the veins have three, and they do not have valves. The outer walls of the sinuses of the brain are formed by a division of the dura mater, while the inner wall is the continuation of the inner wall of the vein.

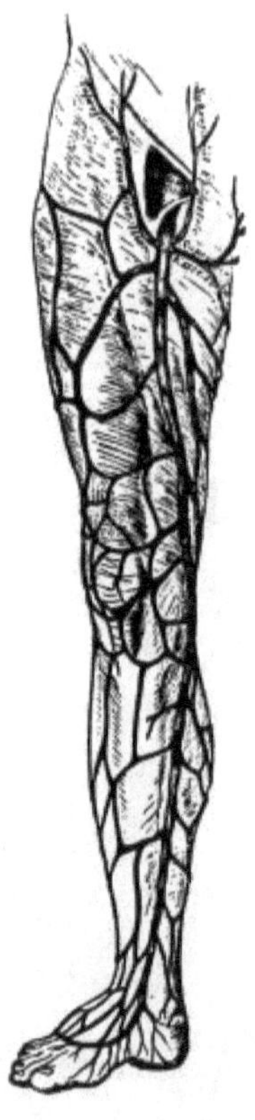

FIG. 37—THE INTERNAL LONG SAPHENOUS VEIN. (GRAY)

They are of little interest to embalmers, except for the fact that when the brain is injected by any of the so-called needle processes, the fluid is quickly conveyed through these vessels to the tissues of the brain, and that organ is thoroughly preserved.

The vessels starting at the foot are the anterior and posterior tibial veins, which unite just below the knee to form the popliteal vein, in the popliteal space. Another vein starts from the foot and runs into the popliteal vein called the external short saphenous. Starting also at the foot and running into the posterior tibial vein is the peroneal vein.

The popliteal vein after leaving the popliteal space is known as the femoral vein as it passes up the leg, to Poupart's ligament. Another vein, the internal long saphenous, starts at the foot, and runs into the femoral vein about an inch below Poupart's ligament. After passing beneath Poupart's ligament the vessel is called the external iliac. Coming from the organs of the pelvic cavity is the internal iliac, which joins with the external iliac vein to form the common iliac vein. The right and left iliac veins join opposite the umbilicus to form the ascending vena cava. The ascending vena cava passes upward to the right of the vertebral column through the diaphragm and enters the right auricle of the heart by means of the eustachian valve.

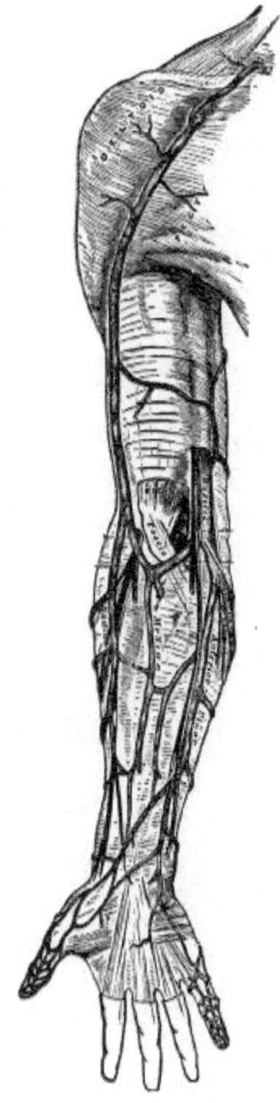

FIG. 38—THE SUPERFICIAL VEINS OF THE ARM. (GRAY)

In the forearm are the radial veins on the thumb side of the hand, the ulnar veins on the little finger side of the hand, and the median vein just between the radial and ulnar veins. The median vein divides into the median cephalic vein and the median basilic. The median cephalic vein unites with the radial vein to form the cephalic vein, which runs up the back part of the arm and finally empties into the subclavian vein. The median basilic unites with the ulnar vein to form the basilic, which runs up the inner part of the arm between the biceps and triceps muscles. The deep brachial veins or the vena comites, two in number, which follow the brachial artery, run into the basilic vein. When the basilic vein arrives at the axillary space it takes on the name of the axillary vein, and as the vessel passes beneath the subclavian bone, it becomes the subclavian vein. The right and left subclavian veins with the right and left internal jugular veins from each side of the head form the right and left innominate veins, which unite to form the descending vena cava, which runs into the right auricle of the heart.

Starting at the head, the superior longitudinal sinus begins at the fore part of the brain and runs backward between the two hemispheres of the brain and empties into the wine press or Torcular herophili. The inferior longitudinal sinus begins at the fore part of the brain, but rung deeper down in the pia mater between the two hemispheres of the brain, terminates in the straight sinus which empties into the wine press. Beginning at the base of the cerebellum are the two occipital sinuses which run together and terminate in the wine press. After all the blood has been gathered together in the wine press, it leaves by means of the right and left lateral sinuses which pass down as far as the jugular foramen. Beginning at the base of the brain in front are the right and left cavernosus sinuses, which run into the inferior petrosal sinuses, which pass down as far as the jugular foramen, where they join the lateral sinuses to form the right and left internal jugular vein. The superior petrosal sinus is between the lateral sinus and the cavernosus sinus uniting them. Joining the right and left cavernosus sinuses is the circular sinus and joining the right and left inferior petrosal sinuses is the transverse sinus. The right and left internal jugular veins pass down through the jugular foramens and down the neck to where they with the right and left subclavian veins form the right and left innominate veins. The right and left innominate veins unite to form the descending vena cava which empties into the right auricle of the heart.

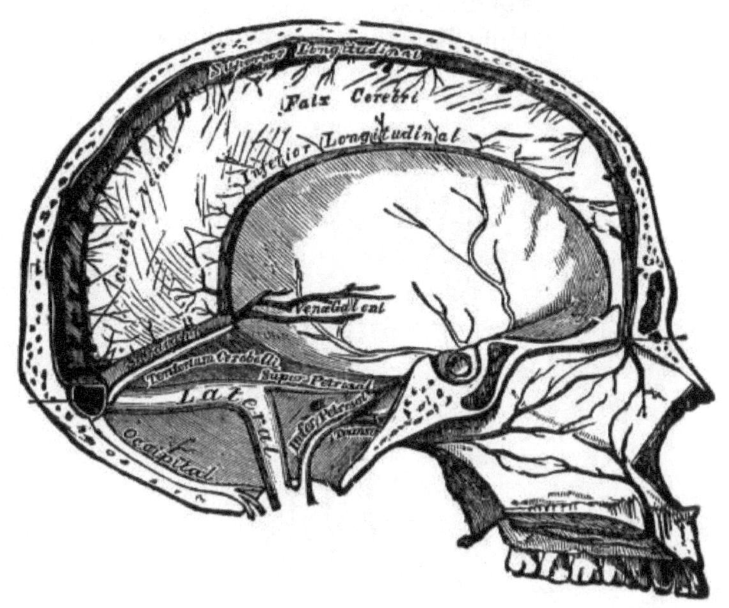

FIG. 39—VERTICAL SECTION OF THE SKULL, SHOWING THE SINUSES OF THE DURA MATER. (GRAY)

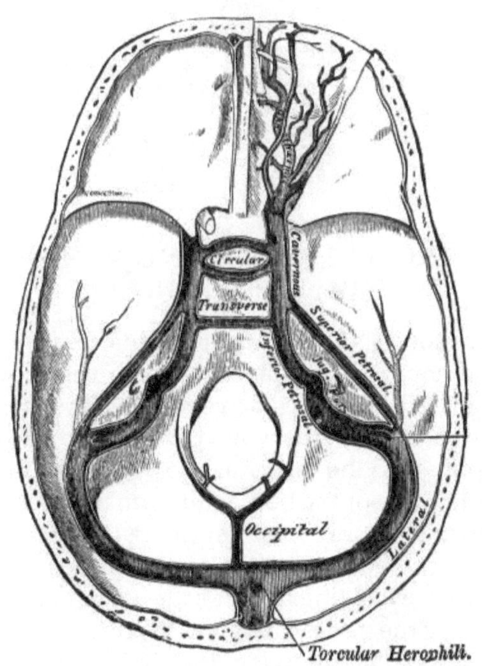

FIG. 40—THE SINUSES AT THE BASE OF THE SKULL. (GRAY)

Beginning in the tissues of the heart are the coronary veins, which terminate in the coronary sinus and then into the right auricle of the heart through the coronary valves.

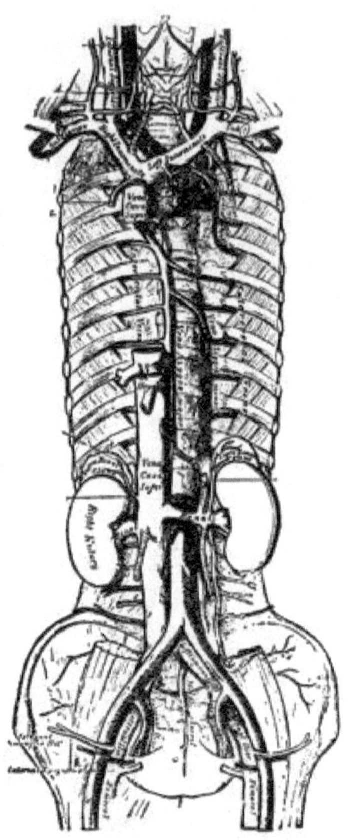

FIG. 41—THE AZYGOS SYSTEM AND VENAE CAVAE WITH BRANCHES. (GRAY)

The azygos system consists of the major azygos vein, which starts at the right external iliac vein and empties into the descending vena cava; the minor azygos vein which starts at the left external iliac vein and empties into the major azygos vein back of the heart; and the tertiary azygos vein, which starts at the left sub-clavian vein and empties into the minor azygos vein. The azygos veins collect all the blood from the side walls of the body and form a perfect collateral circulation between the superior and inferior caval systems, and thoroughly equalizes the blood pressure all over the body. The major azygos vein receives the following: the right intercostal veins, excepting the first; the azygos minor; the right bronchial vein; the esophageal vein; the pericardiac; and the posterior mediastinal veins. The minor azygos vein receives the following: the tertiary azygos vein; the lower five left intercostal veins; the small left mediastinal veins; the lower left esophageal veins. The tertiary azygos receives the following: the fifth, sixth and sometimes the seventh intercostal veins; the lower end of the lower left superior intercostal vein; and the left bronchial vein. The inferior vena cava receives the following veins: the lumbar veins; the hepatic veins; the phrenic veins; the renal veins; the right suprarenal vein; the right spermatic or ovarian vein. The left spermatic or ovarian vein and the left suprarenal vein empty into the left renal vein.

THE PULMONARY CIRCULATION.

—This is the circulation existing between the right ventricle of the heart through the lungs back to the left auricle of the heart.

The pulmonary artery takes its origin from the summit of the right ventricle. It is about two inches in length, and is directed upward, backward and slightly towards the left, and beneath the arch of the aorta it divides into the right and left pulmonary arteries. These end in a system of capillaries in between the air cells of the lungs, where carbon dioxide is thrown off and oxygen taken on.

The pulmonary veins are four in number, two passing from the root of each lung to the posterior surface of the left auricle of the heart. Each vein is formed at the root of the lung by the union of a number of smaller vessels which take origin ultimately from the capillary net work formed from the branches of the pulmonary artery, and to a certain extent from that formed by the bronchial arteries. Each pulmonary vein is about six inches in length.

THE CORONARY CIRCULATION.

—The heart receives its blood supply through the two coronary arteries which arise from the aorta immediately above its origin, the return flow being by the coronary veins which open into the right auricle of the heart by the coronary sinus. The branches of the coronary arteries upon the surface of the heart are, as a rule, all end arteries; that is, arteries which form no direct anastomosis with their neighbors. Practically no blood can be carried directly, therefore, by the left coronary artery into the territory supplied by the right one, or vice versa.

The coronary sinus is a short venous trunk a little over an inch in length, which occupies the right half of that portion of the auriclo-ventricular groove which lies between the left auricle and ventricle. At the right end it opens into the right auricle, its orifice being guarded by the Thebesian valve.

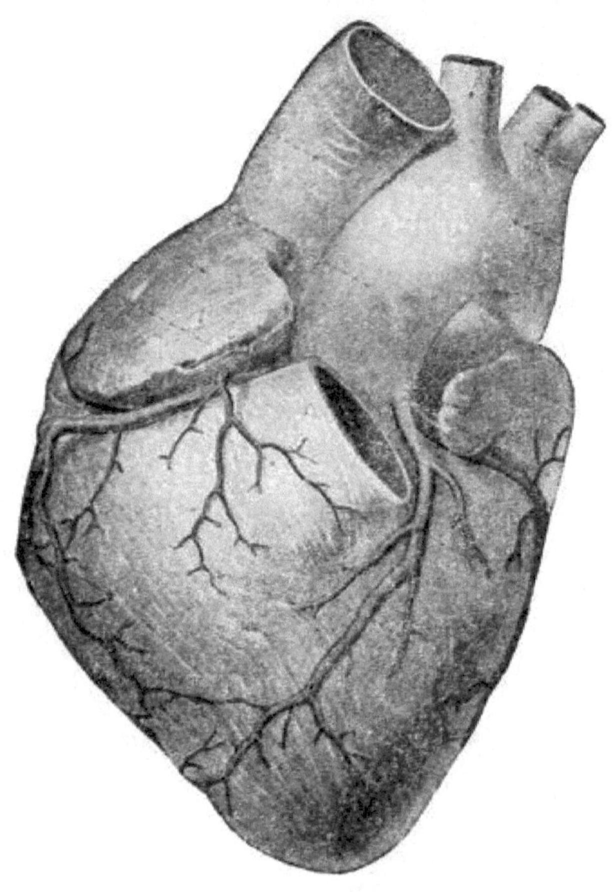

FIG. 42—A FRONT VIEW OF THE HEART SHOWING CORONARY
ARTERIES. (SPALTEHOLZ)

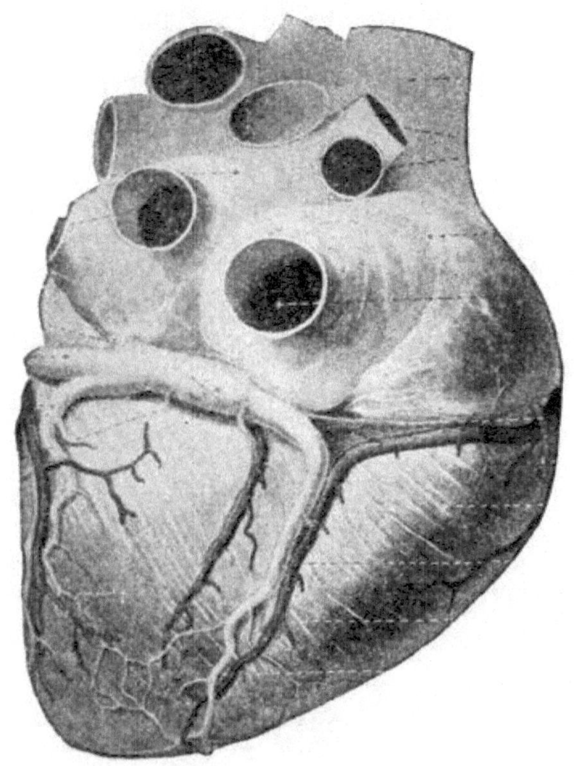

FIG. 43—A BACK VIEW OF THE HEART SHOWING THE CORONARY SINUS, AND VESSELS ENTERING AND LEAVING. (SPALTEHOLZ)

THE PORTAL CIRCULATION.

—This circulation is of little or no value to the embalmer, as no part of it is directly required to supply any of the tissues with embalming fluid.

The portal circulation is formed by the superior mesenteric vein and the splenic vein uniting to form the portal vein. The inferior mesenteric vein runs into the splenic vein; the gastric and cystic veins run into the portal veins. The portal vein ends in capillaries in the liver, where certain important changes take place, namely, the taking out of the bile.

The portal vein and its tributaries are unlike the veins in the general circulation, as there are no valves. Their function in life is to gather up food or nutrition for the blood, and to the embalmer is of no special importance, only to know how this circulation is made up. The vessels that convey blood to the liver in life and the fluid in death are discussed under the liver.

After death, about one-fourth of the blood of the body is to be found in the portal system. This blood can in no way be removed, and this is one of the reasons why the embalmer is not able to draw more blood than he does.

THE FOETAL CIRCULATION.

—The foetal circulation is that circulation existing between mother and un-born child.

The placenta constitutes, from the third month of intra uterine life, the nutritive and respiratory organ of the foetus. The placenta consists of a maternal portion and a foetal portion. *The maternal portion* is that portion of the placenta next to the uterine wall of the mother. In this are intervillus blood spaces, which may be regarded as derivations from the eroded maternal blood vessels. In the non-pregnant state the uterus is supplied with branches from the internal iliac artery, which end in capillaries in the wall of the uterus. In the pregnant state the numerous branches of the arteries supplying the uterus do not end as capillaries, but pierce the basal plate of the placenta, where the arterial vessels lose their muscular coat and open directly into the intervillus or intraplacental blood spaces. Maternal capillaries are wanting within the placenta, since they become early replaced by the intervillus spaces. The maternal blood is carried away from these spaces by wide venous channels, forming networks from which proceed the larger venous trunks.

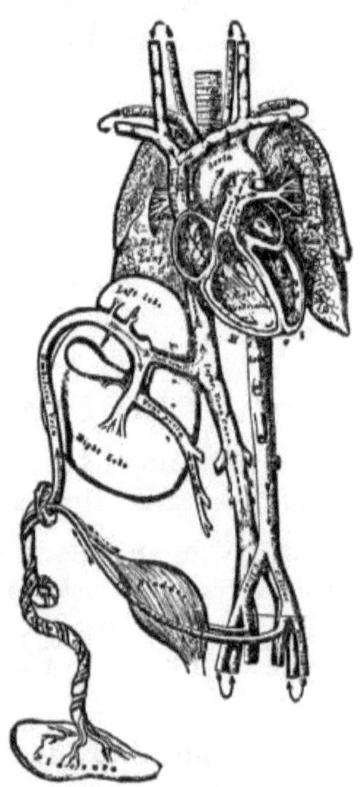

FIG. 44—PLAN OF THE FOETAL CIRCULATION. (GRAY)

The foetal portion of the placenta is that portion next to the child. Here end the terminal loops of the foetal blood vessels, the blood being conveyed to and from the placenta along the umbilical cord, by the umbilical arteries and vein. Although coming into close relation, the blood streams of the mother and of the child never actually mingle, because of the delicate septum which intervenes. The delicate septum, however, allows the free interchange of gases necessary for the respiratory function as well as the passage of nutritive substances into the foetal circulation.

The umbilical cord connects the body of the foetus with the placenta, and conveys the foetal blood to and from the placenta to the child. This blood is carried by means of two umbilical arteries and one umbilical vein.

The umbilical vein originates by means of capillaries in the placenta, traverses the cord and enters the body of the child at the umbilicus. The umbilical vein now enters the substance of the liver and passes from that organ to the ascending vena cava by means of the ductus venosus. The blood now enters the right auricle of the heart and the eustachian valve is so placed that this blood is thrown directly into the left auricle of the heart, from there into the left ventricle, and out into the aorta to find itself in the general circulation of the child. The blood coming from the upper extremities of the child finds its way into the right auricle of the heart by means of the descending vena cava, thence into the right ventricle, and out into the pulmonary artery. This artery after birth will lead the blood to the lungs, but before birth, in as much as the lungs are not functioning, the lungs can not accommodate this amount of blood, so it passes directly into the arch of the aorta by means of the ductus arteriosus, and thence into the general circulation. The umbilical or hypogastric arteries leave the internal iliacs, pass one on each side of the bladder to the umbilicus, and thence down the cord to the placenta, end there in capillaries, where the blood is now purified, and nourished for its return flow.

THE COLLATERAL CIRCULATION.

—By collateral circulation is meant the anastomoses of arteries, or veins through a side branch. There are three great arterial collateral circulations in the body. One is in the arm, the deep brachial artery, and the anastomotica magna, coming off of the brachial artery and anastomosing with the recurrent radial and ulnar artery. One is in the leg, the deep femoral artery, and the anastomotica magna coming off of the femoral artery and anastomosing with the recurrent anterior and posterior tibial arteries. One over the front part of the body, the superior and inferior mammary arteries branches of the subclavian artery and anastomosing with the superior and inferior epigastric arteries, branches of the external iliac and femoral arteries.

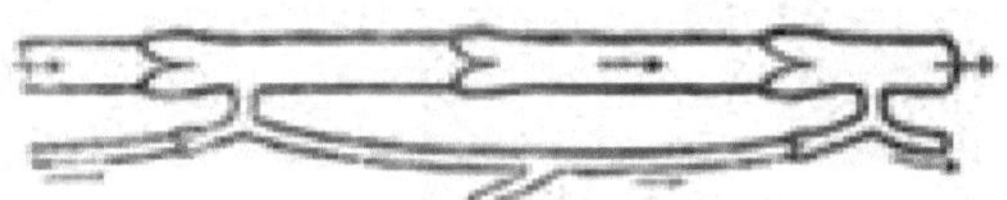

FIG. 45—COLLATERAL ANASTOMOSIS OF VEINS (POIRIER AND CHARPY)

THE LYMPHATIC CIRCULATION.

—The lymphatic system is a system of vessels which occurs abundantly in almost all portions of the body and converge and anastomose to form two or more main trunks, which open into the subclavian veins just before they are joined by the internal jugular. The vessels contain a fluid termed lymph, usually colorless and containing numerous white blood corpuscles known as lymphocytes.

In those vessels which have their origin in the wall of the small intestines, the contained fluid has, especially during digestion, a more or less milky appearance, owing to the lymphocytes being loaded with particles of fat which they have taken up from the intestinal contents. On this account, these vessels are usually spoken of as lacteals, although it must be recognized that they are merely portions of the general lymphatic system.

In certain respects the vessels of the system strongly resemble the veins. They arise from a capillary network, their walls have a structure closely resembling that of the veins, they are abundantly supplied with valves, and it may be said that the fluid which they contain flows from the tissues towards the subclavian veins. With these similarities there are combined marked differences. One of the most import-ant of these consists in the fact that the capillaries of the lymphatics are closed and do not communicate with any other set of vessels as the venous capillaries do with the arterial; and another important difference is to be found in the frequent oc-currence upon the lymphatic vessels of characteristic enlargements, the so-called lymphatic nodes or glands, quite different from anything occurring in connection with the veins.

Throughout the body spaces of varying size are found, containing a clear, more or less watery fluid, which are called lymph spaces. These spaces do not communicate with the capillaries of the lymphatics, but are in such close rela-tionship with them that the fluid easily finds its way into the lymph capillaries by osmosis, absorption, lymphocytes going out into these spaces and returning filled with the lymph fluid.

The lymphatic capillaries, which are arranged in the form of networks of very different degrees of fineness and complexity, closely resemble in structure the blood capillaries, their walls consisting of a single layer of endothelial cells. They differ from those of the blood vascular system not only in their ultimate branches being closed, but also in their general appearance. They are of greater caliber.

The lymph vessels, which issue from the capillary networks and convey the lymph ultimately to the subclavian veins, have the arrangement closely resem-bling that of the veins; the larger ones are usually situated alongside and accom-pany the course of the blood vessels. Just as the veins unite to form larger trunks as they pass from the capillaries toward their termination, so, too, the lymphatics, but the lymphatics present two peculiarities which distinguish them from the veins. They do not anastomose as abundantly as veins and there is not the same propor-tional increase in the size of the lymphatic vessel. The left trunk or thoracic duct is much larger than the right, beginning in the abdominal region and traversing the entire length of the thorax to reach its destination. It receives all the lymph returned from the lower limbs, the pelvic walls and viscera, the abdominal walls and viscera, the lower part of the right half and the whole of the left half of the thoracic viscera, the left side of the neck and head, and the left arm. The other trunk, the right lymphatic duct, is very short and sometimes wanting. It receives the lymph from the upper part of the right side of the thoracic wall, from the right half of the thoracic viscera and the upper surface of the liver, the right side of the neck and head, and from the right arm. The structure of the larger lymphatic vessels is similar to the veins, but, as a rule, their walls are thinner than those of the veins of corresponding caliber and their valves are more numerous. The walls of the most robust trunks, particularly those of the thoracic duct, consist of three coats. From within outward these are: (a) the intima, composed of the endothelial lining and the fibro-subendothelial layer; (b) the media, made up of involuntary muscle interspersed with fibro-elastic tissue; and (c) the adventitia, consisting of fibro-elastic tissue and longitudinal bundles of involuntary muscle.

Lymphatic nodes are scattered along the course of the lymphatic vessels, found in various regions of the body as elliptical flattened nodules of varying size. The embalmer will meet with these in the axillary and inguinal regions, or when he is raising the axillary or femoral arteries.

PART III.
EMBALMING

EMBALMING

The central thought of the modern funeral director in the care of the dead and in all the arrangements of the funeral is to remove so far as may be all that is necessarily painful to those who must place out of sight the body through which the soul of the dear one has expressed itself, in all the ways that are prompted by affection. This does not seem to have been the case in the former days when the methods were in striking contrast to those of today and were such as would intensify the suffering of the living. Beginning with the arrangement of the body in the room made cold by nature in winter or by the ice box in the summer and ending by lowering the body into an unlined grave, each detail seems to have been made with little thought of lessening the pain caused by those things which necessarily have to be done. Perhaps the central thought in the old days was the same as that which was the comfort offered upon funeral occasions by a former local pastor which was "death is a horrible thing." If this was not the controlling thought, it is certain that many details of former funeral customs would be considered horrible today. Today the aim is to lighten the burden and to cheer the hearts of those who mourn.

The introduction of embalming in the seventies has been of untold benefit in improving the environment of the dead prior to interment. Recollections of the use of the old ice box, the crude and cumbersome cooler, the ice water to be cared for and the thought of the chilled body are not pleasant now, and were far from pleasant then to those into whose homes death had entered in hot weather. In winter natural cold was depended upon, the body being placed in the coldest place possible. With the best of care the results were uncertain and far from satisfactory. Modern embalming has changed all this. Its results are with rare exceptions certain and satisfactory and the embalmed body may be dressed and placed in a warm and comfortable room.

CHAPTER X.

MODES, SIGNS AND TESTS OF DEATH.

Just as surely as we are born, just so surely must we die, and just as it is the physician's duty to care for the living body, if possible to keep it in a strong and healthful condition, so it is the embalmer's duty to care for the body after death, not so much for the body itself, but from a sanitary standpoint, namely, to see that the body is well disinfected and embalmed so that there will be absolutely no chance for the spread of disease.

Any one who is familiar with hospital work must know that all do not die in the same way. For some it is the long lingering disease, chronic in form, which after a long and tedious course the thread of life is finally broken, and we hardly know the instant at which the change was completed. For others, it is the short, acute attack, which snaps the life away in a very instant, only after a very short duration. For some it is to die from accidental causes, while for others it is only the passing out from the period of old age. For some the mind may be active and the intellectual faculties useful up to the last moment, while for others the contrary is all but too true.

Although there may be many different kinds of disease infecting the human race, yet we find that death ultimately results from the stoppage of any one, or maybe, all three of the vital organs, namely the heart, brain or lungs. Anything whatsoever which plays upon the body, to such an extent, as to affect the functions absolutely, of either the heart, brain or lungs, will result in the death of that body. And since these organs are of such vital importance to us, and since the stoppage of any one of them will result in death, they have been termed the vital organs.

MODES OF DEATH.

—There are, then, only three modes of death: syncope, or the stoppage of the heart; coma, or the failure of the brain to perform its functions; apnea, or the stoppage of the lungs.

Syncope.—For the heart to properly perform its function, namely that of propelling the blood to all parts of the body, it must first be properly nourished itself. If for any reason the heart does not get this proper nourishment, say the coronary arteries should become clogged, or a fatty infiltration, or a lack of red blood corpuscles, we would have a condition in the body known as anemia.

The heart must also have a proper nerve supply from the brain, and if because of any disease, the vaso-motor or the vaso-constrictor fibers should become affected, the heart would cease to contract and expand, and hence the complete stoppage of the heart. A condition of this kind is known as asthenia.

But whether it is death by anemia or asthenia, the state of suspended animation, common to both these forms is expressed by the single term—syncope.

Coma.—In cases of apoplexy, where we have the blood escaping from the ruptured vessels, compressing the brain, we find death ensuing. Also in accidental cases such as fracture of the skull, the injury will often cause death. These are examples of coma, and can be explained in this way, viz.; the power of the brain becomes inactive either through the result of an injury or a disease, and when this inactivity occurs the respiratory apparatus subsides and the heart deprived of its normal stimulus through the vaso-motor and constrictor fibers, soon ceases to beat, and death is the result.

Apnea, Asphyxia.—If for any reason the supply of oxygen is cut off from the lungs, we will have the body dying the result of asphyxia or apnea. The most common forms found of this mode of death are those of hanging, drowning or coal gas poisoning.

SIGNS OF IMPENDING DEATH.

—The signs of impending death are those conditions which exist on the body or the peculiar features of the body which aid the physician in ascertaining the exact condition of the body. These signs assume many different forms and in no two instances may they be found alike. They of course, are not positive in themselves, but are sufficient to guide us in forming an opinion as to the approach of death.

One of the first signs to be noticed is the coldness of the extremities. In this case the coldness begins at the extreme tips of the fingers and toes and gradually extends toward the trunk. This, of course, is due to the gradual diminishing activity of the heart to propel the blood to the extremities.

The brain also fails to receive its proper blood supply and becomes weakened and we find the mind wandering. This wandering results in the patient going through movements representing the playing with flowers, or picking at the bed clothing. A further result of this weakness is that the patient may have visions of angels and heaven.

Speech begins to grow thick, and a large lump of phlegm gathers in the throat.

The hands now feel cold and clammy, and if they are raised they instantly fall. One cannot detect the act of respiration, as the movements of the thoracic walls are so slight as to be scarcely perceptible.

The heart loses its power to propel the blood and the stoppage of every organ in the body ensues.

The eyes become fixed with a staring look as though they were not focused on anything directly. The eyes lose their lustre on account of the lachrymal glands refusing to secrete.

The vital organs, the heart, brain and lungs come to a halt, and we find the body passing from life to the great beyond.

TESTS OF ACTUAL DEATH.

—From the large number of statistics that have been gathered together for our purpose, we find that the time of greatest mortality is in the early morning hours between three and six A. M., for it is between these hours that the body is in a perfect state of relaxation, and at the lowest ebb of vitality.

The time of least mortality is between the hours of eleven and two P. M., as the body is in a relatively high state of vitality during these hours.

The tests of actual death can be placed in two classes, the common tests and the expert tests.

The common tests are those that have long been used by the inexperienced to ascertain the fact of death. They are not necessarily conclusive in themselves, but when all are taken together there can not be much doubt.

(a) *The Feather Test.*—In this test a feather is held to the nostrils to observe whether it moves. The feather being so light, the slightest respiration of the lung would be apt to move it.

(b) *The Mirror Test.*—In this test a mirror is held to the mouth and nostrils. If moisture collects on the mirror it is evident that respiratory movements are going on. If there is an absence of moisture we are quite safe in saying that the patient is dead.

(c) *The Bandage Test.*—In this test a bandage is placed around the arm and then twisted very tightly. If there is the slightest circulation existing in the body the blood will accumulate back of the bandage in the venous system and thus demonstrate the fact. There will also be no swelling or discoloration beyond the ligature.

(d) By placing the ear to the chest over the heart, no sounds will be heard.

(e) If the ear is applied over the lungs, no sounds will be heard.

(f) If a cup of water is placed on the chest there will be no movement of rays or ripples on the surface.

(g) If the skin is cut, no blood will flow, nor will the wound close.

(h) If heat, say for instance a burning match be applied to the skin it will not blister, or if ammonia is hypodermically injected under the skin there will be no redness, but rather the skin will turn to a yellowish color.

(i) The living hand when held to the light shows pink through the inner edges of the fingers, but with the dead hand it shows opaqueness.

(j) When a strong light is brought before the eye the pupil of the eye will not dilate or contract.

(2) The expert tests are those which a doctor or coroner might use to ascertain the fact of death. These tests are made with the stethoscope and the ophthalmoscope.

(a) By the use of the stethoscope the physician can hear the sounds of the heart and if there is the slightest sound he can detect it. In the absence of any sound the body is pronounced dead.

(b) By the use of the ophthalmoscope the physician is enabled to look into the pupil of the eye and if there is life he can see the blood circulating through the tiny capillaries of the retina. If he does not see this capillary circulation he is quite safe in saying the body is dead.

(c) Another method consists in the hypodermic or intravenous injection of certain substances, and ascertaining whether these substances have been dispersed throughout the body. If they have, then a circulation exists and life continues, although the pulsation of the heart may not be detected by auscultation. Among the substances recommended for injection are fluorescin, sodium iodide, lithium iodide and potassium ferro-cyanide. The injection of the small quantities as used will not cause death should the patient still be living.

Fluorescin is usually injected, one gramme dissolved with an equal weight of sodium carbonate in eight cubic centimeters of water, and the whole quantity injected hypodermically. If the circulation is persisting, the skin and the mucous membranes after a very few minutes assume a greenish color; about twenty minutes after the injection, the portion of the eye within the iris assumes a green color from penetration of the fluorescin into the vitreous and aqueous humors, and in the blood the fluorescin may be detected by the following method: One or two threads of cotton are passed under the skin in the form of a seton, and when saturated with blood are transferred to a test tube, and boiled with a little water. As the liquid clears the green color of the fluorescin becomes evident, if that substance has been absorbed into the blood.

(d) Another method for the distinction of real from apparent death consists in picking up a fold of the skin and compressing it with a pair of artery forceps. If the skin does not completely settle down, and if the fine furrows produced by the teeth of the forceps continue indefinitely, then death has occurred. Whereas, if the circulation is continuous, the fold and the marks of the forceps would disappear. Moreover, if death has occurred the portion of the skin compressed by the forceps assumes a parchment-like appearance.

(e) The electrical current affords a means of determining death. It is now known that the muscles, after cadaveric rigidity has set in, do not respond to electric stimuli. The faradic current will cause, when death has occurred, muscular contractions until a short time before post-mortem rigidity occurs. The faradic stimulus is lost first and the galvanic stimulus soon after. We may be enabled to approximate the time at which death occurred, for, if we find any response to either the faradic or the galvanic current, we know at once that post-mortem rigidity has not yet occurred.

No person should be buried as long as the muscles contract when stimulated by either the faradic or the galvanic current. If the electrical test were always applied before a death certificate was signed, there would be absolutely no possibility of a person being buried alive and the public would soon lose the morbid fear of such an occurrence.

LATER AND MORE POSITIVE SIGNS.

—(a) After a few hours the blood gradually sinks to the dependent parts of the body giving a reddish-blue discoloration, known as post-mortem discoloration, or cadaveric lividity.

(b) The eyes become sunken in the sockets, the eye balls become flattened, the cornea opaque and the pupil irregular in shape.

(c) The eyelid loses its elasticity, and the white transparent color of the conjunctiva is lost, often becoming black or gray.

(d) Rigor mortis may or may not be present.

(e) The body gradually cools to the temperature of the surrounding atmosphere.

(f) On opening an artery it is generally found to be empty after death.

(g) The latest and most positive sign of all is putrefaction, and when this is found to be present all other signs may be ignored.

(h) Skin slip present on the body is only another manifestation of putrefaction, and also signifies that the body is dead.

CHAPTER XI.

PREMATURE BURIAL.

PREMATURE BURIAL.

—In this enlightened age, with our knowledge of respiration and the circulation of the blood, with our complete mastery of the phenomena of death with scientific tests, it is absolutely impossible to have such a thing as a premature burial.

Nevertheless from the earliest times the fear of premature burial has been felt by many, and curious and strange methods have been adopted to prevent the possibility of individuals being consigned to their graves before life was extinct.

Tradition records many cases where, in spite of their precautions, such unfortunate actions have happened. It may be that tradition is an uncertain and erring guide. And yet underlying all tradition, as Dieulafoy said, is a solid substratum of truth which the thoughtful investigator must take into consideration. The tale of the Cologne goldsmith's wife, that survives in the legend of the neighing horses, may be weird, bizarre, and from a scientific point of view, demonstratively ludicrous, but its germ is to be found in the recorded fact that in times of epidemics, when the dying were huddled away with the dead, mistakes did occur, and one or two were rectified by the resurrection of the "dead." In cases where burial took place in commodious family vaults, the changes in the position of the coffin, produced by atmospheric and other physical factors and were startlingly disclosed when the vaults were opened to receive new bodies, doubtless gave an impetus to the belief in the comparative frequency of such mistakes. The medical man remembers that on occasions he has found it difficult, without applying some of the common and finer tests, to certify death in a patient dying of a lingering disease, but his knowledge forbids him believing that such difficulties as he may have experienced in his own practice can ever have caused his fellow practitioner to make so grievous a mistake in a similar case. The public has no such knowledge; it relies on the exceptional cases and glibly credits the statement—true enough in a limited sense that there is no certain proof of death. While it is certainly true that no single sign can be absolutely relied upon to prove that life is extinct, all practitioners will agree that several signs taken in combination and methodically applied are sufficiently accurate to obviate the possibility of mistake. Much has been made of the cataleptic condition and the probability of mistaking it for death, which has formed the basis of one of Poe's narratives. As a matter of fact, catalepsy, of such a nature as to be confounded with *tota exitus*, is extremely rare—so rare that we doubt if any practitioner with a large experience of nervous conditions has met with more than one or two instances. Further, even in such extremely rare conditions, the usual tests are applicable and to the trained medical man at least clearly prove the nature of the case. The stethoscope and the mirror held in front of the patient's mouth are usually sufficient to demonstrate that the patient is alive and we should want more conclusive evidence than such as has been brought forward up to the present, to feel that cataleptic patients have been consigned to their coffins before life was totally extinct.

Newspaper writers delight in the fictitious and marvelous, and without any regard whatever to the scientific phase of the subject, frequent mention of cases of premature burial is to be found almost daily in the press of the country. But upon investigating these newspaper stories, it will be found that they have been either originated in the fertile brain of some reporter or were merely published to consume space.

·CHAPTER XII.

THE CHANGES IN THE BODY AFTER DEATH.

COOLING OF THE BODY.

—The internal temperature of the healthy living being is about 37 degrees centigrade. But it may be increased several degrees in consequence of disease. After death the chemical changes upon which the maintenance of this temperature depends rapidly diminishes, and the body gradually cools to the temperature of the surrounding atmosphere. This usually occurs in from about fifteen to twenty hours, but the time required depends upon a variety of conditions. Immediately after death there is, in nearly all cases, a slight elevation of internal temperature, owing to the fact that the metabolic changes in the tissues still continue for a time, while the blood ceases to be cooled by passing through the lungs and peripheral capillaries. After death from certain diseases yellow fever, cholera, rheumatic fever, and tetanus, a considerable elevation of internal temperature has been repeatedly observed.

The time occupied by the cooling of the body may be prolonged after sudden death from accidents, acute diseases, apoplexy, and asphyxia. A number of cases is reported in which the body retained its heat for several days without known cause.

After death from wasting chronic diseases, and in some cases after severe hemorrhage, the cooling of the body is very rapid, the internal temperature being reduced to that of the surrounding air within four or five hours.

Fat bodies cool less quickly than lean ones, the bodies of well nourished adults less quickly than those of children or old persons. The temperature of the surrounding atmosphere, the degree of protection of the body from currents of air, of course, modify the progress of cooling; and the internal organs naturally retain their heat longer than the surface of the body. The rate at which cooling occurs is most rapid as a rule, during the hours immediately following death, notwithstanding the postmortem rise which may ensue.

CADAVERIC LIVIDITY.

—This means the black and blue discoloration from the effects of the congestion or contusion of the blood.

After life becomes extinct, and before the blood coagulates, it changes its position chiefly in two ways: First, it is driven by their contraction out of the arteries and into the veins; second, it settles in the veins and the capillaries of the more dependent parts of the body, inducing, usually within a few hours after death, a mottling of the surface with irregular livid patches. These patches may coalesce, forming a uniform dusky red color over the back of the trunk, head and extremities, and sometimes over the ears, face and neck. The same effect is noticed on the anterior aspect of the body if it has lain on the face. At points of pressure, from the folds in the clothing, and from the weight of the body on the bed or the cooling board, the red color is absent or less marked. This to the undertaker and the embalmer is known as postmortem discoloration. These changes occur before putrefaction sets in. This cadaveric lividity should not be mistaken for the antemortem ecchymoses from which it may usually be distinguished by its position and extent by the fact that the surface of the skin is not elevated, and by the fact that on incision no blood is found free in the interstices of the tissues. Not infrequently the subcutaneous tissue in the neighborhood of these postmortem discolorations become infiltrated with a reddish serum. Very soon after death, particularly in warm weather, the tissues immediately around the subcutaneous veins of the neck and the thorax and in other situations, may become stained a bluish red color from the decomposition and escape from the vessels of the coloring matter of the blood. This to the undertaker and the embalmer is known as postmortem discoloration.

PUTREFACTIVE CHANGES.

—As soon as the body dies, it becomes as any other inanimate object, subject to putrefaction and decay.

The tissues of the body undergo various changes as to consistency of the solids, semi-solids, fluids, and as to color.

Putrefactive changes are caused by the presence of putrefactive germs normally present in the tissues or gaining access to them, which in their effort to satisfy their own nutrition, break down those complex molecules of which the tissues are composed into simpler compounds.

Putrefaction then is organic decomposition or decay the result of putrefactive bacteria. Putrefaction may also be defined as the separating of the constituent elements of the body due to the presence and growth of bacteria.

Although septic changes may take place before the death of a body, yet the term putrefaction is not applied until after the death of a body, and denotes those changes in color, consistence, and smell so clearly perceptible.

Usually in from one to three days, depending upon circumstances, a greenish discoloration of the skin occurs at first upon the middle of the abdomen, over which it gradually spreads, assuming a deeper hue, and often changing to greenish purple or brown. Greenish patches may now appear on the different parts of the body, earliest upon those overlying the internal cavities; this discoloration is probably produced by the action on the haemoglobin of gases developed by decomposition.

The eyeballs now become placid and if the eyelids are not closed the conjunctiva and cornea become brown and dry. The pressure of gases developed by decomposition in the internal cavities not infrequently forces a greater or less quantity of frothy, reddish fluid or mucous from the mouth and nostrils, distends the abdomen, and, if excessive, may lead to changes in the position of the blood in the vessels and even a moderate amount of displacement of the internal organs.

After five or six days, under ordinary circumstances, the entire surface is discolored to a green or a brown. After this the epidermis becomes loosened through the formation of gases and separating of fluids beneath, and the tissues become flaccid.

The abdomen and the thorax may be greatly distended, and the features distorted and scarcely recognizable from swelling, and the hair and nails loosened.

On the interior of the body, those soft and less compact tissues, or those tissues in which there is a great amount of fluid, are the first to decompose. This may be noticed by examining the walls of the trachea, esophagus and the intestines and noting the change in color.

Decomposition of the soft and liquid portions of the body take place almost immediately after the death of the body, and then follow in rapid succession the decomposition of the semi-solids and finally the solids. Beyond this stage of putrefaction, the consecutive changes can scarcely be followed with accuracy.

The putrefactive changes can not be said to begin at the same place in all bodies, as the conditions under which death occurred will regulate that. The rapidity with which these changes follow one another depends upon a variety of conditions such as temperature, moisture, access of air and the diseases which have preceded or caused death.

Various temperature relations will effect greatly the more or less rapid decomposition of the body. Bodies dying in mid-summer are decomposed much more quickly than those dying in mid-winter.

Moisture added to the temperature relation will hasten the rapidity of the decomposition as can be noticed in those localities with a high temperature but moist climate that the decomposition takes place very quickly. In those climates with high temperature, but dry or absence of moisture, the tendency is to dry up the tissues, and instead of putrefaction we have mummification as the result. This last statement then serves to explain the reason for the high state of preservation in the forms of mummification as exists in those countries like Egypt with their extremely hot and dry climates.

Exposure added to the temperature and the moisture relations adds greatly to the rapidity of the decomposition. A moist climate with a hot temperature and free exposure favors rapid decomposition. We notice that putrefaction progresses much more rapidly in the air than in the water and in the earth its progress is slower than in the water. The more exposed a body is then, to the elements, especially the air, the more rapid will be the decomposition.

An elevated temperature and the presence of air and moisture hasten the advent and progress of putrefactive changes.

Bodies dying in high fever and edematous subjects are much more quickly decomposed than those dying with the ordinary wasting away disease.

The bodies of infants usually decompose more rapidly than those of adults, fat bodies more rapidly than lean ones.

The infectious diseases, intemperance, and the puerperal condition promote rapid decomposition as also does death from suffocation.

Poisoning from arsenic, alcohol, antimony, sulphuric acid, strychnine and chloroform may retard the progress of decay.

It is impossible, then, to say how long a body will keep without the use of preservatives, as it depends partly upon temperature, partly upon moisture, partly upon the amount of exposure and partly upon the conditions existing in the body before death.

We can easily understand the reason for all this if we understand the bacteriology relating to the subject.

In the first place, bacteria require for their best and most rapid growth the proper temperature, moisture and media relations. By this we mean that the temperature should be moderately warm, ranging from about forty to one hundred degrees Fahrenheit, the optimum being about the body temperature 98.6 degrees Fahrenheit or 37 degrees on the centigrade scale. With this optimum temperature, the element of moisture should always be present, as we find that nothing in nature will germinate without the necessary moisture. Then the bacteria must have the proper media, meaning that they must have the right substance on which to grow. Inasmuch as the cause of putrefaction is the host of putrefactive bacteria which abound trying to satisfy their own nutrition, and since these bacteria require a moderately warm and moist media on which to grow, it is only natural that putrefaction and decomposition should occur much more rapidly in warm moist climates than in dry cold climates.

In regard to exposure we learn that certain putrefactive bacteria are aerobic in character, i. e., that they need a great quantity of oxygen for their growth, and for this reason a body in water or buried in the earth does not decompose as rapidly as one exposed to the air. But although they do not decompose as rapidly yet we find that they do decompose in time. This is due to the fact that there is another class of bacteria, called anaerobic, i. e., which do not need oxygen for their growth. In the case of the body in water these anaerobic bacteria exist and develope slowly in the alimentary tract, and eliminate gases sufficient to bring the body to the surface, where the aerobic bacteria enter, and putrefaction progresses much more rapidly.

The starting point of decomposition is usually at the seat of the disease the subject had before death, but it soon spreads to all the various tissues of the body.

Putrefaction is always accompanied by a great amount of odor, which is caused by the generation of gases the result of bacterial action. The obnoxious gases, offensive to the smell are sulphureted hydrogen, nitrogen, carbonic acid and ammonia.

The material actually present when the body is actually decomposed has been determined as being water, nitrogen, methane, carbon dioxide, etc.

Treatment by the Embalmer.—Putrefaction always means that there is present a great amount of putrefactive bacteria and if you are to arrest this condition you must resort to the most thorough embalming. By placing some preservative fluid in the arteries and having a thorough circulation all the tissues of the body can be reached and hence the complete destruction of those bacteria causing the putrefaction.

If all the tissues are properly bathed with embalming fluid there need be no further danger of putrefaction; but what seems sometimes at first a thorough circulation, proves afterward to be only a partial one. If after several days the body still shows signs of decomposition it is best to reinject or if the decomposition only occurs in spots a simple hypodermic injection will prove adequate.

SKIN SLIP.

—To properly understand the causes of skin slip a thorough knowledge of the structure of the skin is necessary. It would be best then to turn to the chapter on the tissues of the body and study the minute structure of the skin.

Skin slip is caused by a putrefactive softening of the epidermis. There is a watery infiltration from the minute capillaries and the surrounding tissues between the dermis and the epidermis, causing the latter to loosen and if touched to slip and tear away from the dermis or true skin.

Many embalmers have been led to believe that the slipping of the skin is due to the use of certain fluids used in injecting the arterial system. This error should be corrected, as it is most generally the absence of the fluid from the part which results in the slipping of the skin.

Diseases of the heart, liver, kidney and dropsical conditions predispose to the early skin slip. The immense amount of water occurring in the minute capillaries of the skin prohibits the embalming fluid from reaching the tissues.

Skin slip then is due to putrefactive changes occurring in the skin, and if it should occur after embalming, it is positive proof that the part or parts have not received a sufficient quantity of a preservative fluid.

Treatment by the Embalmer.—In the average case you will never see skin slip, because you will be called comparatively soon after death has occurred and the body will be embalmed and buried before this later form of putrefaction will manifest itself. But in some few cases you will have to keep the body for a greater length of time, say to await the arrival of some friend living abroad, or it may be a coroner's case. In cases like this the body being kept for a period of weeks, will if it is not perfectly embalmed show signs of skin slip. As has been stated above, cases that die from diseases causing dropsical infiltration in the subcutaneous tissues should also be handled carefully. If you are aware before hand that you are to keep the body for a great length of time or that you have a dropsical subject, a little formaldehyde should be added to the fluid that is injected, about two or three ounces to each quart of fluid. Zinc compounds might be added, but formaldehyde is better because of its great affinity for water.

If skin slip occurs after the body is embalmed it is best to place a layer of cotton over the part where the skin slip occurs and saturate the cotton with equal parts of alcohol, formaldehyde and glycerine.

In drowned cases where all the skin is slipping it is best to envelope the whole body with a layer of cotton saturated with formaldehyde.

RIGOR MORTIS.

—Rigor mortis is the stiffening condition which occurs on the body after death.

When the muscle substance dies it becomes rigid, or goes into a condition of rigor; it passes from a fluid to a solid state. The rigor that appears in the muscles after somatic death is designated usually as rigor mortis, since its occurrence explains the death stiffening in the cadaver. It is characterized by several features: the muscles become rigid, they shorten, they develope an acid reaction, and they lose their irritability to stimuli.

After the death of an individual the muscles enter into rigor mortis at different times. Usually there is a certain sequence, the order given being the jaws, neck, trunk, upper limbs, lower limbs, the rigor, therefore, taking a downward course. The actual time of the appearance of the rigidity varies greatly, however; it may come on within a few minutes or a number of hours may elapse before it can be detected.

Death after great muscular exertion, as in the case of hunted animals, or soldiers killed in battle, is usually followed quickly by muscle rigor. Death after wasting diseases is also followed by an early rigor, which in this case is of a more feeble character and shorter duration.

Certain drugs such as veratrum, hydrocyanic acid, caffeine and chloroform, will hasten the development of rigor.

People who die in full habit, meaning that there has been no muscular exertion or wasting processes before death, usually have the rigor developing more slowly and of a longer duration.

After a certain interval, which also varies greatly, from one to six days, the rigidity passes off, the muscles become soft and flexible; this phenomenon is known as the release of the rigor.

The usual explanation that is given of rigor is that it is due to a coagulation of the fluid substance, the muscle plasma, of which the fibers are constituted. During life the fluids exist in a liquid or viscous condition; after death they coagulate into a solid form.

Rigor mortis is not a sign of death, as there is rigidity of the muscles following apparent death, as in cases of asphyxia and trance. If the body is rigid, in a case in which there is a doubt that death is present the rigidity may be broken up. If it is a case of trance or that of the contraction of the muscles following drowning, it is likely to return, especially in case of trance; but if death is actually present it will not return.

The chemical changes occurring, the result of rigor mortis can be briefly stated:

(a) There is a coagulation of the proteid material of the muscle plasma.

(b) There is an increased acidity, which is doubtless due to the production of lactic acid.

(c) There is a production of carbon dioxide.

(d) There is a consumption of glycogen.

Treatment by the Embalmer. — Many times when called to embalm a subject you will find the body in a state of rigor. In cases of this kind the rigor mortis should be broken up. This can be done by taking each of the joints and gradually bend them a little at a time until they become perfectly lax. Once a joint is bent the stiffening disappears and the embalmer can proceed.

FERMENTATION AND THE PRODUCTION OF GAS.

— A molecule is the smallest portion of a compound which can exist by itself.

An atom is one of the ultimate particles composing a molecule. A complex molecule is one in which two or more elements have been combined. Example: water molecules are formed by two atoms of hydrogen and one atom of oxygen.

A ferment is a substance causing fermentation in other matter with which it comes in contact. There are two kinds of ferment expressed by the names organized and unorganized.

Unorganized ferments are chemical substances having the power to produce or assist in the production of fermentation.

Organized ferments are bacteria having the power to produce fermentation.

Fermentation means the process through which complex molecules are decomposed and their ingredients disassociated by the action of ferments. As an example of fermentation, we can take proteid food substances, the molecules of which are always of complex form, and by subjecting them to the action of organized ferments (bacteria), decompose them, and separate each gas ingredient, obtaining therefrom a variety of gases from what was formerly a substance of perfect chemical union. Fermentation is present in most of the natural processes whereby chemical changes are produced in animal and vegetable matter. Fermentation is taking place all the time in all the climes excepting possibly the frigid zones. The organized ferments (bacteria) are subject to the same temperature limits that govern the reproduction and the growth of all bacteria.

Fermentation is divided into spirituous fermentation, digestive fermentation, metabolic fermentation, and putrefactive fermentation.

SPIRITUOUS FERMENTATION.

— Spirituous fermentation is that process of fermentation by which forms of yeast cells, by their growth and reproduction in such complex substances as grapes, fruit, apple juice, grains, etc., extract alcohol from these substances and by this process produce wine, cider, spirits, etc. Many times in the dead body, spirituous fermentation occurs. Spirituous fermentation is caused by a vegetable parasite called yeast.

DIGESTIVE FERMENTATION.

—Digestive fermentation is that process by which digestion and nutrition in the living body is assisted through the action of ferments called enzymes, acting on the food substance. This process is mainly one where each food particle is split up by a particular ferment or enzyme. After death this process may continue for a certain length of time and result in the formation of gas. Digestive fermentation is mostly chemical.

Enzymes are unorganized ferments and are cast off the living body within the living body.

METABOLIC FERMENTATION.

—Metabolic fermentation is that process by which enzymes in the tissues of the living body destroy the dead cells, and reduce them to the following gases: nitrogen (N), carbon-dioxide (CO_2), ammonia (NH_3), uric acid, and other materials. In the living body these gases and other products are eliminated from the tissues, by the sudoriferous glands and ducts through perspiration, by the lungs with the expired air, by the intestines with the feces and by the kidneys with the urine. In the dead body the enzymes become active agents in tissue gas production, unless they are kept in restraint by being brought in contact with germicidal embalming fluids.

PUTREFACTIVE FERMENTATION.

—Putrefactive fermentation is the process by which undigested food substances (principally proteids), under the influence of ferment bacteria, yield gases. This change rarely takes place in the small intestines of the living body as the germs are held in restraint by lactic acid and acetic acid bacteria in those parts. There is little restraint to their activity in the large intestines, however, and the intestinal gases along with putrefactive changes in fecal material are a natural consequence.

Intestinal fermentation is hastened in the dead body by the presence of much undigested food and the absence of any restraining organisms. The gases produced in the intestines of either the living or dead body by the action of putrefactive ferment bacteria are: carbon-dioxide (CO_2), hydrogen (H), nitrogen (N) hydrogen sulphide (H_2S), methane (CH_4). The continued fermentation in the stomach and the intestines causes a coffee colored material of a frothy character to purge from the mouth.

When the hollow needle or trocar is used to reach the scene of ferment activity, the gases mentioned are released from the effected organs. As these gases are extremely odorous, they should be passed through a pledget of cotton saturated with formaldehyde, before being allowed to pass into the open air. Germicidal fluids when directed against the bacteria in an intelligent manner should destroy them and prevent their becoming active again.

Putrefactive fermentation is divided as follows: abdominal fermentation, gastric fermentation, and intestinal fermentation.

ABDOMINAL FERMENTATION.

—Abdominal fermentation is putrefactive fermentation as it effects the tissues and necrotic substances of the abdominal cavity itself (excepting the digestive organs), caused by the action of zymogenic bacteria. Perforations of the intestines or appendix, inflammation of the mesentery or peritoneum, may allow putrid material to escape into the cavity proper, where bacterial action will produce noxious gases. You will recognize a condition of this kind by the following illustration: As soon as the point of the trocar has penetrated the peritoneum and the rod has been withdrawn, there will be an escape of gas. This escape is due to the internal pressure being greater than the atmosphere pressure. This explains the swollen condition of the abdominal wall and its subsequent relaxation as the gas is allowed to escape.

Certain diseases predispose to abdominal fermentation as inflammatory diseases which effect the peritoneal covering of the organs, and cause a swollen abdominal wall after death.

Treatment.—In the treatment of these cases it is always advisable that the operator be familiar with the location of the disease, so that direct trocar application can be made to the affected part. The location of the affected part is not always the same, as it varies with the location of the particular tissue or organ affected. In appendicitis, where death has occurred without surgical attempts to remove the appendix, the operator should spray the right inguinal space with enough fluid to neutralize the cause of the gas. Where the cause of death has been typhoid, the umbilical, hypogastric and epigastric spaces should be sprayed. Where the cause of death is puerperal fever, the right and left inguinal and hypogastric spaces should be sprayed. The gas itself, will be eliminated from the cavity of the body by simply inserting the trocar and allowing the gas to escape until the internal pressure approximates that of the atmospheric pressure. This though does not prevent the reformation of gas, as the origin of the gas is the living and growing fermentative and putrefactive bacteria. To prevent a recurrence the bacteria must be killed, and this is done by spraying a germicidal fluid around the affected part. Abdominal fermentation and gas is much easier to treat than gastric or intestinal fermentation.

GASTRIC FERMENTATION.

—This is recognized by a frothy coffee colored purge from the mouth or nose caused by pressure in the stomach, due to putrefactive bacteria, and their action on proteid food substances which are present in the stomach. Where the cause of death has been principally from inflammatory processes, or where the deceased has died shortly after eating a full meal, this condition must be looked forward to. The swollen condition directly over the stomach is another visible sign of value in diagnosing the condition.

Treatment.—When the body is placed in your care, the embalmer should make a careful and thoughtful survey of the condition of the body and the cause of death. Any inflammatory disease of the abdominal tissues or a full meal eaten shortly before death will almost always predispose to the formation of gas. The treatment would be to take proper care of the stomach contents.

(a) Insert the trocar at a point two inches to the left of the median line, half the distance from the ensiform cartilage and the umbilicus. Direct the trocar downward and diagonally to the left to a depth of three to four inches. Remove the trocar rod and allow the gas to escape into a fluid bottle, containing a small amount of fluid, so that the gas may be deodorized. Before removing the trocar, inject not less than one pint of normal fluid into the stomach, so that the fermentable materials and the bacteria may be destroyed.

(b) Make an incision in the median line of the body, three inches long, from the tip of the ensiform cartilage downward toward the umbilicus, and proceed as directed for the direct incision described on page 257.

The treatment for gastric fermentation demands the specific treatment as directed above. No short treatments can be depended upon for certain results. Cotton placed in the mouth only delays the time for the purging to begin from the mouth. Gastric fermentation can be prevented in all cases by the use of the specific treatments as described in (a) and (b).

If in your practice, you receive a body from a shipping undertaker, which unfortunately was not treated in the correct manner, and which is purging from the mouth, arrange to puncture the stomach in the manner described in treatment (a). This can be done without disturbing the position of the body in the casket, by opening the clothes above the stomach. After puncturing the stomach and allowing the gas to escape, inject not less than one pint of fluid therein, cleanse the mouth with absorbent cotton by the use of the lock forceps and a recurrence of the purge will not be possible.

If in your practice you have overlooked the possibility of gastric fermentation, and find, either by advice from the family or from your own observation, that purging is going on, use either the treatment (a) or (b), neutralize the fermentable material, cleanse the mouth and no recurrence will be possible.

INTESTINAL FERMENTATION.

—Here we have the fermenting gases in the intestines and the colons. The pressure of the gases will bear upon the stomach and there may or may not be purging from the mouth depending upon the fact of presence or non presence of material in the stomach. The abdomen though will be greatly distended, and when palpated will give a drummy note.

Treatment.—(a) Insert the trocar through the umbilicus, and direct the point downward into the right inguinal region so as to relieve the gases from the caecum, then inject a small quantity of fluid; then direct the point of the trocar upward into the left inguinal region so as to relieve gases from the sigmoid flexure, and inject a small quantity of fluid; then direct the point of the trocar upward into the right hypogastric region so as to relieve gases from the hepatic flexure, and inject a small quantity of fluid; then direct the point of the trocar upward into the left hypogastric region so as to remove gases from the splenic flexure, and inject a small quantity of fluid; and if at this time it is thought that the stomach contains gas, relieve it, and inject therein a small quantity of fluid; now place some fluid directly into the abdomen around the small intestine and with this treatment you are assured that your intestinal fermentation is taken care of.

(b) Intestinal fermentation may also be treated by the direct incision, as described on page 257.

CHAPTER XIII.
DISCOLORATIONS.

DISCOLORATIONS.

—Discolorations should be treated as a separate and independent subject because they are causes of great annoyance and embarrassment to the operator, and their treatment is of utmost importance. Just think of the possibility of having a body properly injected, and the preservation complete, and something along the line of a discoloration coming to the front and ruin the results of the work. If there is any condition possible in the dead body that can cause more trouble to the embalmer than discolorations in general, it has not as yet been discovered. You have only to realize what the appearance of a body would be in the casket, if any discolorations were present on an exposed surface, to know that too much can not be said on the subject.

Discolorations may not occur in conjunction with tissue changes, so when they do occur we should look for the cause of the same before deciding just what the name of the discoloration is, or what treatment should be given to eradicate it.

For convenience in study, and for the proper classification of the various conditions, the subject has been divided into those discolorations occurring before death, and those discolorations which may occur in the body after death.

DISCOLORATIONS OCCURRING BEFORE DEATH.

—Those discolorations occurring before death and which would remain on the body after death would be:

(a) Yellow jaundice,

(b) Pigmentary atrophy,

(c) Cancerous spots,

(d) Gangrene,

(e) Ecchymosis or ante-mortem staining,

(f) Wounds, fractures, scars and tattoo marks.

YELLOW JAUNDICE.

(a) **Yellow Jaundice.**—In the study of the liver you have heard that the liver secretes a digestive juice called the bile.

Bile acts as the natural antiseptic of the intestines in life, and aids with the digestion of fatty food substances along with other actions. The principal coloring matter of the bile is a yellow substance called bili-rubin. Biliverdin, green, is precipitated by alkalies.

The course of this bile in life is from the liver to the gall bladder, which acts as the reservoir, into the cystic duct and then into the common bile duct and into the cavity of the duodenum (first section of the small intestines). It sometimes happens that there may be an obstruction of the bile ducts with the result that the bile is backed up into the gall bladder, and from there into the liver again, throwing it into the blood vessels of the liver and out into the tissues of the body along with the blood. As the blood traverses the entire area of the body, and as the yellow coloring matter of the bile acts as a stain, it is only a matter of course that the tissues will be stained the characteristic color of the bile.

This stain will be found all over the body from the outer layer of the skin to the membrane covering the bone (the periosteum) and will adhere very closely to the tissues, rendering the removal practically impossible.

Ordinary arterial injection of a body of this character will have absolutely no effect, no matter what preservative fluid may be used and regardless of whatever any one may say, as it stands to reason that when the discoloration is not located in the blood vessels, that the removal of same can not be accomplished by flushing the blood vessels alone.

Of course, the washing of the blood vessels with a solution will aid the removal of the discoloration, but it is necessary to employ a strong bleaching solution on the outer surface of the exposed parts in order to better the conditions so that the body may be made presentable.

In addition to this treatment, it would be advisable to color the lights in the room in which the body is to be shown, so as to make every thing in the room about the same color of the body, including the persons viewing the remains. This will have the effect of lessening the apparent bad color of the body, and will add to your reputation as an embalmer.

PIGMENTARY ATROPHY.

(b) **Pigmentary Atrophy.**—Here is another instance of the work of bile pigments or coloring matters, in which not only the yellow, but the green colors are deposited in the tissue cells. In addition to this, the cells all over the body atrophy (contract or reduce in size). The contraction of the cells may be due to imperfect nutrition or perhaps anemia or some other action causing great emaciation of the body.

You will see very readily that the main point of difference between yellow jaundice and pigmentary atrophy is in the color, and also in the fact that the cells in yellow jaundice are in their normal state and in pigmentary atrophy are in a contracted condition. The treatment given for yellow jaundice as follows: injecting and washing the blood vessels with a mild solution and the application to the affected parts of a strong bleaching solution, should be given for pigmentary atrophy.

The suggestions as regarding the lights to show the body under, should also be noted and used in these cases.

CANCEROUS SPOTS.

(c) **Cancerous Spots.**—What is intended for this particular discoloration, is not the ordinary cancer that has eaten through the skin, but that form sometimes noted in aged persons where the cancer is just about to come through the skin. In other words, a yellowish brown color showing in any of the exposed parts of the skin before death.

As cancer is in fact a rottening or mortification of the tissues, the injection with a hypodermic outfit of a strong hardening and bleaching solution will harden and bleach out the color of the cancer to a great extent, and thus improve the appearance greatly, the ordinary cosmetic powders will finish the preparation.

For the hypodermic injection we would suggest the following:

> R Alum, 10 gr.
>
> Corrosive sublimate, 5 gr.
>
> Zinc chloride, 5 gr.
>
> Grain alcohol, 4 fluid oz.
>
> Formaldehyde, 2 fluid oz.

The cancerous spot should not be confounded with the color of dessication which will resemble it somewhat. The main point of difference would be that the cancer would be present before death, and the dessication could not possibly occur until after the body is embalmed. This caution is advised on account of the tendency the solution to be injected hypodermically would have to make a dried spot worse in color than better.

GANGRENE.

(d) **Gangrene.**—Gangrene can best be described as the death of certain areas of tissue of the living body. The death of the tissue may be brought about by very many causes; by vascular obstruction and arrest of the blood supply to a part, or of the outflow from a part; by enfeebled circulation; temporary stoppage of the circulation of a part or organ; acute infection; and by burns.

Gangrene with its peculiar color, a dark green, is not often found on the exposed surfaces of the body, but will more often be found on the lower extremities and then only on the bodies of aged persons. For this reason it will be unnecessary to treat it for the removal of color.

ECCHYMOSIS, OR ANTEMORTEM STAINING.

(e) **Ecchymosis, or Antemortem Staining.**—Ecchymosis is an extravasation of blood into the areolar tissues, forming a bruised place caused principally by a blow from a heavy instrument or missile.

This form of discoloration is mostly seen in accident cases, where death was due to mechanical causes.

In ecchymosis the blood capillaries being ruptured, the blood permeates the bruised tissues surrounding the ruptured vessels and thus gives the characteristic color of venous blood. There seems to be no positive treatment, but in some cases it can be remedied to some degree by a hypodermic injection of a good bleacher, and then massaging the part with a strong bleaching solution. Spots of this kind can sometimes be covered with flesh tints.

It is often important to determine whether violence has been inflicted on a body before death. In regard to this point, we must remember, first, that blows and falls of sufficient violence to fracture bones and rupture the viscera may leave no marks on the skin, even though the person has survived for several days; and, second, that there are postmortem appearances which simulate antemortem bruises. A severe contusion during life may present, at first, no mark or only a general redness. After a short time the injured part becomes swollen and of a red color, this color may be succeeded by a dark blue, and this in turn fade into a greenish yellow or yellow; these later appearances are due to an escape of blood from the vessels and to a subsequent decomposition of the hemoglobin. If, therefore, we cut into such an ecchymosis after death, we find extravasated blood or the coloring matter of the blood, in the form of pigment granules, free in the tissues. Postmortem discolorations, on the other hand, although their external appearance may resemble that of antemortem ecchymosis, are not formed by an extravasation of blood, but by a circumscribed congestion of the vessels or by an escape of blood stained serum. If you cut into such discolorations, therefore, we find no blood outside the vessels. Care should be taken not to mistake the lesions of hemorrhagic infection for traumatic ecchymosis.

Blows on the skin of a body which has been dead for not more than two hours may produce true ecchymosis with extravasation of blood, such as can be distinguished with great difficulty or not at all from those formed during life. If putrefactive changes be present, the difficulty of distinguishing between antemortem and postmortem bruises is greatly enhanced.

Hanging and strangulation are attended with the formation of marks on the neck which are described in works on forensic medicine. These marks must not be confounded with the natural creases of the skin of the neck. Many adults during life have creases of the skin of the neck, one or more in number, running downward from the ear under the chin or encircling the neck. After death these creases may be much more evident than during life, and may be rendered more decided by the position of the head, or if the body be frozen. They usually persist until the skin putrefies.

WOUNDS.

(f) **Wounds.**—The embalmer should notice the situation, extent and the direction of a wound, the condition of the edges, and the surrounding tissues. If it be a deep, penetrating wound, its course and extent should be ascertained by careful dissection rather than by the use of a probe.

If the edges of a wound be inflamed and suppurating, or beginning to heal, it must have been inflicted some time before death. In a wound inflicted a short time before death the edges are usually everted; there may be more or less extravasation of blood into the surrounding tissues, and the vessels contain coagulated blood; but sometimes none of these changes occur. The chief characteristics of a wound inflicted after death are absence of a considerable amount of bleeding, non-retraction of edges, and the absence of extravasation of blood into the tissues. But a wound inflicted within two hours after death may resemble very closely one received during life. In general, unless a wound is old enough for the edges to present inflammatory changes, the embalmer must be very careful in asserting its antemortem or postmortem character.

FRACTURES.

(g) **Fractures.**—It may be important to determine whether a bone was fractured before or after death. This point can not always be decided. Fractures inflicted during life are, as a rule, attended with more extravasation of blood and evidences of reaction in the surrounding tissues; but fractures produced within a few hours after death may resemble these very closely. Usually a greater degree of force is necessary to fracture bones in the dead than in the living body.

SCARS AND TATTOO MARKS.

(h) **Scars and Tattoo Marks.**—The presence and character of these should be noted. Scars produced by any considerable loss of substance may become very much smaller and less conspicuous, but never entirely disappear. Slight and superficial wounds, however, leave marks which may not be permanent.

The discoloration produced by tattooing may, although it rarely does, disappear during life. The embalmer should not try to remove it.

CHAPTER XIV.

DISCOLORATIONS.—CONTINUED.

DISCOLORATIONS OCCURRING AFTER DEATH.

—Those discolorations occurring after death would be as follows:

(a) Desiccation.

(b) Greenish tinge of putrefaction.

(c) Chemical action.

(d) Postmortem discoloration.

(e) Postmortem staining.

(f) Capillary or venous congestion.

DESICCATION.

—This is a brownish color caused by the drying of the skin. Various conditions might cause this color of which a few are considered here:

Natural evaporation, the drying action of formaldehyde, freezing the skin, feverish conditions of the body before death, absence of a normal amount of moisture in the skin of the dead body.

Natural Evaporation.—The passage of moisture from the skin into a dry atmosphere reduces the normal amount of moisture in the skin, thereby producing an altered color. The extent of the moisture reduction governs the color produced. When evaporation begins, the skin loses its softness and becomes slightly yellow in color. As evaporation continues the skin becomes more hard and the color changes from yellow to brown. At this time nothing can be done to restore the original color as in the absence of the blood circulation, the pigment of the skin will not take up moisture, nor will moisture penetrate the skin itself.

Treatment.—The only treatment for a condition of this kind is necessarily a preventive one. While embalming a body, the operator should apply either water or one of the commercial face solutions to the skin of all the exposed portions of the body. If the condition within the skin is one in which there is a predisposition toward dryness, the face solution or the water by being present on the skin will reduce evaporation from the skin itself; in this way maintaining the natural degree of moisture. Should a hard, dry spot appear in the absence of any preventive treatment, the operator can only coat the spot with grease paint and thereby hide it.

The Drying Action of Formaldehyde.—Formaldehyde is derived from methyl spirits, which in itself has an active affinity for water. The amount of water ordinarily mixed in formalin in the compounding of a formaldehyde fluid is not sufficient to satisfy the appetite of the formaldehyde for more water. When a formaldehyde fluid comes in contact with moisture laden skin, there will be a movement of moisture from the skin toward the formaldehyde fluid, thereby reducing the degree of moisture in the skin and in that way causing it to become dry. When the skin becomes dry, it changes in color the same as in natural evaporation.

Treatment.—There are three conditions in the skin met by the operator. The first is where there is a predisposition toward dryness and this is where the skin does not contain a normal amount of moisture to begin with. In old age cases, tubercular, and anemic bodies, the ordinary embalming fluid should be diluted at least one half for the first part of the injection, thus reducing the appetite for moisture on the part of the fluid. In addition to this, water or a face solution should be used externally to prevent outward evaporation from further reducing the moisture in the skin. The fluid exhibits a tendency to draw water into the pores, thus maintaining to a large degree, the normal moisture percentage.

The second condition met with is one in which the skin contains a normal amount of moisture. In this case it would not be necessary to reduce the strength of the standard fluid at any time during the injection, but it is necessary to apply water or a face solution externally to limit outward evaporation and to provide a source whereby moisture could be drawn into the pores by the appetite of the formaldehyde, thus again maintaining the normal percentage of moisture in the skin.

The third condition is one in which the skin along with the balance of the body, will contain more than a normal percentage of moisture. This condition may be looked for in edematous or dropsical cases. The injection in these cases should be normal in strength unless the dropsy is very pronounced, when an overnormal injection can be given without reducing the moisture percentage in the skin below the normal point.

Should the above precautions not be used and the skin be dried through the appetite of formaldehyde for water, no treatment can be given which will restore the moisture to the skin. When moisture is drawn from the skin and the percentage is below normal, the skin will shrink and will draw tight against the bones and subcutaneous tissue. This frequently gives rise to the sharp nose and to the drawn appearance so common in those cases. Prevention is the only remedy.

Freezing the Skin.—When the body is subjected to a temperature of 32 degrees Fahrenheit, the moisture in the skin freezes, thereby removing it from its usual consideration, as the element that is responsible for the usual softness and flexibility of the skin.

In the cold months, bodies are sometimes left in cold rooms with the windows open. The embalmer did this in the past, thinking that subjecting the body to the influence of a cold atmosphere would simplify preservation.

From the standpoint of preservation alone, this theory is correct, but in accomplishing the above result the moisture of the skin may be frozen. The resulting color is light yellow. The texture of the skin is changed from soft to a slightly hardened condition.

Treatment.—Never allow the room temperature to approach the freezing point. Should the above treatment be disregarded, and the yellow color become present, have the room warmed, and the color will slowly disappear.

Feverish Conditions in the Body Before Death.—Fever is the name usually given to the rise of temperature that goes with inflammation. In severe inflammatory diseases, the tissues lose much of their moisture through the arrest of the saturating power of the blood stream and the disturbance of circulation. The skin contains a sub-normal amount of moisture when the embalmer reaches these cases, which may be further reduced by outward evaporation and the dehydrating power of the embalming fluid. Small brown spots resembling the fever blister in the living body may be present around the mouth.

Treatment.—Use half strength fluid for the first part of the injection, followed by normal fluid for the second, third and fourth parts. Apply water or a commercial skin or face solution while the injection is going on.

Absence of a Normal Amount of Moisture in the Skin of the Body.—The normal amount of moisture in the skin has been determined to be an amount equal to seventy-five per cent. of the weight of the skin. Any percentage less than seventy-five per cent. is considered subnormal. This condition can be expected in all fever cases, in anemics, and in old age.

Treatment.—When the skin appears rather dry, the injection of fluid should be half strength for the first and second parts, normal for the third and fourth. The skin of the exposed parts of the body should be dampened with an application of water or a commercial face or skin solution, while the injection is being made.

GREENISH TINGE OF PUTREFACTION.

—Putrefaction discolorations are those which are produced when putrefactive bacteria become active in the skin or subcutaneous tissue.

This discoloration appears generally about the second day, unless preservative fluids have been applied to prevent it. It first begins in the ileocaecal region or lower part of the abdomen. The skin covering these parts assumes a brownish color which shades to yellow, yellowish green, and finally a green color. This green discoloration will in a few days spread all over the surface of the body.

Among the putrefactive bacteria is the bacillus fluorescens, a chromogenic germ, which produces a greenish color when it becomes active in the tissues. One of the first external evidences of putrefaction is the production of a greenish color in the abdominal wall. This, of course, could not occur when embalming had been done with any degree of completeness. Should an insufficient circulation be encountered when embalming a body, the part which does not receive the fluid, being unprotected, may be affected by the color producing germ mentioned above. The most likely to be affected by an insufficient circulation will be located somewhere in the extremities of the circulation, that is to say, in the skin. We can place the affected part more definitely in the skin of the face, particularly the nose, which has a rather poor circulation. This condition will not make its presence known until three or four days after embalming has been done, making it almost entirely absent in bodies embalmed in ordinary practice. Should several days elapse between the time the body died and embalming, allowing the discoloration to appear, the following treatment would be advisable:

Treatment.—Inject a very small portion of the following solution just under the skin, using a hypodermic needle.

Alum	10 gr.
Corrosive Subl.	10 gr.
Zinc Chloride	5 gr.
Grain Alcohol	4 fl. oz.
Formaldehyde	2 fl. oz.

Just a small portion of the above solution is all that will be necessary, working it under the skin with the finger tip, so as to avoid destroying the features by swelling the tissues.

This treatment being a chemical one, it is necessarily slow in its action of bleaching the green color. Should haste be necessary, inject a very small quantity of embalming fluid to arrest the putrefactive process and then cover the spot with theatrical grease of the proper color to match the surrounding skin.

CHEMICAL ACTION.

—Chemical action is any discoloration of the skin or tissues of the body which may be caused by the action of opposing chemicals. There is only one known discoloration occurring in the body after death as a result of the presence of a chemical in the body, which, when coming in contact with formaldehyde, produces a discoloration. This particular discoloration, greenish in color, is the result of the work of the drug methylene blue in contact with formaldehyde.

Often, in cases of chronic malaria, or diseases of the liver, or again as a general antiseptic, methylene blue will be administered by the attending physician, and you should learn this fact beforehand, for if methylene blue has been administered it is advisable not to use a formaldehyde fluid. There is a chemical action set up between the formaldehyde and the methylene blue, which gives the tissues a greenish color, which is quite objectionable.

In this case you would use some fluid which does not contain formaldehyde, benzoate of soda, or borax, or peroxide solution should be used.

Another good formula to use is the following:

Rx

Carbolic acid	5 oz.

Borax	12	oz.
Glycerine	1	oz.
Water, sufficient to make	1	gall

or

Rx

Carbolic acid	5	oz.
Oxalic acid	12	oz.
Boracic acid	2	oz.
Water, sufficient to make	1	gall

POSTMORTEM DISCOLORATION.

—This is a general expression, and refers to any discoloration which might occur on the body after death.

What is usually meant, though, when this term is used is *the settling of the blood to the dependent parts of the body after death.* If the body is lying on the back, the blood will naturally gravitate toward the back, into the azygos system and cause a bluish discoloration, or the same condition will result, if the body is found lying on the face and stomach, in which case the discoloration will be in the face and the anterior chest and abdominal walls.

POSTMORTEM STAINING.

—This condition is caused by changes in the blood while in the veins. The blood becomes more fluid in character and the red blood corpuscles become granular and give off their oxygen which escapes through the walls of the veins and carrying with it the haemoglobin or coloring matter of the blood, stains the tissues over the superficial veins a purplish red color. This discoloration only appears on the ventral surface of the body and along the course of the large superficial veins. An excellent example of this discoloration is seen in the drowned subject where almost always all the superficial veins can be easily traced by this discoloration.

CAPILLARY OR VENOUS CONGESTION.

—This term includes those discolorations either caused by gas distension or by the unskillful injection of fluid into the vascular system. Gas forming in the abdominal or thoracic cavities will so press upon the heart as to empty it of its blood, which will be forced upwards into the large venous trunks of the head, neck and axilla. All embalmers are familiar with the flushed face which often appears when the arterial system has been injected in a too hasty manner. It causes the veins and capillaries of the face and neck to become congested the same as that caused by the formation of gases in the cavities.

CHAPTER XV.

ARTERIAL EMBALMING.

MAKING THE FIRST CALL.

—There are some pertinent points to consider regarding the procedure at the time the call is received. Many embalmers have some particular rules that govern their inquiries at this time. It is the consensus of opinion among professional men of all kinds that a rule is a good thing to have to cover any regular procedure. It matters not so much as to what the rule is, just so the necessary information can be acquired in a uniform manner, thus systematizing that part of the work and enabling the embalmer to properly prepare for the case at hand before leaving the establishment.

The habit of inquiring about the sex, and age of the person, as well as the cause of death, should be cultivated. The importance of knowing the sex of the person lies in the fact that in some communities different styles of door badges or decorations are more appropriate for one sex than for the other. When the ruling decoration is some form of fresh flowers, this should be ordered before the embalmer leaves for the house of mourning if possible, unless the call should be received at night or in the early hours of the morning, when this item is usually left until the earliest business hour. The age of the person also determines to a great extent the style of decoration which is to be used.

The cause of death is vitally necessary. In some cases, the ordinary contents of the embalmer's grip or hand bag are sufficient for the usual needs. In other cases, extra material of various kinds are necessary, for instance, the rubber floor covering for the carpet in dropsical cases; the sanitary clothes in eruptive contagious diseases; the fumigating outfit in the same diseases, (providing this duty is not performed by the health authorities); and other articles needed only in the treatment of special cases.

After obtaining the above information, examine your grip or hand bag to see that you have all the equipment needed to care for the case in the proper manner. This saves many cases for those who follow these rules, as they are enabled to have just what is needed, and prevents the slighting of a case for which there may be some excuse if the proper materials are not in the outfit. From a professional standpoint, it should be necessary for the embalmer to carry anything he may need, otherwise carelessness may dictate his procedure and disaster may result.

An ordinary case can be attended with the following material[1]:—

The couch embalming board.
The slumber robe, and face cover.
A rubber or oil cloth cover for the board.
A suit case grip, or hand bag.
Concentrated fluid (at least 4 bottles).
One or two empty 64-oz. bottles (for mixing fluid).
One bottle for blood drainage.
One injecting outfit (pump, tubes, etc.)

One blood drainage outfit.

One instrument wallet, containing:—

2 scalpels, 1 bone separator, 2 aneurism needles, 1 spool linen thread, 1 grooved director, 3 arterial tubes (assorted diameters), 1 bistoury, 1 lock forceps, 1 spring forceps, 1 artery forceps, 1 case needles, 1 6-inch child's trocar, 1 12 or 14-inch trocar, 1 chin rest, 1 hypodermic outfit, 1 roll absorbent cotton, 1 sponge, 1 box face powder, 1 nail file, 1 hair brush, 1 bottle bichloride of mercury tablets, 1 shaving outfit.

For special cases it would be well to have on hand the following articles:—

1 small can plaster of paris.

1 tube lip cement.

2 rubber bandages.

1 can hardening compound.

1 bottle Platt's chlorides or any other good deodorant.

1 outfit of formalin and permanganate of potash, or any other standard gaseous germicide preparation for fumigating.

1 small bottle of tincture of iodine as a preventive to infection should you cut yourself.

After the outfit has been found correct for the case at hand, place everything in the conveyance, and leave for the house. Upon arriving at the house, enter alone and meet the member or members of the family who have been delegated to talk to you. At this time it will be well to ascertain the position of the body, the wishes of the family in reference to where the body is to be placed after embalming and to where the body is to rest in the casket until the time of the funeral.

If you meet with any objection as to embalming, it will be well for you to consider the sanitary aspect of the case in speaking to those interested. In this case the sanitary aspect should always take precedence over the preservative aspect, since

[1] NOTE—Many embalmers get along, some way, with much less in their outfit than enumerated here. The authors believe that the embalmer should have all the material needed to properly carry out his work, and anything of necessity left from the outfit only reduces the efficiency of the embalmer, and leaves him, at times, without the proper assortment of material.

you can count on the assistance of the physicians in supporting embalming on that account. Should your wishes be overruled after you have presented the facts in the matter, it would be well for you to place the entire responsibility for the condition of the body upon the family, since without embalming you are unable to know the final condition of the body, and should not be held responsible for it regardless of what the condition may be in that case.

After this short talk with the family, return to your conveyance and carry your outfit to the room of death. Everything that you carry should be properly covered, as there is nothing quite as indecorous as the display of an embalming board without a cover. When you have placed the outfit in the room, call for everything that you will need from the family, which will include such things as a pail, warm water, soap, towels, etc. Do all of this before touching the body; and after securing all the necessary items, close the door, and do not open it again until the work has been completed.

Should unforeseen circumstances cause you to re-open the door, present yourself with a coat on, and never, under any circumstances, appear before any one in your shirt sleeves, as that is another indecorous procedure. After the preservation has been completed, dust a little face powder on the face and hands, to remove the moist, clammy appearance which may have been left on those parts. Place the undergarments on the body and then any other garments which may have been given to you by the family. Cover the body with the slumber robe, and then call in as many members of the family as may wish to view the body, asking them to criticize your work. Before calling in the family it would be well to put everything out of sight and not have any grips open.

If favorable comment is heard from the family, your work is done for the time being. If unfavorable comment is heard, ascertain the cause of the comment and do not leave the house until the proper appearance has been secured. If your work has been pleasing to the family, you can rest assured that the case is a success and that you have done your work well. When you are satisfied in your own mind that all is well with the body, make arrangements for the selection of the casket, and then retire from the house. If the door decoration has not been placed in position before you leave, you will place it in position yourself.

Some funeral directors set the time for the funeral during the first call, and some wait until later. The same for the other arrangements, such as newspaper notices, minister, singers, church or chapel services, number of conveyances, etc. Whatever method you choose to use in your community should be carried out systematically so that at no time, will anything be left undone to cause confusion at some inopportune time.

THE POSITION OF THE BODY ON THE EMBALMING BOARD.

—The position of the body on the embalming board is regulated by the adjustment of the movable head end of the board.

After much experience with various classes of bodies, we find that the adjustment mentioned is a very valuable aid in securing the best results both as to completeness of the circulation and amount of blood drained.

In anemic, tubercular, cancer of the stomach and exhaustion cases, together with other conditions resulting in emaciation, the head end of the board should be raised to the height that seems suitable for the position of the upper part of the body when placed in the casket during the injection of the first bottle of fluid. When the first bottle of fluid has been injected, lower the head end of the board until the entire board is level, and leave it in that position until you have completed the injection, when you will again raise the end of the board until the position of the body is just as it will be in the casket.

When pneumonia and other non-emaciated bodies are to be injected, with drainage, use the same procedure as is stated above for the emaciated bodies.

In dropsical cases, raise the head end of the board only for the first bottle of the injection; then for the second bottle, lower the head end to about half of its first height, and set the foot end of the board on some object that will raise it five and six inches. In this way you will have a slight elevation at both ends of the body, and drainage can better be obtained from the center of the circulation. When the operation is complete, lower the foot end again and raise the head end so that the body occupies the proper position for the casket.

These adjustments are practical methods of overcoming gravity handicaps in the distribution of the fluid, and of accelerating the amount of drainage obtainable by keeping the level of the drainage tube below the blood level in the body, thus accomplishing a universal distribution of fluid, and securing a greater quantity of undiluted blood from the vein.

It is very important to remember when you are through injecting the body that you are to place the body in the exact position on the cooling board which you want it to have in the casket. After a little time the body will become more or less rigid due to the action of the preservative fluid used, and will set in the position you have placed it which condition will be hard to change later.

SELECTION OF AN ARTERY.

—Great care should be taken in the selection of an artery. Never make a practice of using the same artery on all cases. Acquaint yourself with the location of them all, and on different occasions, as different conditions arise, use the artery most likely to give the best results for the condition in hand.

Convenience usually governs the operator as to the artery he is to use. If blood is to be removed it is best to raise one of the larger blood vessels, such as the carotid artery and the internal jugular vein, or the femoral artery and femoral vein, or the axillary artery and axillary vein. If it is desired to draw the maximum amount of blood, the femoral artery and vein should be selected, as they are more dependent, and control more of the blood, when the body is placed on an incline. A drainage tube sufficiently long to reach above Poupart's ligament as far as the common iliac is all that is necessary as there are no valves intervening between the bifurcation of the common iliac and the right auricle. However if you can, extend the tube up through the ascending vena cava and eustachian valve into the right auricle. This will give you a chance to draw blood from the right auricle and is a much better procedure than tapping the right auricle with the trocar.

If the body is already dressed and the hands or feet need to be re-injected, the radial or posterior tibial likely will be most convenient as their use will not necessitate the removal or cutting of the clothing.

Oftimes there is but a single window to admit light and the operator should be so skilled as to be able to raise the arteries either on the right or left side without having to turn the cooling board.

In emaciated subjects the linear and anatomical guides are always plain but in fleshy subjects this is not always the case. Look over the subject and see which artery will be the most convenient to raise. Usually in fleshy subjects the femoral is hard to raise as there is a great amount of fat in Scarpa's triangle making the artery lie very deep, but in these subjects the guide for the brachial is quite plain, a distinct groove being seen between the biceps and triceps muscles.

In a short necked subject it is never advisable or convenient to raise the carotid as there is not much room to work and the incision is very liable to show. Another artery will be found much more advantageous in these subjects.

In accident cases the seat of injury will determine the artery to be raised, using the one through which you can give the body the greatest supply of fluid to all parts. Often it will be necessary to raise several arteries to complete the injection.

There is no necessity for undue exposure in either sex, however it is hardly ever advisable to inject the femoral in the female, as some mischief-maker might without any real cause influence others in the community against your methods.

When selecting the brachial and femoral arteries always raise them at a place below the point where collateral circulation is given off or in other words raise them in the middle third. By so doing the fluid will reach, by means of collateral circulation, the tissues of the arm and leg below the point of injection.

As far as the injection of fluid is concerned, one artery is just as good as another. All arteries are parts of the same channel branches of the aorta. No valves exist in any part of their course.

HOW TO RAISE AN ARTERY.

—With the scalpel make an incision an inch long in the average size arm, cutting through the skin and then through the fat. Reverse the blade and at each end of the wound cut forward and upward to make it clean. Take the grooved director and with the small end puncture the deep fascia, then reverse ends of the director and force the blunt end up the wound, underneath this deep fascia, one-fourth to one-half an inch longer than the wound. Now take the scalpel with the edge of the blade upward and split the fascia as far up as the needle extends and cut the tissue (fascia and fat) up to the skin, being careful not to cut the skin. Reverse the needle and cut the lower end of the wound the same way. This will give you an incision one inch long on top and one and one-half or two inches at the bottom of the wound, and none of the vessels will be injured.

With the handle of the aneurism needle separate the tissues between the muscles, artery, vein and nerve, then use the hook end of the aneurism needle, pass it under the artery and raise it to the surface, passing the bone separator or the forceps with the closed end underneath. Remove the individual sheath surrounding the artery. Likewise raise the vein to the surface.

If the artery and vein lie side by side and it is desired only to raise the artery, hook down between the two, away from the vein, sliding the hook forward and backward underneath the artery, then raise to the surface.

If the artery and vein lie side by side and it is desired to raise both, pass the hook around the vein first, as by hooking around the artery toward the vein the point of the hook will often rupture the vein.

HOW TO TELL AN ARTERY FROM A VEIN OR A NERVE.

—Raise the suspected vessels to the surface, placing a bone separator underneath to form a bridge, which will cause the blood to recede on every side. If you are in doubt which is the artery, remove the individual sheath from each one.

The nerve will appear as a glistening white cord, very solid to the touch and showing bands of nerve fibres which can be separated by the aneurism hook. It will not have any central opening.

The vein will appear as a dark blue color and collapsible because of the fact that they have thinner walls than the arteries, lacking the middle circular layer of fibres. Veins have a central opening. As a rule the vein contains blood after death, which gives it the dark blue color but should it not contain blood, it resembles the artery very closely as to color.

The vein contains valves which can be seen distinctly, if the blood be pushed the opposite way from which it runs in life.

The artery is of a creamish white color and non-collapsible because of the fact that it has heavy walls and a middle circular layer of fibres. The arteries feel firm to the touch while the veins are soft and velvety. Arteries have a central opening and as a rule do not contain blood after death. They likewise do not have valves. The artery is usually more constant than the vein.

Should all these not convince you, raise the one you think is the artery with the hook, pass the forceps underneath, spread these and pass the bone separator under for a bridge and with the scalpel incise the artery about one-fourth the way. Attach the arterial tube and if there is blood present, allow it to drain by lowering the arm. When it has ceased to flow, inject very gently and slowly. If you get a half-pint of fluid in the body, you may be assured of its being the artery.

Another way to tell the artery from the vein is to roll them lightly between the fingers. If it feels like a thin rubber tube, and does not roll together in a little bundle, the supposition is that the vessel is an artery. This however is not certain, as phlebitis, or some other diseased condition of the veins may result in the thickening of the walls of those vessels, to such an extent as to make it impossible to distinguish in this way between the artery and the vein.

The anatomical and the linear guides for the arteries and veins, and their relation to the accompanying nerve, will help also to tell them, one from the other.

HOW TO CUT AN ARTERY FOR INJECTION.

—After the artery has been located it should be freed from the surrounding tissues and then raised to the surface. After it has been raised to the surface the bone separator which is to act as a support while cutting the artery, should be placed underneath the artery.

The artery may be cut in several ways as follows—a T shaped incision may be made. This is a very old method, one of the first to be used for this purpose. To make this kind of an incision in the artery, the scalpel is placed point down about one-fourth the distance from the edge of the artery, and then by forcibly bearing down on the scalpel cut the artery crosswise. Rotating the artery the cut will now be on the upper surface. Now from the middle of the crosswise cut, extend a longitudinal cut lengthwise of the artery, for almost one half inch. We have no comment to make on this kind of an incision, excepting to say that the method is old and obsolete, and no longer used, and that a much better method is now used.

Another method suggested by some authors is the longitudinal incision. With the belly of the scalpel cut the artery lengthwise for a distance of a little less than one half inch. The disadvantage of this kind of a cut is that the operator does not know when he has cut to the center of the artery and no more than the center. If the cut has been made to a distance beyond the center, then the inside wall on the opposite side will be cut and if the wall is in the least diseased, the arterial tube when it is inserted may get between the walls which will mean that no fluid can be injected.

Another method is to cut the artery crosswise, placing the point of the knife on the artery about one fourth the distance from the edge of the artery, bearing down so that the point will come through to the bone separator which is beneath, then forcibly bearing down cut outward with the belly of the knife. Now rotate the artery and the cut will be on the front of the artery.

Another better method is the same as the above, but instead of cutting outward perpendicular to the artery, cut outward diagonally, then when the artery is rotated there will be a V—shaped cut. The point of the V should be made opposite the way the operator is to inject the fluid. With the aneurism hook, pick up the point of the V, which will mean that the hook will have to be inside of the artery, and using the hook as a guide insert the arterial tube. The only disadvantage of this method is that the tensil strength of the artery is to a certain extent weakened, but if the artery is not cut too deep, this is not a serious disadvantage. The advantage is that the operator is always certain that he is in the center of the artery, that if his knife is sharp, that he will always cut all three walls of the artery at once, and thus prevent a ruffling up of the inner wall of the artery should it be diseased.

THE INJECTION OF FLUID.

—One very important point to be taken into consideration when embalming, is the slowness with which the fluid should be injected.

Upon this one thing will depend very largely the success you will have with the perfect circulation of the fluid and cosmetic effects.

Some authorities on the art and science of embalming have made the claim that it makes no difference how rapidly a body is injected as the fluid is so widely distributed through so many branches of the artery that no harm can come from this source. This is very erroneous for when the fluid is forced rapidly through the arteries, it also flows rapidly through the capillaries into the veins, thereby enlarging the quantity of fluid in those vessels and often forcing the blood into the exposed parts of the body, causing serious discolorations.

The capillaries are sometimes ruptured by the rapid injection of fluid, causing spots to appear on the face that would never have been there had the body been injected more slowly.

A further reason for slow injection is that the disinfecting fluid is given an opportunity to be absorbed by the tissues as it passes into the capillaries and not be forced through those little vessels into the veins, as it is by the absorption of the fluid that the body is disinfected. This is especially true when the drainage tube is being used as the fluid, seeking the course of least resistance, passes through the artery, into the capillaries, through those vessels to the veins and out through the drainage tube.

As it takes but little blood to color a large quantity of embalming fluid, many embalmers are led to believe that they are removing large quantities of blood, while in reality perhaps one-half of the colored liquid which flows from their drainage tube is the fluid which is being injected. Many failures have resulted from this error.

Fluid should always be injected into the body very slowly, and the more slowly it is injected the more perfect will be the cosmetic effect.

If necessary make a second injection. An embalmer who makes the proper charge for his services as a professional can afford to make two injections if necessary. He can let it be known that he will not be content with anything but perfect work, and patrons will not only cheerfully pay for it, but will have a better opinion of his professional standing. Thorough drainage and slow injection are the best safeguards against discoloration.

Dr. Erdman before the Minnesota association suggests that the amount of fluid that fills the arteries is not enough to percolate through the capillaries and into the tissues, and saturate all the parts of the body. He favors the gravity injection by merely allowing the fluid to flow naturally into the arteries from an elevated vessel, and would use no force or pressure in injection. Ideal embalming would be a series of gravity injections at intervals of several hours. While the gravity injection such as the doctor describes will undoubtedly be a sure method of getting a perfect circulation, and while it is the process generally pursued in morgue work where the apparatus is convenient, it is in the majority of cases in the home impractical.

All bodies to be shipped must be thoroughly arterially embalmed, that is, to have introduced into the arterial system sufficient amount of disinfecting fluid to thoroughly sterilize every particle of matter in the dead body. This can only be done by introducing into the arteries an approved disinfecting fluid.[2]

APPROVED DISINFECTANTS.

—This is construed by most states to mean a fluid which is sufficient in strength to kill all the germs on the surface of the body or on the interior. An approved disinfectant for the external surface of a dead body is a solution of 1 : 1000 bichloride of mercury. An embalming fluid which has the official approval should contain 5% formaldehyde.

EMBALMING FLUIDS.

—At the present time only a few states have placed restrictions on fluids. These restrictions are that they contain neither mercury, arsenic, antimony or any of their compounds. These poisons when used to inject a body make it almost impossible to detect from a chemical analysis whether death was caused by a poison or the poison was from the embalming fluid. Iowa recommends a fluid the formula consisting of formaldehyde, glycerine, borax, boracic acid, salt petre and water.

WRAPPING A BODY IN COTTON.

—In certain diseases, when a body is to be shipped, the law compels the embalmer to wrap the body in cotton. This may be the ordinary cotton purchased from a dry goods store. The cotton should be cut in strips at least one to one and one-half feet longer than the body. Two layers are laid side by side upon a sheet, the body then placed thereon and the whole wrapped about the body will envelope the body in a satisfactory manner. This means that the entire body is to be enveloped, so that the face head or feet will not be exposed, and the wrapping should never be removed. Absorbent cotton may be used for this work, but it is more expensive and not as good as dry cotton for this purpose.

[3]THE CHARGE OF EMBALMING.

—This subject is one that has long been forcing itself upon the thought and attention of progressive undertakers, principally because of the many abuses and misunderstandings that have grown out of the manner in which members of the profession regard the value of their services and the careless and indifferent systems used in conducting the business side of our work.

---

[2] The quantity to be injected of course varies, but a fair estimate would be that the quantity should be three-fourths of the capacity of the blood vessels of the body. This would require approximately one and one-eighth gallons of fluid to every 150 pounds of tissue. The latest transportation rules demand the injection of an amount of fluid equal to 10% of the body weight into the arteries.

[3] Extracts from a paper written by F. W. Alexander, Conrad, Iowa.

In order to succeed in a chosen calling one must first have a liking and a natural adaptation for the work; second, he must prepare himself by obtaining a thorough working knowledge of the profession or business he expects to follow. He must educate himself for the work. This is fundamental and has been proven many times with the successes in every profession. It is fair to presume then that the great majority of men entering this profession have considered the probabilities of success and have met the requirements needed to qualify them to follow this calling and to receive the support of any who through necessity need their services.

Without going into the non-essentials showing the rights of individuals holding a license as an embalmer to practice, we may naturally come to the next question in this connection, the value of his services and how they should be charged for. Charge what your work is worth, and do not conceal the amount in the price made on the casket or any other part of the funeral expenses. Make it a specific charge in every instance for there is a good and sufficient reason why you should.

An explanation of these reasons may be summed up as follows: the conscientious effort in qualifying yourself to meet the needs of your calling and the requirements of the state, the cost of your training and education in time and money, the years spent in the hard school of practical experience and self development.

Next your business equipment and investment, the care of the case on which you are called, its peculiar requirements and how it taxes your skill in doing the work, the risk from infection, the distance you must travel and the expense of the trip. All of these considerations enter into the cost and should be the basis on which to formulate a charge for the work.

Just as the well equipped surgeon of wide experience and training skillfully performs operations relieving suffering, saving and prolonging life, naturally allows the difficulties of the case and the distinctive personal service rendered to govern him in the amount of the fee, so in a very similar sense the services of the embalmer should hold a certain ratio of value to the conditions under which he works and the ability he employs in its performance. Therefore let me again urge that you make it a specific charge showing it a distinctive personal service.

In the matter of the value of personal services the question is often raised: "Which is the more important part of the work in our profession, directing and managing the funeral or the embalming and care of the body." In answer to this let me say that the care and the embalming of the body is first importance because the law says so, because the education of the embalmer is paramount to other considerations and so regarded by the national association, because sanitary science demands it, because without a body properly embalmed and prepared for burial the funeral is a failure from whatever standpoint you wish to judge it.

A director may bungle the arrangements and at the most it is but a matter of annoyance to the family. However, let him fail to properly fit and prepare the body so that the relatives can see restored to them the face of their beloved one, beautified in the last long sleep of death, and they will never forgive him. They secured his services first as an embalmer and incidentally as a director of the funeral, naturally, therefore, the greater importance of his work centers around his services to the family in that capacity. Now in all candor, why should he not make a specific charge for his work? He is rendering the greater service in caring for the body, it should be the first item charged for on the funeral bill.

CHAPTER XVI.

THE ANATOMICAL AND LINEAR GUIDES FOR SPECIAL ARTERIES.

HOW TO LOCATE AND INJECT THE CAROTID ARTERY.

—The carotid artery, is not used much, by the average embalmer for several reasons. It is usually a hard artery to raise, partly because the average embalmer does not know the anatomy of the neck. In subjects having short and very fleshy necks it is not advisable to use the carotid, however in subjects where the neck is long and not fat it is with some a favorite. It is always essential to know how to raise and inject the carotid for in accident cases, where the arteries of the lower part of the neck and thorax are ruptured it becomes necessary to raise and inject the carotids to get the fluid into the tissues of the face and brain. In cases of suicide where the arteries of the neck have been cut it is necessary to know where the arteries and veins lie so that they may be tied off. Often the body is so badly mutilated that it is impossible to raise any other artery excepting the carotid. Every practitioner should know how to raise and inject this artery, even though some other artery is the one generally used.

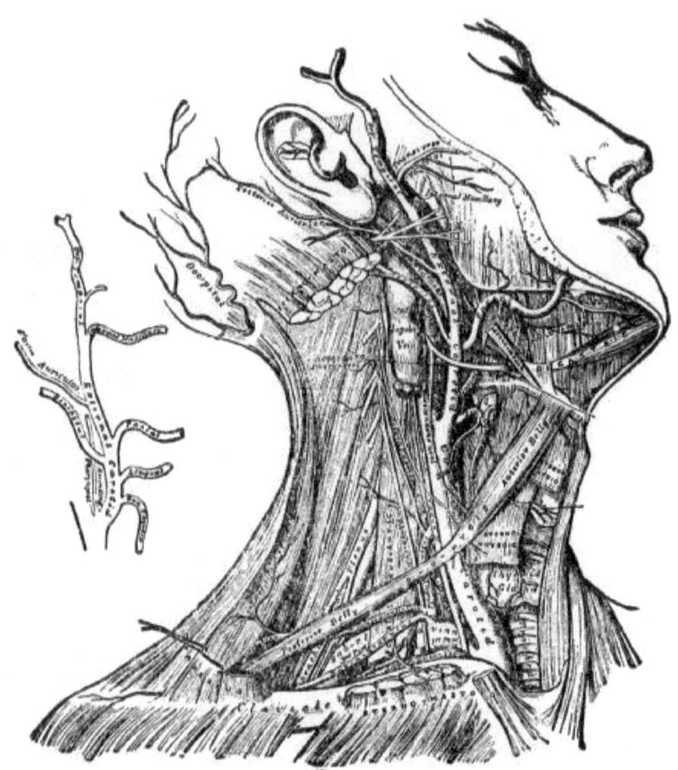

FIG. 46—THE ARTERIES OF THE NECK. (GRAY)

Linear Guide.—By a linear guide is meant that an imaginary line is drawn from a point to a point the same direction the artery runs so that by mentally imagining this line one can be safe to cut on the line and be sure that the desired artery will be reached.

The linear guide for the carotid is represented by a line drawn from the sterno-clavicular junction to a point between the angle of the jaw and the lobe of the ear. (Mastoid process).

As the body lies on the cooling-board place one finger on the sterno-clavicular junction and the other at a point between the angle of the jaw and the lobe of the ear, and by cutting on this imaginary line, the artery will be reached, providing the artery is normal and if the embalmer is thoroughly acquainted with the anatomy about the artery, as is summed up in the anatomical guide.

Anatomical Guide.—By the anatomical guide is meant the relation which the artery bears to the surrounding tissues.

The anatomical guide for the carotid artery is that the artery lies between the sterno-mastoid muscle to the outside, and the muscles surrounding the trachea (wind pipe) and the esophagus, to the inside. In the middle third or sometimes between the middle and upper third the omohyoid muscle crosses over the artery.

Perpendicular Incision. —The artery is divided for the sake of description into thirds. By making an incision on the linear guide in any one of the thirds the tissues that must be passed through are the following:—skin, platysma muscle, superficial fascia, deep fascia, common sheath, and the individual sheath.

The platysma muscle is a broad tissue paper like muscle, placed immediately beneath the skin and a part of the superficial fascia, in the cervicle or neck region. It arises by thin fibrous bands from the fascia covering the pectoral and deltoid muscles on the thoracic wall, and passes upward over the clavicle and inserts the lower jaw. This muscle is so delicate and the fibers so finely divided that it is hardly perceptible. When the skin is cut, the platysma muscle will as a rule be cut too, and because of its thinness it will rarely be seen or does it form any hindrance to the raising of the artery. It is only mentioned here because it forms part of one of the questions so often asked by the State Board in their examination: "What tissues would you pass through in raising the carotid artery?"

Having cut through the skin and platysma muscle, the superficial fascia is next seen. In this part of the body it consists of but a single layer and very thin.

The deep fascia lies next and constitutes a complete investment of the neck. When this is torn or cut through the sternomastoid muscle comes into view.

The sternomastoid, is a large, thick muscle, which passes obliquely across the side of the neck, being inclosed between two layers of deep fascia. It has its origin at the sternum and clavicle and attaches to the mastoid process of the temporal bone. By making the perpendicular incision in the lower third, in as much as the muscle slightly covers the artery, it can either be cut or pushed to the outside of the incision. It is best to push the muscle to the outside with the thumb, and with the handle of the scalpel, work down deep through the areolar tissue. The operator will now arrive at the common sheath, or that part of the deep fascia surrounding the artery, vein and nerve. The common sheath will be very tough and a slit must first be cut, then it can be torn the length of the incision.

The artery will now be seen lying next to the wind pipe and the internal jugular vein to the outside. In the lower third the artery will be about one-half inch deep, while in the upper third it will be about one to two inches deep, owing to the amount of fat in this region. In the upper third, the omohyoid muscle crosses over the artery, which must be either pushed aside or cut in two.

It is always advisable, to raise this artery in the lower third, as it is less apt to show in that third.

Loosen the artery well from the surrounding tissues with the aneurism hook, raise to the surface and place a bone separator beneath the artery.

Now remove the individual sheath, incise the artery and insert the arterial tube.

If it is desired to raise the internal jugular vein for the withdrawal of blood, it is best not to open up the common sheath, but to raise the artery and the vein both at the same time. Having raised them to the surface they can then be separated by the removal of the common sheath and dropping it back into the incision.

If it is desired only to raise the carotid, the hook should always be inserted between the artery and the vein, and directed toward the trachea. If it is directed around the artery in the other direction there is danger of rupturing the vein, and thus getting a bloody incision.

The Circular Incision.—In the circular incision as much of the skin as can be, is pushed above the clavical bone from off the chest wall. The cut is then made from one sterno-clavicular junction to the other following the supra-sternal notch. This method was devised for the use of the "Y" shaped tube, where both sides of the face could be injected at the same time. One precaution however should be noted, which is, that care should be taken that not more than the skin, be incised with the first cut. Just below the incision will be noticed a little branch vein which runs into the arch connecting the two external jugular veins. If the first cut is too deep this branch will be cut, and a flow of blood will result. However by cutting carefully this little branch can be noticed, tied off in two places and cut in between, and thus cause no further trouble. Remembering the linear guide, the artery can be reached by going down at either end of the incision. The tissues to go through will be the same as for the perpendicular incision, and the method of raising the artery will be the same, only, in the circular incision usually both carotids are raised, so as to inject both sides of the face at the same time.

The only advantages derived from the circular incision is that one can by the use of the "Y" shaped tube inject both sides of the face at the same time and get an equal distribution of fluid, and that after the injection is over, and the incision sewed up, the skin can be pulled back in place, making the incision appear much below the clavical, and where it is less liable to show than in the perpendicular incision.

For embalming female subjects, if the carotid is chosen as the artery to use, it will be best to use the circular incision. However for ordinary embalming it will perhaps be best to choose some other artery, which will be less apt to show, and not so deep.

We should be so skilled as to never make a mistake, but the best sometimes do make mistakes. If in raising another artery, a mistake should occur, the operator can raise either above or below the original cut, but with the carotid, the only advisable incision to make is in the lower third, and if a mistake is made the last chance is lost. For this reason then a great amount of care should be taken.

In injecting the body from the carotid, the arterial tube should be inserted first toward the heart, and after the body has received a sufficient amount of fluid, if it is noticed that the side of the face from which you are injecting has not received a supply of fluid, then reverse the tube and inject a few bulbs of fluid upward.

Relation of Artery, Vein and Nerve.—The common carotid artery lies in relation to the internal jugular vein and the pneumogastric nerve. The artery lies to the inside next to the muscles surrounding the trachea (windpipe). The internal jugular artery lies to the outside of the artery. Just back of the common carotid artery and the internal jugular vein and between the two lies the pneumogastric (vagus) nerve. These all as a rule lie in the same common sheath of deep fascia.

HOW TO LOCATE AND INJECT THE AXILLARY ARTERY.

—The axillary in recent years has come to be a much used artery. It not quite as large as the common carotid, but as a rule large enough to admit the large size arterial tube. It has become a favorite with many because it is quite easy to locate and to raise, and because of its proximity to the axillary vein, a vein which is large enough to admit a drainage tube for the withdrawal of blood. Again the axillary artery is in a secluded place, being as it is in the axillary space (arm pit). The artery does not lie very deep, and is not covered by any muscles as you operate, there being practically nothing to hinder the progress of the operation.

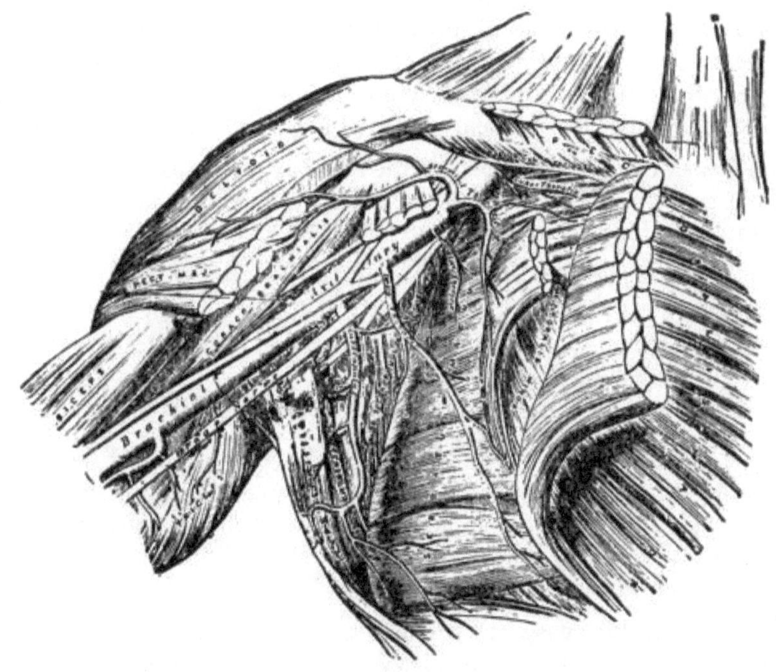

FIG. 47—THE AXILLARY AND ITS BRANCHES. (GRAY)

Then after the operation is completed and the arm placed back in normal position, the casual observer is not liable to see the incision, even though the body be only partially dressed.

Linear Guide.—A line drawn through the center of the axillary space (arm pit), at the anterior border of the hair line.

The Axillary Space.—When the arm is maintained in a horizontal plane, the axilla has the shape of a three-sided pyramid, the apex of which lies above, below the clavicle, and the base of which corresponds to the lower wall, covered only by skin and fascia.

The axilla is filled with blood vessels, lymph vessels, lymph glands, nerves, and masses of fat.

To Raise the Artery.—Make an incision on the linear guide. After the skin is passed through there is a large quantity of fascia, lymph glands, and lymph vessels, which must be carefully dissected through, and at the same time the axillary vein will be discovered. This vein, for the present, should not be loosened from the surrounding tissues. Dissect down to the upper side of the vein, and the common sheath of fascia surrounding the artery and nerves will be seen. By carefully tearing this the length of the incision, the brachial plexus of nerves now is exposed. Now by gently pushing the nerves apart with the handle of the scalpel, the artery will be seen. With a hook loosen the artery from the surrounding tissues and raise to the surface.

If it is desired to draw blood, now proceed to raise the vein to the surface. Open the vein and insert a drainage tube, which should be long enough to reach through the entire length of the axillary and subclavian veins, because they have valves along their entire course nearly to the bifurcation of the innominate.

Inject a few ounces of fluid toward the hand as the axillary is above the point of collateral circulation. Then reverse the tube and inject toward the heart, until a sufficient amount of fluid has been injected.

Relation of Artery, Vein and Nerve.—The vein is quite superficial, just below it and to the upper part of the incision is the brachial plexus of nerves, which surrounds the artery.

HOW TO LOCATE, RAISE, AND INJECT THE BRACHIAL ARTERY.

—The brachial artery is located in the upper arm and extends from the inferior margin of the muscle pectoralis major, or from the shoulder to the elbow. It is one of the most popular arteries known to the embalmer, and is now used, perhaps, more than all others combined.

The anatomy of this vessel is simple, yet, when we take into consideration all the numerous anomalies or irregularities that surround its use to us as embalmers, we feel the necessity of making the description very thorough and complete, in order to raise it under all the various difficulties that attend its use.

The brachial artery has its several branches, the most prominent of which are the artery profunda brachii (superior profunda artery) and the artery collateralis ulnaris superior (inferior profunda artery) and the artery collateralis inferior (anastomotica magna artery).

For the sake of a more correct description we divide the artery into thirds, viz: the upper, middle and lower thirds. The upper third begins at the extreme upper part of the arm and extends one third of the way to the elbow, the middle and lower thirds occupy the remainder of the artery. In the upper third we have the superior and inferior profunda arteries coming off; their position is not always the same, and in the extreme lower third the anastomotica magna artery. These arteries continue down the outer and inner arm and anastomose with the recurrent radial and ulnar arteries, thus furnishing collateral circulation. Thus if the fluid is injected in the middle third, toward the heart, these branches that come off the brachial in the upper third will convey the fluid down the arm, filling the branches below the point of injection, which supply the forearm and the hand.

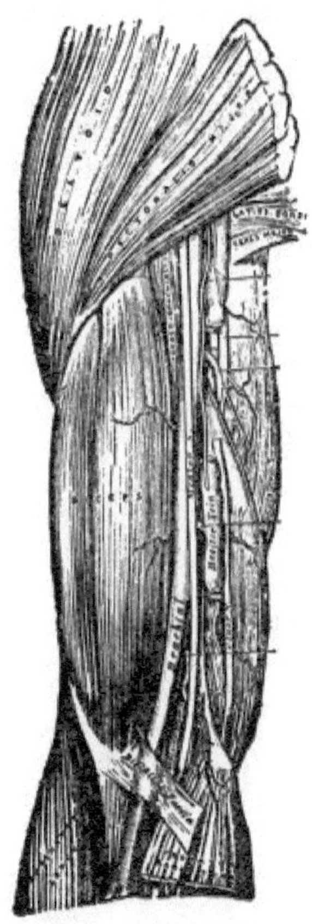

FIG. 48—THE BRACHIAL ARTERY. (GRAY)

The brachial artery is one continuous vessel, the entire length of the upper arm, and varies in size according to the size of the person and the development of the arm. It is accompanied by the venae comites or deep brachial veins, the one to the inner side of the artery about one-third to one-half the size of the artery, the other about one-half its size lies directly underneath. All are encased in the same common sheath of deep fascia that surrounds and holds them together. Great care, then, should be taken to separate the artery from these veins before cutting the artery for injection.

The artery lies along the inner and under border of the large muscle on top of the arm known as the biceps. The biceps is the muscle used when lifting a weight. To those whose occupation is to exercise the muscular tissue of the body liberally, this muscle becomes quite large, and generally the artery is proportionally large.

Linear Guide.—The course of the brachial artery may be marked out by drawing a line from the middle of the axillary space (arm pit) to the center of the elbow, provided the palm of the hand be turned upward. This line will be immediately over the artery, which will be found by cutting through the skin at any point on the line, and dissecting through the subcutaneous tissue toward the center of the arm.

The Anatomical Guide.—In the upper third the artery lies between the biceps and coracobrachialis muscles which lie above the artery, and the triceps muscle which lies below the artery. In the upper third the nerve lies close to the muscle, the artery below and to the inner side toward the body, and the vein a little farther to the inside.

In the middle third the artery lies between the biceps which lies above the artery, and the triceps muscle which lies below the artery. In the middle third the artery will lie beneath the nerve.

In the lower third the artery lies between the biceps which lies above the artery, and the triceps which lies below the artery. In the lower third the artery lies next to the muscle and the nerve to the inner side next to the body, and the vein still farther to the inner side.

How to Raise the Artery.—First trace the inner border of the biceps muscle, feel for the median nerve, which will always be present. The artery in the middle and lower thirds will follow the border of the muscle. The palm of the hand should always be turned upward, and the linear guide, as stated above, will indicate the exact position of the artery. Make an incision through the skin, on the linear guide, pushing the fatty subcutaneous tissue to one side, if there be any, and with the handle of the scalpel, work through the superficial fascia. Reverse the blade, and at each end of the incision, cut forward and upward to make it clean. Now with the scalpel cautiously cut through the deep fascia, and remove this from the vessels below. This will expose to view the median nerve, and with the handle of the scalpel, separate the tissue between the artery and the muscle, and between the artery and the nerve. Having thus freed the artery, use the hook end of the aneurism needle and pass it under the artery toward the muscle, and raise the artery to the surface. Pass the bone separator or the forceps with the closed end, underneath, remove the sheath surrounding the artery and the deep brachial veins. The natural position will be, the artery on top, the larger deep brachial vein to the inner side and the smaller one underneath. It is very necessary to remove these deep brachial veins, for the reason that if they are not, in cutting the artery for injection, they will be cut also, resulting in a flow of venous blood into the incision.

HOW TO LOCATE, RAISE AND INJECT THE RADIAL ARTERY.

—The radial artery is one of the branches of the brachial artery, and extends from about one half inch below the bend of the elbow, along the valley of the forearm, to the thumb part of the hand. It is divided into thirds, viz: the upper, middle and lower thirds. It is accompanied in close relation by the radial veins, but in no way do they interfere with the operation of raising the vessel. The value of this artery is in the embalming of ladies, where the body has been dressed and the sleeve cannot be removed to use the brachial artery without material inconvenience and annoyance. It is especially desirable to those who are just beginning to use the arteries. The radial artery is somewhat smaller than the ulnar, but, on account of the depth of the latter and inconvenience of raising, the radial artery is the one artery in the forearm which is generally used. It is an excellent vessel to employ in cases where the friends are opposed to embalming because of the mutilation of the body, as they choose to call it. Some object to the use of this artery on account of the fact that the mutilation is not easily hidden. The wound can be easily covered by simply pulling the sleeve down to its normal place. The incision necessary to be made is so small and it can be closed so neatly, that no objection on the part of the relatives need be apprehended.

Before the advent of formaldehyde fluids the radial artery offered more advantages to the embalmer than any other artery used for injecting. But at the present time almost all embalming fluids contain large quantities of formaldehyde, and when injected into this artery, which is very small, it is liable to constrict the vessel to such an extent as to sometimes make it difficult to inject the fluid.

Moreover, since both the radial and the ulnar arteries have many branches, a large quantity of fluid is liable to accumulate in the forearm, hardening it more than is necessary and giving the hand an undesirable color.

The radial artery is very superficially located, and can be secured without the possibility of error and with very little mutilation. The expert will, of course, choose that vessel which he believes will at the time and under the circumstances best serve his purpose.

The Linear Guide. —Is a line drawn from the center of the bend of the elbow to the center of the ball of the thumb.

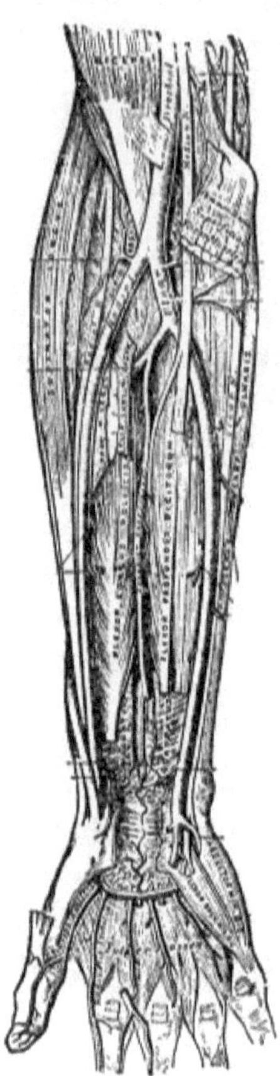

FIG. 49—THE RADIAL AND ULNAR ARTERIES. (GRAY)

The anatomical guide for the radial artery (in the wrist, where it should be raised) is the brachio-radialis muscle on the outside of the artery and the flexor carpi radialis muscle on the inside of the artery.

When about to raise this vessel, the embalmer should hold the arm at right angles with the body, with the palm up, and holding the hand of the body, with the hand, draw the arm tight. In most bodies this will show plainly the tendons of the muscles between which the vessel lies, thus affording an excellent guide for the incision. The arm should never be grasped and the tissues drawn out of their normal position, as that is very misleading. The vessel should be raised at a point about three inches above the wrist joint (the space where you would feel the pulse beat in life). The operator making an incision through the skin, superficial fascia, and fat, about one-half inch in length, will plainly see the artery lying in its sheath between the two tendons of the muscles. The cut should now be opened carefully, by placing the fingers on either side of it, and the fascia dissected from the artery, when it can easily be raised with the aneurism hook. There is no other vessel at this point that can be mistaken for the radial artery. Its two venae comites, or accompanying veins, are usually attached to the artery and need not be removed, as they are very small and can give the embalmer no trouble.

HOW TO LOCATE, RAISE AND INJECT THE ULNAR ARTERY.

—The ulnar is the larger branch of the brachial artery. It crosses obliquely the inner side of the forearm, to the beginning of its lower half, it then runs along the ulnar border to the wrist, crosses the annular ligament on the radial side of the pisiform bone (wrist bone), and immediately beyond this bone into two branches, the superficial and deep palmar arch. In its upper half it is deeply seated, being covered by all the surface muscles. It is crossed by the median nerve, which lies to the inner side for about an inch. In the lower half of the forearm the artery runs more superficially, and is covered only by the skin and superficial and deep fascia, but at that, the ulnar lies a little deeper in the wrist than the radial. The ulnar nerve lies to the inner side in the lower half and the ulnar artery is accompanied by two ulnar veins, one on either side, called the venae comites.

The Linear Guide.—Is a line drawn from the center of the bend of the elbow, to the inside of the pisiform bone in the wrist.

The Anatomical Guide.—The artery lies in a groove in the wrist, made by the flexor carpi ulnaris muscle on the outside, and the flexor digitorum sublimis on the inside.

To raise the ulnar artery, locate the valley in the lower third about one to two inches above the pisiform bone. Make an incision about an inch in length, cutting first the skin, superficial fascia, layer of fat, which will vary in thickness. The deep fascia is now reached, which should be split by means of the fascia needle and bistoury. Then separate with the handle of the knife or bone separator, the artery from its connective tissue on either side. Then with the hook raise it to the surface, and place the bone separator beneath, remove the hook, and tear off the individual sheath.

The two ulnar veins will be separated from the artery by taking away the individual sheath, which should be allowed to drop back into the incision. Proceed now to open and inject the artery the same as you would the radial or the brachial. While this artery may seem just a little more difficult to raise, still at times it has its place in arterial embalming.

HOW TO LOCATE, RAISE AND INJECT THE FEMORAL ARTERY.

—The femoral artery is usually objected to, because, situated as it is, it requires an undue exposure of the limb, especially in ladies. For this reason, then, the femoral artery should never be raised in the female, excepting in accidental case when it is impossible to raise any other artery. In the male, however, the femoral with many is a favorite. The artery should be raised either in the upper or the middle thirds, but preferably in the former, as by raising at this point the artery is not very deep in the tissues as it will be further down, and at the same time one is able to get collateral circulation to the lower leg and foot by means of the deep femoral and the recurrent anterior and posterior tibials.

It is believed quite commonly, that by the injection of the femoral artery, there is a great danger of flushing the face. This belief is erroneous. Flushing of the face will result from the injection of any artery if it is full of blood and if it is found that the femoral artery contains blood, and likewise any other artery, this blood should be removed before injection takes place, and what little then remains, will not discolor the face, since it will be greatly diluted.

The internal long saphenous vein is mistaken frequently for the femoral artery. It is a superficial vein and is usually found empty after death. It lies a short distance to the inner side of the femoral artery in Scarpa's triangle. This vein is taken up frequently, not only by the younger members of the profession, but by the older as well, when the guides are not followed closely, and when this mistake does occur, and fluid is injected through it, flushing of the face results.

Next to the common carotid artery the femoral artery is the largest branch artery used in embalming. The femoral artery commences immediately behind Poupart's ligament and is a continuation of the external iliac artery.

FIG. 50—THE FEMORAL ARTERY. (GRAY)

It passes down the forepart and inner side of the thigh, terminates at the opening in the adductor magnus, at the junction of the middle with the lower third of the thigh, where it becomes the popliteal artery. In the upper third the artery is contained in a triangular space called *Scarpa's triangle* and in the middle third of the thigh it is contained in an aponeurotic canal called *Hunter's canal.*

At a point about one and one-half to two inches below Poupart's ligament, the femoral artery gives off a branch to the outer and under side, known as the deep femoral artery, or the profunda femoris, which courses the thigh downward, and connects with branches coming off the popliteal and the anterior tibial arteries, thus forming the collateral circulation to the lower leg and foot.

As the femoral artery leaves the body, it is accompanied by the femoral vein, which for two inches down, lies along side the femoral artery to the inner and under side. At about this juncture, however, it passes underneath the artery and continues its course in that position until it passes below where we have occasion to use the artery.

The femoral artery can be used all the way from where it leaves the body at Poupart's ligament until it reaches Hunter's canal. At Poupart's ligament the artery is very superficial, being covered only by the skin, superficial fascia and superficial lymphatic glands, but it gets deeper further down, being covered not only by the above named tissues, but also by muscles, making it very difficult to raise in the middle and lower thirds of the thigh. About five to seven inches below Poupart's ligament the artery passes under the adductor magnus muscle, and enters what is known as Hunter's canal. Because this artery does get deeper as it courses down the thigh, it is generally raised in the upper third.

A knowledge of the anatomy of the vessels of the thigh and leg will be of value in treating accidents when this member is injured.

Scarpa's triangle is a triangular space, the apex of which is directed downward, and the sides formed externally by the sartorius muscle, internally by the inner border of the adductor longus muscle, and above by Poupart's ligament. The floor of the space is formed from without inward by the ilio-psoas pectineus and the adductor longus muscles. The space is divided into two nearly equal divisions by the femoral vessels, which extend from the middle of its base to its apex, the artery giving off in this situation the superficial and profunda branches, and the vein receiving the deep femoral and the internal saphenous veins. Besides the vessels and nerves this space contains some fat and lymphatics.

Hunter's canal is the aponeurotic space in the middle third of the thigh, extending from the apex of Scarpa's triangle to the femoral opening in the adductor magnus muscle. Hunter's canal contains the femoral artery and vein inclosed in their own sheath of areolar tissue, the vein being behind and on the outer side of the artery, and the long saphenous nerve lying at first on the outer side and then in front of the vessels.

Linear Guide. — The guide for the femoral artery is represented by a line drawn from the center of Poupart's ligament to the inner side of the knee joint.

Poupart's ligament extends from the crest of the ileum bone to the top of the pubic bone. To determine the center of Poupart's ligament for the right leg, get on the right side of the body and with the left hand, place the second finger on the top of the pubic bone and the thumb on the crest of the ileum bone, then let the index finger drop down between the two which will represent the commencement of the femoral artery.

Anatomical Guide.—The artery runs through the center of Scarpa's triangle from the center of its base to its apex. In the middle third of the thigh the artery passes beneath the vastus medialis muscle and enters Hunter's canal.

Relation of the Artery, Vein and Nerve.—The femoral vein at Poupart's ligament lies close to the inner side of the artery, separated from it by a thin fibrous partition; but two inches down the vein runs behind the artery and then to its outer side.

There is no nerve in relation to the artery in the upper third, the anterior crural nerve lies about half an inch to the outer side of the femoral artery, being separated from the artery by the ilio-psoas muscle. In the middle third of the thigh the internal saphenous nerve is situated on the outer side of the artery, but not usually in the same sheath with the artery.

To raise the femoral artery in its proper place, is to measure down from Poupart's ligament from one and one-half to two inches in the linear guide, and there begin the incision, making it two inches or less in length. This will bring the incision below the point where the collateral branches are given off. Cut through the skin, then the fat, which will vary in thickness with the subject. Underneath the fat are several layers of deep fascia, which must be split the length of the incision.

The femoral artery will then be seen, and underneath it will be the femoral vein. Both will be in the same common sheath of fascia, which may be removed with a hook by gently tearing the sheath loose over the artery. When the artery has been loosened the length of the incision, raise it to the surface, placing a bone separator underneath for a bridge.

If it is desired to remove the blood, the femoral vein should then be raised.

CHAPTER XVII.
CAVITY EMBALMING.

CAVITY EMBALMING.

—In shipping a body, cavity embalming must always be resorted to and consists of introducing a trocar into the abdominal and thoracic cavities and injecting sufficient fluid over the contents of these cavities to thoroughly preserve them.

The scientific work in the embalming of to-day is being done on the arteries, but cavity embalming should still hold an important place with those embalmers who desire to get the best results. Although the arteries have been injected, yet we find that sometimes the fluid does not reach the cavities. Any cavity may contain gas or material for decomposition, such as blood, pus, lymph, or as in perforation of the intestines, feces in the abdominal cavity. Besides these we always have the bacteria of decomposition, called saprophytes, which have thoroughly invaded the organs and tissues of the body as soon as sixteen hours after death. Then, if for any reason the fluid has not reached a certain part, fermentation, and putrefaction will immediately set in.

THE CEREBRAL CAVITY.

—Gases may be generated in the cerebral cavity soon after death, especially in drowned cases, where the gas forming bacteria, the aerogenes capsulati, are distributed all over the body. These bacteria work much more rapidly in fresh or shallow water, or in the summer when the water is warm, than in the winter when the water is cold, or the body is in salt water. The gases may penetrate every tissue in the body, particularly the tissues about the eyes, which gives the eyes their bulged appearance. The gases that are formed in the brain and forced out into the tissues surrounding the eye do not enter the eye ball. In these cases the eye ball may or may not be pushed out of its socket, depending, of course, upon the amount of gases that have been produced.

These gases may be removed by inserting a trocar inside the head at the inner angle of the eye or in the nose through the turbinated process of the ethmoid bone.

After the gases have been removed from the inside of the skull, about one-half pint of strong formaldehyde fluid should be injected.

Another method of inserting the trocar into the brain would be to pass it through the foramen magnum. This can be done by inserting the trocar in the neck a little below and behind the lobe of the ear, directing the needle upward and inward toward the opposite eyebrow, when the needle will enter the subarachnoid space (Barnes Method).

In cases of hydrocephalus (water on the brain) where there may be from one to two quarts of water inside the cranium, the water may be removed by any of the above processes.

For ordinary cases we do not feel that it is necessary to make a cavity injection in the head for the reason that the circulation there is complete, only in rare instances do we find an obstruction.

PURGING.

—By purging, as the embalmer uses the term, is meant, the fluid which emerges from the mouth and nose of the cadaver. If this fluid is a brownish coffee-like substance, it signifies it is coming from the stomach, but if it is a bloody frothy mixture it signifies it is coming from the lungs.

The real cause of purging is the living and growing saprophytic bacteria, which were normally in the body, or having gained access later, produce as a result of their development, gas formations. These gases confined as they are, press out from the stomach and lungs the contained fluids of the color mentioned above.

Purging from the stomach may either be due to the presence of gases in the stomach itself, or in the intestines or in both. If the gases have formed in the intestines, they would dilate the canal sufficiently to fill the entire abdominal cavity, thus pressing the stomach against the diaphragm with enough force to cause the contents to escape through the upper end of the alimentary canal.

Purging from the lungs is due to the presence of bacteria of putrefaction, which begin to develope in the diseased portions. These cause liquefaction of the lung substance and the formation of gas. The gas will force the liquefied matter, of a bloody, frothy color out through the respiratory tract.

Before embalming of the chest and the abdominal cavity is begun the trachea and the esophagus should be treated in order to prevent purging. There are two ways of doing this:

The first method consists of placing a ligature about the trachea and the esophagus, this is done by making an incision through the skin and tissues over the left edge of the trachea, one-half inch above the top of the sternum. Insert the right forefinger, passing it to the right side behind the trachea and the esophagus to separate the tissues from them. In doing this great care should be taken so as not to injure the carotid on the left and the innominate artery on the right side. Pass the aneurism hook threaded with narrow tape (this must be very strong tape) along the inner side of the finger, below the trachea and the esophagus, to the point of entrance on the left side. You will have no difficulty now in tying securely both the above tubes, and there will be no possibility of purging from either the lungs or the stomach.

The second method of preventing purging from the lungs and stomach consists in plugging the pharynx through the mouth, there-by plugging the trachea and the esophagus. The only disadvantage of this method is that it can not be done successfully after the body has been embalmed arterially. And for this reason, after arterial embalming, the lower jaw will be firmly set and to use this method, it would mean that the lower jaw must be pried back in order to gain access through the mouth. Then it will be found very difficult and in some cases impossible to set the lower jaw again in its proper position. If this method is to be used at all, it is advised that you do the plugging of the pharynx before the arterial embalming has been done.

To do this, take your position at the head of subject on the right side, and open the mouth wide enough to admit two fingers. Roll several pieces of dry cotton, the size of an English walnut, and holding the corner of the mouth back with the left hand, insert a ball of cotton with the right hand and shove it hard down behind the tongue (this can best be done with a pair of clamp forceps). Continue to do this until the pharynx is well and firmly filled, but avoid bulging out the side of the cheek. If properly done this plug will prevent an ordinary amount of purging and dry cotton seems much better to use for this purpose than absorbent. It must be borne in mind that simply filling the mouth is of no use; nothing is plugged by this procedure, as it leaves the opening into the nose open.

If you had not anticipated purging in the beginning, and the body has been embalmed arterially it will be necessary to stop the purging by the first method.

A third method of preventing purging from the lungs and stomach is in the use of plaster of paris. In this method the plaster of paris is mixed thinly, then by means of a paper funnel, pour the liquid into the nose and mouth, then plug tightly with absorbent cotton as in method two. It requires only a short time for the plaster of paris to set and it has been found quite successful. Probably the only disadvantage of this method is that it is mussy and because of the rapid drying qualities of the plaster of paris the operator must work very quickly.

THE THORACIC OR CHEST CAVITY.

—Cavity embalming must be resorted to frequently in the chest or thoracic cavity for the reason that in certain diseases, especially tuberculosis, fluids cannot enter the diseased cavities, as the capillaries and small vessels are destroyed by the disease and the ends of the arteries securely plugged. If this were not so, the patient would have died of hemorrhage of those arteries, a thing which seldom takes place.

Again in certain other diseases, especially pneumonia, the fluid cannot reach the diseased lung, either through the nutrient arteries or by the respiratory tract, because of the resistance offered. The nutrient arteries will be filled with coagulated blood and the bronchi, to a certain extent, with a bloody mucous.

This being the case, the bacteria of putrefaction will begin to develop within the diseased portions of the lungs, and will be the cause of the purging so much dreaded by the embalmer.

The thoracic cavity may be treated by one of several methods.

A first method consists in passing a curved trocar into the trachea just above the sternum and injecting a strong embalming fluid into the bronchi. In cases of gangrene of the lung, the sputum has a very offensive odor, which may be disinfected by this method. But it must be remembered that the ends of the bronchioles which enter the diseased parts of lungs will be closed (from the nature of the disease), so that any fluid injected into the bronchi from the trachea will not reach the diseased part of the lungs. You will thus see that it is absolutely necessary to use a method in treating the thoracic cavity, whereby any mass of rotten tissue, which may be present, may become thoroughly saturated with the disinfectant.

A second method written about the Robbins, is accomplished by inserting the trocar on both the right and left sides at the tops of the lungs, and at the bases. At the top of the lungs the trocar is introduced two inches outside the sternum just below the clavicle. The trocar may then be pushed in any direction, except toward the sternum, without injury to any of the larger vessels.

The arch of the aorta passes a little to the right of the sternum and as high as the lower border of the first rib, then makes a turn to the left and goes directly back to the left side of the fifth dorsal vertebra. The superior vena cava lies a little to the right of the arch of the aorta. The advantage of inserting at this point rather than above the clavicle is that there are no vessels in the location in danger of perforation. If the trocar is inserted above the clavicle on either the right or the left side there is danger of perforating the subclavian artery or vein, while if the insertion is made next to the sternum, the aorta may be perforated, in either case breaking the circulation. Disease fluids are seldom found at the top or apexes of the lungs, but in consumption, breaking down of the lung substance usually begins at this point, especially in young cases. To insure a perfect embalming of the lungs, you should inject at the apexes, about a half-pint of strong formaldehyde on each side. It should, however, be remembered that the injection at the tops of the lungs, as suggested, gives no fluid to the lower parts of the lungs where it is often most necessary.

It is not an unusual condition to find a whole lobe rotten and broken down at the base of the lung, and when such a diseased condition exists the lungs become firmly attached to the chest walls, and unless fluid is placed below these adhesions it does not reach the diseased parts. The intelligent embalmer, will never trust to the fluid passing from the tops of the lungs to the base, as in almost all cases the adhesions between the lungs and the walls absolutely prevent this taking place.

It is necessary first to draw off by aspiration, at the bases of the lungs, the fluids which have accumulated and which may be either water, pus or blood. This is done by inserting a curved trocar of small size, between the fifth and sixth ribs on the axillary line. The thoracic cavity extends in the back as low as the last rib and the twelfth dorsal vertebra and it may be necessary to pass the trocar down into this part of the cavity in order to remove the fluids.

As soon as the fluids are removed, inject from a pint to a quart of strong formaldehyde on either side. By so doing the gangrenous and decomposed part of the lung will be put to soak in the embalming fluid, which will insure perfect disinfection and an absence of bad odors.

ABDOMINAL CAVITY.

—Often it will be found necessary to do cavity work in the abdominal cavity. Gases may arise causing a distention of the abdominal wall, resulting in purging from the mouth and nose. This gas is the result of putrefaction and fermentation in the alimentary canal. When one of the principle arteries is injected, the fluid finds its way to the minute capillaries of the organs of the abdominal cavity, including the stomach and the intestines. It must be remembered that often there is a great amount of undigested food and fecal matter in the stomach and intestines. The only way the fluid which is in the minute capillary circulation of the stomach and intestines, is able to reach the inside of those organs and come in contact with the undigested food and the fecal matter is by soaking through the mucous wall. No doubt a certain quantity of the fluid does soak through, and when it does, if there is not much undigested food or fecal matter in these parts, disinfection will be accomplished and it is in these cases that we do not have any trouble with distentions of the abdomen. When however, there is a great amount of undigested food and fecal matter inside the stomach and the intestinal tract, it is only obvious that enough fluid can not possibly soak through to disinfect, and consequently a host of putrefactive, and fermentative germs will begin their work, with the formation of gases and the distended abdomen, and perhaps purging from the mouth and nose.

To prevent the formation of gas now which has arisen, a second injection will do no good. More drastic measures will have to be used. One method that has long been in vogue is the use of the trocar.

The Trocar Method.—In this method a trocar varying in length from six to fourteen inches is used. It may either pierce the abdominal wall through the umbilicus, or two inches above and two inches to the left of the umbilicus. Then after the trocar has entered the abdomen the secret of removing gases successfully depends very largely upon the operator having a very correct idea of the location of all the abdominal organs. It is difficult to know when the trocar has pierced the interior of the stomach, or in fact even to make it pierce the stomach at all for the peritoneum which is a covering for all the organs of the abdominal cavity contains a serous fluid which makes the organs slippery, and even the sharp pointed trocar often does not take hold as it should. Again it must be remembered that the stomach is a hollow organ, and for example let us try to pierce a soft rubber ball, containing air and a small opening, a condition resembling the stomach, with a trocar, we know that the one wall, will have to be pushed up against the other wall, and then placed against something firm, before the trocar will pass through. Just this condition happens with the stomach when the trocar tries to pierce the arterial wall of the stomach there is nothing solid to bear against and consequently the front wall will be pushed up against the back wall and then if enough pressure is now used to push the trocar through, it is very liable to pass all the way through both walls.

Again it must be remembered that the descending aorta passes very close behind the stomach and should the trocar go all the way through the aorta might be pierced and the circulation in a measure ruined. The one main disadvantage of this trocar method is that the operator is always working blindly, it is always impossible to tell just how much damage may be done to the internal organs and the circulation, and again should the operator desire to place fluid in a certain part—say the inside of the intestines or the inside of the stomach or the colons, will the operator have assured knowledge that he has actually placed the fluid in the part desired. From the number of experiments that have been carried out in our anatomical rooms, the proof seems to be in every case that the fluid has not reached the part it was supposed to reach.

The advantage of this method is the fact that by introducing the trocar into the abdominal cavity two inches above and two inches to the left of the navel that after the abdomen has been treated that the trocar then can be directed upward into the thoracic cavity and fluid there distributed to the several parts, but this is seldom necessary. After the trocar has been removed or better, just before the trocar is entirely pulled out the operator should sew a circular stitch about the wound and then as soon as the trocar is pulled out, pull the stitch closely together as if it were a draw string, and tie. This will prevent any further leakage from the part.

THE DIRECT INCISION.

—Sometimes before the body is embalmed or a day or two after the body has been embalmed, there is a distention of the abdominal wall indicating gases and there may or may not be purging from the mouth and nose. From the great number of cases that have been posted in our anatomical laboratories, it has been found that the gas that has accumulated is as a rule located in either the stomach, the transverse colon, or the colons in general, but rarely in the small intestines to the extent that it would do much damage. By the use of the direct incision, make a cut with a sharp scalpel, about three inches long in the median line of the body over the abdomen. Start the cut about one inch below the ensiform process of the sternum and cut toward the navel. After a cut has been made three inches in length on the skin, direct the scalpel downward so that it enters the abdomen. Place the index and second finger in the incision thus made pressing the organs from the abdominal wall, and carefully cut upward between the two fingers. This will prevent the operator cutting any of the underlying intestines.

The incision having been made, it is evident now that the part containing the gas will come up into the incision. If the stomach contains the gas it will come up, if the transverse colon contains the gas it will come up, but that makes no difference, for it is the part with the gas that the operator is after. Usually the transverse colon will be the first to come up into the incision, now take hold of the part with your artery forceps and with a pair of scissors make a clip through the wall, this will let the gas escape. Do not let the gas escape into the room not deodorized, so place over the hand quickly after you have made the clip, a towel, or absorbent cotton that has been saturated with formaldehyde, this will both deodorize and disinfect the gas. Keep hold of the part until all the gas has escaped, and then pick up the arterial tube and inject a small quantity of fluid in the colon, and then sew up with the circular stitch. Then locate the stomach, which can easily be found if it contains gas and treat it in the same way, relieving the gases and then placing a small amount of fluid inside. Treat the other several parts of the intestines in the same way if gas be present and it is remarkable how quickly the abdomen sinks to its normal level. After this has been done place hardening compound or common salt in the cavity, and placing a layer of absorbent cotton in the abdomen under the incision, sew up neatly.

The one great advantage of this method is that you can actually see what you are doing, you can see the part that contains the gas and treat that part particularly, the operator is not working blindly, but is able to place the fluid in the part that he desires and is assured of the fact that it is in the part for his eyes do not deceive him as the sense of feel and touch sometimes do. By this method the operator is able to surround the parts of the abdominal cavity with a hardening compound, and thus feel sure that his case if it is to be shipped, will be received in proper condition, at least it will be as far as the abdomen is concerned, if it is treated under this method. This method is one sure cure for purging, for the gases once properly relieved from the stomach and the contents disinfected, there is no chance for them to recur. If the stomach is found to be full of liquid as well as of gas, as is the condition during purging, the liquid can be taken from the stomach with a drainage tube or a stomach pump, and lastly every part is deodorized and disinfected properly.

A seeming disadvantage might be that a critic might suggest that you are mutilating the body with your abdominal incision. Let a fair question be asked. If it were your sister that was to be embalmed and gases had to be removed, which would you rather see some operator running a trocar here and there through the abdomen, relieving gases and injecting fluid here and there, or, the use of the neat surgical incision, made as a surgeon would make it.

EMBALMING OF THE SUBCUTANEOUS TISSUE.

—It is not always possible to fill the tissues of the body through the arterial system, the arteries may be full of blood in a coagulated condition so that it can not be removed, the walls of the arteries may be diseased, or they may be severed at many places the result of accidental death, such as railroad accident, etc. If any of the above conditions be present or other similar conditions, it will be impossible to inject the arterial system, or it may be that arterial injection is only partly possible. In order, in arterial embalming, to have the tissues embalmed the fluid must reach the capillaries, and to fill the capillaries it is first necessary to fill the larger arteries. So if for any reason it is impossible to reach all or certain tissues by arterial embalming, it becomes necessary to resort to some other means.

With these difficulties then in view, the best operation for filling the tissues, that is the subcutaneous tissue covering the bony framework of the body, is the direct injection of fluid into the part by means of (1) the hollow needle trocar, and (2) the hypodermic needle.

The hollow needle trocar is to be used for the rough work, so called. Inserting the trocar into the center of the popliteal space it can be pushed through the tissues of the foreleg, and fluid injected; then reversing, push the trocar through the tissues of the leg proper, and inject fluid. Inserting the trocar into the center of the bend of the elbow it can be pushed into the tissues of the forearm, and fluid injected; then reversing, push the trocar through the tissues of the arm proper and inject fluid. Turn the body over so as to trocar the back. Insert the trocar above the sacrum bone in the middle line of the back, and push the trocar through the fleshy parts of the gluteal regions, and inject fluid. Again insert the trocar in the middle line of the back between the two scapulae bones, and inject fluid into the region of the shoulders and the small of the back.

After each puncture, before the trocar is removed a circular stitch should be thrown around the trocar and when the trocar is removed draw the puncture shut, the circular stitch acting as a draw string.

A large amount of fluid may be injected in this manner, it being possible to inject several gallons into a body of average size. The fluid transudes through the tissues very readily filling them up completely, but of course, not as certainly as if the fluid were injected arterially. It is an easy matter to inject from two to three gallons of fluid into the soft tissues on the outside of the skeleton of a body weighing from 130 to 140 pounds.

This procedure is only to be used if it is impossible to inject the body by the ordinary arterial embalming. The cavity work in the cerebro-spinal, the thoracic, and the abdominal cavity, should be done first, and then follow with this subcutaneous tissue outside the bony framework.

This procedure may be used in dropsical cases and in certain cases, where for some reason the fluid does not reach a certain part, or where a certain part is not completely supplied with fluid, by the arterial injection.

The hypodermic needle is to be used for the more delicate work, such as the hands and the face. Insert the needle at the wrist and direct it into the palm of the hand, inject a very small quantity of fluid; then into the back of the hand and inject a small quantity of fluid.

To reach the tissues of the face insert the needle into the muscles and tissues of the face from the inside of the mouth. The region about the temple can be reached by inserting the needle into the tissues in the hair line, which will hide the puncture.

With the use of the hypodermic needle fluid can be placed in contact with all the tissues of the hands and face, and the cosmetic effect will be almost perfect if the operator is careful as to the amount he injects, and is careful to see that, the fluid is equally distributed throughout the part.

PLUGGING ORIFICES OF THE BODY.

—The proper manner in which to plug the orifices of the body is to use a pledget of absorbent cotton dipped in your embalming fluid and forced into all the orifices, following this up with a pledget of dry absorbent cotton. In this the fluid disinfects the surface with which it comes in contact and the dry cotton prevents the outgoing of the germs from the body or the passage inward of bacteria. It must be understood that absorbent cotton filters out germs from the air, even though air passes through it, they become entangled in the meshes of the cotton and there remain.

REMOVAL OF URINE.

—As a rule, in the last throes of death, the bladder is emptied, but in some instances this is not done and then it becomes necessary for the embalmer to remove the urine. This may be done in two ways. Use the steel catheter, insert it in the bladder through the urethra, and draw off the urine, or use the trocar and insert it through the abdominal wall in the median line just above the pubic bone, directing the end of the trocar into the bladder which lies just below the pubic bone and draw off the urine. It is seldom necessary to inject the bladder with fluid, as after the urine has been removed, we find from general experience that it is well supplied with fluid from the arterial injection.

In the male it is wise to tie a string about the penis just back of the head, or glans, while in the female it is best to plug the meatus of the urethra and the vagina with cotton.

CHAPTER XVIII.

THE REMOVAL OF BLOOD.

THE REMOVAL OF BLOOD.

—In November 1882, Prof. J. H. Clarke and Dr. C. M. Lukens, while instructing a class in Philadelphia, in taking up the carotid artery, the internal jugular vein was injured and a flow of blood followed much to their dismay. This however turned out to be one of the greatest events that ever happened for the embalming profession, as it marked the beginning of the practice of the removal of blood from the body.

There are some very important reasons why blood should be removed from the body.

(1) There may be discolorations on the body, especially the face. This discoloration may be due to the presence of blood in the minute capillary system and other vessels which are near the surface skin. This discoloration may be due to the presence of the bile pigments in the blood, which would tend to give the body a yellowish hue. This discoloration may be due to the breaking up or disintegration of the blood corpuscles after death, which would tend to give the tissues of the body a light, pale, yellow color. Or this discoloration may be due to the presence of chromogenic bacteria, or color producing bacteria, in the blood, which might give to the tissues a characteristic green color.

(2) There may be blood in the arterial system after death, which certainly will have to be removed or else it may be pushed into the tissues of the face during the injection of the fluid and cause a discoloration. Besides if the arteries are congested with blood, this will have to be removed to make room for the embalming fluid, so that it will reach the capillaries and the tissues of the body.

(3) There may be the formation of tissue gas, and there is no doubt but that the removal of blood will greatly facilitate in the treatment, for without the blood, the fluid will have more chance to act on the parts containing the gas. This gas may be in the blood vessel itself, and the removal of that blood then will relieve the gas and the pressure exerted by the gas, which will aid in the injection of the fluid.

(4) To prevent a hasty decomposition. It may be that our subject is very heavy and fleshy which will mean that there is more tissue to be preserved and necessarily more fluid will have to be used. To make room for this increased amount of fluid, blood should be removed.

It may be that the body is in a hydropic condition. The tissues and the blood vessels will be filled with water. This will mean a hasty decomposition. The watery blood should be drawn from the blood vessels in order to make room for more fluid than ordinarily.

It may be that the body has died of a fever, which will also mean a hasty decomposition. This will mean that the blood will soon coagulate after death, and therefore the sooner it is removed, the better for the general cosmetic effect.

We do not however believe that blood should be removed from every subject, in order to get good cosmetic effect. Rather there are times when blood should not be removed, the conditions which are as follows:

(1) In the thin emaciated subject where there is no discoloration. An example of this condition would be in the tubercular subject, where before death the body has become very thin and emaciated. We would not remove blood when the subject is in this condition, for as a rule the body will take plenty of fluid, the arteries are as a rule empty after death, and besides we desire to leave the blood in the body, in order to give the skin of the face a more filled out healthy cosmetic effect.

(2) In the pale, marble-like, anemic subject. We would not remove blood in this case, first because it is not necessary, for there is a lack of blood in the surface capillaries showing that the arterial system is completely empty, and there is no congestion of the veins; secondly, experience teaches us that in these cases, you probably would not get any blood if you did try to remove it, and thirdly what little blood is in the surface capillaries is needed to build up a more healthy cosmetic effect.

There are times when blood should be removed from the subject after death which are as follows:

(1) Whenever blood is found in the arterial system. An example of this might be found in those cases of sudden death, such as drowning, suffocation, electric shock, or general heart failure. Whenever there has been a case of sudden death, the operator may expect to find blood in the arterial system. The last contraction of the heart normally would drive all the blood out of the arteries and arterial capillaries into the venous capillaries and veins, but this is not accomplished in the cases of sudden death. Whenever, on incising an artery, you find blood in the artery, and it runs freely, it indicates that there is a considerable quantity of blood in the arterial system. This blood then should be removed, because, were fluid to be injected into the artery, when it is full of blood and in this congested condition, all of this blood would be pushed ahead of the fluid toward the center of pressure, and from there large quantities would be pushed back into the tissues of the face, which would result in a greatly discolored face and a very poor cosmetic effect. DO NOT FORGET. Always remove blood when you find it in the arteries. The regular blood drainage tube should be placed in the artery, and all the blood removed that is possible, before attempting to inject. If this blood is not removed, the operator need not be surprised if he causes a decided blood discoloration of the face and a bad cosmetic effect. In these cases blood should be removed from the veins too, for that procedure will help to make room for what blood does remain in the arteries and capillaries, so that it can be pushed by the fluid into the veins

rather than the tissues of the face.

(2) When the venous blood vessels are congested with blood and gas. An example of this might be found in almost any case. When the operator makes the incision to disclose the vessels and finds the venous channels congested, or when over the body the surface veins show signs of congestion and distention with gases, then blood should be removed.

(3) In dropsical cases. Often in these cases the tissues throughout the body are in a hydropic condition (filled with water), the arteries as well as the veins are filled with a watery, bloody colored fluid. It will be best for the operator to remove all this watery blood from the arteries, veins, and the tissues also, in order to get the greatest amount of preservative action from his fluid.

(4) In heavy, fleshy subjects. Experience teaches us that these bodies are as a rule difficult to handle from a cosmetic, as well as from a preservative standpoint. It seems advisable to draw blood from these subjects whenever possible, and by so doing bring about a clear non-discolored cosmetic effect; also the removal of blood will give more room for a greater supply of fluid, and thus the tissues will be better preserved.

(5) When the face is discolored. Whenever the operator takes charge of a body and finds the face discolored, no matter what the cause of the discoloration may be, it is a good indication to remove blood from that body.

By removing blood from the larger venous channels, the operator will make room for the blood to leave the face, and in this way better cosmetic effect is assured. Massage the face toward the internal jugular vein, and push the discoloring blood from the tissues of the face, out into the larger channels, that have been emptied by the removal of blood.

(6) In fever. Whenever a body dies in a high state of fever, it indicates a hasty coagulation of the blood, and a tendency to a discoloration of the face. Whenever the operator knows that the subject has died of a fever, or when there has been considerable fever on the body before death, then blood should be removed.

(7) To make room for fluid. The average embalmer only injects a gallon to a gallon and a half of fluid into a body. There are times when the operator desires to use more fluid. It may be that the body will have to be shipped a long distance, perhaps to another country or a distant state. After a certain amount of fluid has been injected the vessels become filled up and there is a great resistance established. If the operator disregards this pressure, and forces still more fluid into the arterial system, the fine capillary network will be broken, especially in the lung where the result will be a leakage of fluid through the mouth and nose from the ruptured air cells in the lung, or in the tissues of the skin, where the result will be a leakage into a certain area of tissue later causing a condition known as leathery skin. To have prevented this the operator should not have forced the fluid beyond a certain maximum resistance. He could, though, have reduced this resistance by removing the blood from the venous system, and then succeeded in the further injection of fluid.

There are times when blood ought to be removed from a subject after death, but for some reason it seems impossible to remove any. The reasons may be stated briefly as follows:

(1) The blood may already be in a coagulated condition, owing to the fact that the body has died in a state of high fever.

(2) The blood may be in a coagulated condition owing to the fact, that the bacteria of decomposition and putrefaction, have so altered the blood as to make its removal impossible.

(3) Certain drugs may have been previously given, or taken during life which would cause a hasty coagulation of the blood.

(4) The body may still be in a condition of rigor, and although the operator may have released the rigor in the joints, still all the tissues are in that condition, a condition which might prevent the blood from draining from the veins no matter what method was used.

Arterial blood is removed from the aorta indirectly, and from the arteries, only when the arterial system contains blood after death.

Venous blood is removed from the right side of the heart directly or indirectly, and the veins, only when it is deemed necessary by the operator.

There are two methods of removing this arterial or venous blood from the body. These two methods are aspiration and drainage. Besides these two methods some modified methods or combinations of the two, are given.

Aspiration consists in actually pumping the blood from the heart, arteries or veins. In this method, if blood is to be taken from the heart directly, the trocar is used; if the blood is to be taken from the heart indirectly or from the arteries or the veins one of the drainage tubes is used. Either the trocar or the drainage tube is connected by rubber tubing, to the goose neck on the blood bottle, which in turn is connected by rubber tubing to the aspirator side of the aspirator and injector pump. When the air is drawn from the blood bottle, there is a vacuum formed, which will aspirate or draw the blood from the heart directly or indirectly from the arteries or veins. The one great disadvantage of this method is that if the vacuum is made too great, the artery or vein will collapse ahead of the drainage tube and thus prevent the successful aspiration of the blood.

Drainage or gravity consists in opening one of the principle arteries or veins of the body, inserting a blood drainage tube into the artery or vein as far as it seems practical, and then connecting the blood drainage tube to the blood bottle by means of rubber tubing. The blood bottle should be placed considerably lower than the body in order to have the blood drain successfully. If the femoral artery or vein is used, the body ought to be on a considerable incline, the head at least one foot higher than the feet in order to get the maximum amount of blood.

If the axillary, brachial, or carotid, or their corresponding veins are used, the body ought to be on a level or turned to the side of the opening veins.

Simple drainage in itself is not a very successful method of getting the maximum amount of blood from the body.

The process can be modified in three ways which are as follows:

(1) By placing the blood drainage tube in the vein and the arterial tube in the corresponding artery. Inject fluid into the arteries which will tend to push the blood in turn from the capillaries into the veins, and out into the drainage tube into the blood bottle. This modified method has been called by Robbins "Displacement." This is a good name and one which should be generally adopted.

(2) By placing the blood drainage tube in the artery or vein, preferably the femoral, and connect it by means of rubber tubing to the blood bottle. The operator now stands at the head of the subject, he reaches over, takes hold of each hand of the subject, raises the arms of the subject to right angles with the subject, then crosses the arms and with a steady gentle pressure bears down on the chest of the subject over the heart region.

If the axillary is used the operator is able to manipulate but one arm, the one opposite. Raise this arm to right angles with the body then fold down on the chest, exerting an even steady pressure. By raising the arms the blood will leave the hands, and each time pressure is exerted on the chest blood begins to flow from the artery or the vein, and will continue to flow as long as the even pressure is exerted.

(3) By the combination of number one and two. The operator opens the artery, preferably the femoral, inserts the arterial tube, and injects a pint of fluid to exert a pressure on the venous system. He then opens the vein, inserts the blood drainage tube which is connected with the blood bottle. With the pump in his right hand (granting that he is using the aspirator and injector pump), he stands at the head of the subject and slowly injects the fluid. If at any time the blood ceases to flow, by taking hold of the hands, raising both arms at right angles to the subject, crossing, and while in this position injecting a few ounces of fluid, then bear down gently on the chest with a steady pressure. If the blood will not flow by this method and the operator is using either the axillary or the femoral, there is hardly any use of trying any other method. The operator will be able to draw the maximum amount of blood with this method, if it is at all possible to draw blood.

Often when the blood stops flowing, there is a blood clot formation ahead of the drainage tube. By injecting just a few ounces of fluid or salt water through the tube into the vein, the clot may be pushed to one side, and the blood will continue to flow.

REMOVAL OF BLOOD FROM THE RIGHT AURICLE OF THE HEART. DIRECT METHOD.

—Insert the trocar in the third intercostal space, just to the right edge of the sternum or the breastbone. The trocar should be inserted obliquely, the point of the trocar is to pass in the general direction of the left hip joint, while the open end of the trocar is to point in the general direction of the right ear. A general knowledge of the anatomy as far as the location of the heart is absolutely necessary to master this procedure. The object is to have the point of the trocar pierce the right auricle of the heart. When the trocar has pierced the right auricle, which the operator will have to judge through practice, attach rubber tubing to the gooseneck of the blood bottle and by the use of the aspirator pump, draw the blood from the heart into the blood bottle. This is removal of blood by aspiration.

REMOVAL OF BLOOD FROM THE RIGHT VENTRICLE OF THE HEART. DIRECT METHOD.

—Insert the long thin twelve or fourteen inch trocar two inches above and two inches to the left of the navel and pierce the abdominal wall, pass the trocar keeping the point close to the abdominal wall, in the general direction of the right shoulder as far as the lower border of the third intercostal space, without fear of breaking any circulation. The right ventricle will thus be reached from which blood can be aspirated as in the previous method. Here again a general knowledge of the anatomy as far as the location of all the organs in the upper abdominal and thoracic cavity is necessary to perform a successful operation. This is removal of blood by aspiration.

REMOVAL OF BLOOD FROM THE RIGHT AURICLE OF THE HEART. INDIRECT METHOD.

—Make the incision for the femoral artery and vein.

Raise the artery and inject about a pint of fluid in order to cause a pressure on the venous system. Open the vein and insert the flexible rubber drainage tube, known on the market as the Red Seal drainage tube or the Worsham drainage tube. Push this tube up through the femoral, external iliac, the ascending vena cava, through the eustachian valve, and into the right auricle of the heart.

In order to determine when the tube is inside the right auricle, the operator should have laid the tube on the external surface of the body from the point of entrance to the point where the right auricle normally should be, allowing for the bend of the vein in its course. Mark the tube, then when it has been pushed into the vein to that point the operator is reasonably sure that the end is in the right auricle.

In order to make the tube slip easily it should be greased with a liquid solution of vaseline.

After the tube has reached the right auricle the blood may be allowed to drain, or it may be aspirated.

Either femoral may be used, but the left femoral is preferable owing to the fact that, the angle at the bifurcation of the ascending vena cava is more obtuse.

If the operator desires to remove blood from the heart, we believe that the indirect method is the better way. By the use of the direct method to draw blood from the right auricle by means of the trocar there is always danger of rupturing the circulation. The aorta may be accidently pierced. When the trocar is inserted from below to reach the right ventricle the stomach may be punctured and the liver and diaphragm will have to be pierced which, too, may mean an injured circulation. If any accidental damage has been done, it can not be remedied. The direct method is a blind procedure and is always uncertain. On the other hand if the flexible rubber drainage tube is inserted into the vein it must follow the channel of that vein. It is more certain than the trocar method and there is no danger of rupturing the circulation.

The basilic or axillary vein may be used to remove blood from the heart instead of the femoral. These veins should be used on the left side of the body owing to the fact that the angle at the junction of the subclavian and internal jugular veins is not so acute as on the right side.

REMOVAL OF BLOOD BY THE USE OF THE FEMORAL VEIN.

—The use of the femoral vein is considered by some operators a very good method. The femoral should be employed in the upper third. Make the incision in the center of Scarpa's triangle, just below Poupart's ligament. The incision should be about two inches in length, the length of the incision usually depends upon the size and thickness of the thigh and the depth of the vein in the tissue. Expose the artery and the vein. The vein at this point will lie to the inside of and a little below the femoral artery. Open the artery and inject about a pint of fluid to cause a pressure on the venous system.

Have all the blood drainage outfit in readiness then open the vein and quickly insert the drainage tube. Any of the drainage tubes now commonly sold on the market are good. For the femoral, though, the flexible rubber drainage tube seems to be the best, because the femoral vein dips deep down into the posterior part of the abdomen after it leaves the Poupart's ligament. The flexible rubber drainage tube will follow this bend and can be pushed as far as is desired by the operator, in contrast the steel drainage tube could only be pushed into the vein for a few inches.

Blood ought to drain out into the blood bottle, if it does not, inject a little more fluid to cause more pressure on the venous system, and if it will not flow by the drainage method or any of its modifications try the aspirator. If blood still will not flow, it may mean that there is a clot ahead of the drainage tube. Pump some fluid through the drainage tube into the vein, to see if the tube is open, then let the fluid drain out which usually will bring some blood. After you have tried all the methods, if blood still does not flow, it will indicate that the blood is either in a coagulated condition, or there is not very much blood in that particular vein, which in this case is the femoral. The blood may be more in the dependent parts of the body.

REMOVAL OF BLOOD FROM THE AXILLARY VEIN.

—The axillary vein is of large size, and is formed by the junction of the venae comites or deep brachial veins with the basilic. The axillary vein begins at the lower part of the axillary space, increases in size as it ascends by receiving tributaries corresponding in name with the branches of the axillary artery and terminates immediately beneath the clavicle at the outer margin of the first rib where it becomes the subclavian vein. To remove blood from the axillary vein, raise the vein to the surface, and insert the drainage tube. The Eckels-Genung steel drainage tube will perhaps be the best tube to use. Insert the drain tube high up in the arm pit, pass through the subclavian, to beyond the valve located in the subclavian vein outside the point at which the internal jugular vein unites with the subclavian to form the innominate. There being no more valves the blood should pass out freely. If the blood does not flow, raise the axillary artery, begin the injection of fluid which will tend to cause a pressure through the capillaries on the venous system pressing the blood back to the right auricle of the heart as in life, and as there is no obstructed passage the blood should flow freely from the tube. The vein tube is of metal having a plunger rod within, and a Y attachment at the upper end. The blood runs from the Y shaped attachment into a rubber tube which is connected with the blood bottle. A flexible arterial tube should be used in the artery, which will measure eight to ten inches in length and constructed with a shut-off valve. The tube will reach the innominate artery close to the arch of the aorta. With these arterial and drainage tubes the arms can be folded and placed in position, with the hands over the abdomen and the tubes will extend out over the upper border of the arm. This method will enable the operator to inject the body and have the arms in their natural position. If a short circuit through the internal mammary vessels occurs, and this will be evidenced by the premature flow of thin blood, close the vein tube now and then during the operation, continuing the injection until the proper results are obtained.

REMOVAL OF BLOOD FROM THE BASILIC VEIN.

—To withdraw blood from the basilic vein the left arm should be employed, because of a more direct route to the right auricle. Make the incision in the middle or the upper third of the arm. The basilic vein lies in the upper arm and extends from the elbow to the shoulder, and can be found a short distance from the brachial artery, either above or below, but generally below and toward the body. Its position is not always the same, owing to the many anomalies that might occur. As a rule the vein is quite large and prominent and when secured, raise to the surface freeing it from the surrounding tissues.

Prepare two ligatures, make the incision in the vein and pass gently the basilic drainage tube upward toward the heart. Either a steel or rubber tube may be used. If the flexible rubber tube is used, it will find its way to the right auricle of the heart, its course is through the basilic, axillary, sub-clavian, innominate, superior vena cava, to the right auricle. Either the aspiration or the drainage methods may be used. If these fail try the displacement method.

The use of the basilic for the removal of blood is fast disappearing from general practice. Larger veins can be used, which will always insure greater success.

THE REMOVAL OF BLOOD FROM THE INTERNAL JUGU-
LAR VEIN.

—The internal jugular vein is the largest tributary vein in the body, and accompanies the carotid artery. The operator will cut through the skin at a point from one half inch above the clavicle or collar bone and in the valley formed by the sterno-mastoid muscle to the outside and the muscles of the wind pipe to the inside, cut upward making the perpendicular incision. Raise both the artery and the vein according to the usual method. It seems best to raise the artery and the vein together, and by so doing this will tend to give added strength to the vein which is very large but has quite thin walls.

Direct the hook around the vein first then around the artery toward the wind pipe or trachea, raise both to the surface, place on the bone separator, and remove the sheaths. Use any of the drainage tubes. Insert the vein drainage tube and the arterial tube, the point of both tubes being directed toward the heart. The injection should be made slowly, which will cause the blood to flow from the vein through the tube and into the blood bottle.

This vein is not as much used as the axillary or the femoral for the removal of blood.

It is true that it is very close to the center of circulation and a gateway for the blood from the face. The chief disadvantage is that the vein lies quite deep, is very large and has such thin walls, that it is almost impossible to raise it without a rupture.

About one-thirteenth of the body's weight is calculated to be blood. Granting for the sake of argument that the average body that we would desire to draw blood from would weigh 208 pounds, then that average body would contain 16 pounds of blood. One pound of blood is practically equal to one pint, making the average body to contain about 16 pints of blood.

After death about one-fourth of the blood of the body is found in the portal system. The portal system has capillaries at both ends so that it is impossible to draw this blood.

After death about one-fourth of the blood of the body is found in the tiny capillaries and tissues, blood which by the ordinary methods used today the embalmer is unable to draw.

After death about one-fourth of the blood of the body is found in the azygos system, and points dependent in the body, which blood, too, it is impossible to draw.

This leaves about one-fourth of the blood of the body, which we are able to draw. One-fourth of 16 pints, is 4 pints which is the maximum we can draw from the average body.

The point of this argument is that if from the average body you have taken from two to four pints of pure undiluted blood, then you should be satisfied. If the majority of this blood has been taken from the face you will get the desired cosmetic effect. The claims by some that they are able to draw a gallon or more of blood is in our judgment erroneous, as we feel the blood has been greatly diluted. We have tested this out many times with the aid of control solutions and have found that what the embalmer would ordinarily call thin blood was composed of from 10 to 30% blood and from 70 to 90% fluid.

PART IV.
TREATMENTS

INFECTIOUS DISEASES

CHAPTER XIX.

TREATMENT OF SPECIAL DISEASES.

ANTHRAX.

—Synonyms.—Malignant Pustule; Splenic Fever, Wool-sorter's Disease; Carbuncle; Charbons.

Definition.—An acute infectious, non-contagious disease, caused by the bacillus anthracis, and characterized by the formation of a boil with a circumscribed, infiltrated base and dark center, and a systemic infection of a severe type, the toxemia being of the gravest character.

Pathology.—The blood is dark, thick, diffluent, and rich in the spores of this disease.

Treatment.—Wash the body with 1 : 500 bichloride of mercury or 5% carbolic acid. Inject the arteries, using 64 ounces of half strength fluid followed by enough normal fluid to secure preservation. Inject the cavities with normal fluid. Drain blood from the veins, and disinfect the blood before disposing of it. Close the openings of the body. For transportation, govern yourself according to the provisions of the transportation rules.

CEREBRO-SPINAL FEVER.

—Synonyms.—Spotted fever; Cerebro-spinal meningitis; Typhus syncopalis; Malignant purpuric fever.

Definition.—An acute, infectious non-contagious disease, occurs sporadically, epidemically and endemically characterized by hyperemia of the brain and spinal cord, and sometimes attended by a petechial eruption.

Cause.—The meningococcus intracellularis of Weichselbaum.

Pathology.—In those cases that speedily prove fatal, there are little, if any, changes in the blood or tissues after death. Where the disease has continued for several days, however, we find the characteristic suppurative exudation. The sinuses of the brain contain blood clots. Sometimes pus is found in the internal ear, and the chamber of the eye. The liver, spleen and kidneys are usually slightly engorged and somewhat softened. There occurs in quite a number of cases a petechial eruption; the purpuric spots may be quite profuse, or but one or two may be seen.

Treatment.—As the means of ingress and egress of the infectious material is not known, it is best that we give these cases a thorough treatment; which should include a full arterial injection, drainage from the vein, injection of the cavities, and full care of the exposed portions of the body by washing same with a 1 : 500 solution of bichloride of mercury. The ears should be treated by packing them with absorbent cotton saturated with the fluid or with bichloride of mercury solution. The eyes should be carefully cleansed with a soft cloth or with cotton saturated with bichloride of mercury solution. The arterial injection should consume an amount of fluid equal to 10 per cent. of the body weight. Give full cavity injection. Govern yourself by the regulations of your district for transportation of these cases.

ERYSIPELAS.

—*Synonym.*—St. Anthony's fire.

Definition.—An infectious, non-contagious disease, characterized by an acute and specific inflammation of the skin and subcutaneous tissues, attended by a shining redness, which spreads rapidly, marked swelling and pain, and which finally terminates in desquamation.

Cause.—This disease is supposed to be caused by the streptococcus erysipelatis.

Pathology.—The blood vessels are dilated and distended with blood, the cell infiltration may extend into the deeper tissues with suppuration. The cocci are found in the lymph spaces of the affected area, also in the lymph vessels. There is a true dermatitis, involving the skin, subcutaneous, and mucous surfaces.

Treatment.—Operator should wear rubber gloves. Wash the body externally with 1 : 500 solution of bichloride of mercury using absorbent cotton in the process. If crusts have formed bathe the spots with sweet oil, which will soften them and which will allow you to remove them; destroying them by burning would be the best means of disposal. If the face be the part affected, treat as above and then apply the following solution to the part with lintine (Moadinger) or by simple saturation: boric acid, one drachm; glycerine, one ounce; water, three ounces.

Inject the first 64 ounces of fluid at half the normal strength, gradually strengthening the fluid until the tissues become firm. Drain blood freely from a large vein and disinfect the drawn blood before disposing of it. Allow the softening solution mentioned above to remain on the face until you are ready to place the body in the casket, when the face can be dried and the usual cosmetic powders applied. Should the peritoneum or the pleura be affected, inject the proper cavities with very strong fluid. For transportation, govern yourself according to the provisions of your district rules.

GLANDERS.

—*Synonyms.*—Farcy.

Definition. —A specific, infectious, non-contagious disease of the horse, communicable to man by inoculation, and characterized by the formation of nodules in the mucous membrane of the nose-glanders; and also beneath the skin and lymph structures—farcy.

Cause. —In 1882, Loeffler and Schütz discovered the bacillus mallei which is the exciting cause of this disease. The infectious material is transmitted directly from horse to men, usually through an abraded surface, and occurs most frequently among hostlers, veterinarians, farmers, and those who come in contact with horses. It has been communicated from man to man, but this is rare.

Pathology. —There are found nodules located in the nose, in which case the disease is called glanders; or beneath the skin, in which case it is called farcy. These nodular masses discharge a yellow pus, which will infect any abraded surface.

Treatment. —Disinfect the oral and nasal openings, and wash the body with a good germicide. Give a thorough arterial injection, using half strength fluid in the first bottle and normal thereafter. Drain blood from a large vein, disinfecting the blood before disposing of it. Give a complete cavity injection. Close openings. For transportation, govern yourself according to the provisions of the transportation rules.

HYDROPHOBIA.

—*Synonyms.* —Rabies.

Definition. —A specific infectious, non-contagious disease peculiar to animals, especially the dog, and communicable to man by inoculation, generally by a bite. It is characterized in many by melancholia; great fear of water; violent spasms of the pharynx and larynx, rendering deglutition and respiration very difficult; great prostration, a stage of paralysis, which generally terminates in death.

Cause. —The specific cause has not been determined, though bacteriologists agree that it is of microbic origin.

Pathology. —The blood vessels of the cerebrospinal system are congested.

Treatment. —Wash the body with 1 : 500 solution of bichloride of mercury, or 5% carbolic acid. Inject half strength fluid into a large artery for the first part, followed by enough normal fluid to secure preservation. Drain blood from the veins and disinfect the blood before disposing of it. If circulation to face and head is impaired through the cerebral congestion, open the common carotids and inject upward, draining from the internal jugular vein. Give thorough cavity injection. Close all openings of the body. For transportation, govern yourself according to the transportation rules.

RELAPSING FEVER.

—*Synonyms.* —Typhus recurrens; Bilious fever; Famine fever; Hunger pest; Spirillum fever.

Definition. —An acute, infectious and non-contagious disease, characterized by a series of exacerbations and remissions, each lasting from five to seven days, and prevailing epidemically.

Cause.—The spirillum of Obermeier.

Pathology.—There is no characteristic change in the solids of the body. There is sometimes icteric discoloration during the disease and the tissues are stained after death. The liver, kidneys and spleen are somewhat enlarged. The heart becomes soft. The body retains its heat a long time after death and the blood coagulates slowly if at all.

Treatment.—Arterial injection with half strength fluid, followed, in the second and third parts, with normal fluid. Drainage of blood. Spray fluid over abdominal viscera, through the usual puncture.

For transportation of bodies dead of this disease, govern yourself according to the provisions of the transportation rules.

SYPHILIS.

—Synonyms.—Pox; mal-venereal; lues venereal.

Definition.—A specific infectious, non-contagious disease, weeks or months are occupied in its development; contracted by inoculation which is known as acquired syphilis, or hereditary, which is congenital syphilis, and is characterized by three distinct stages; primary, secondary, tertiary.

History.—"In all probability syphilis is as old as the human race; for we can readily believe that illicit intercourse was practiced in the cities of the ancient world when the morals of the people were more lax than those of today. Our knowledge of the disease, however, dates from the fifteenth century. Breaking out among the troops of Charles VIII, King of France, it rapidly spread over Europe. From then to the present day our knowledge of the disease has grown, till today we are able to classify and separate the various lesions resulting from illicit and promiscuous intercourse. All forms of venereal disease were included under the name of syphilis till Ricord, in 1831, demonstrated that gonorrhea and syphilis were two distinct diseases."

Etiology.—Predisposing causes are injuries or abrasions of the mucous surfaces of exposed parts, for the disease can originate in only one way, by inoculation.

Modes of Infection.—There are three modes of infection; illicit intercourse, heredity and accidental. Of these the embalmer need only consider the accidental form of infection.

Pathology.—The initial lesion is the chancre, the secondary lesions are ulceration of the mucous surfaces and cutaneous eruptions, and the tertiary lesions are inflammatory products known as gummata, and are found upon the bones and periosteum, or in the skin, muscles, liver, kidneys, lung, heart, brain; in fact in any of the viscera of the body.

Treatment.—Wash body thoroughly with 5% carbolic acid or 1 : 500 solution of bichloride of mercury. Work with rubber gloves. Inject half strength fluid for the first 64 ounces of fluid and follow that with normal fluid until disinfection and preservation are assured. Give the body a complete cavity injection with normal fluid. Drain blood from a large vein, and disinfect the blood before disposing of it. Close all openings of the body with absorbent cotton saturated with normal fluid. Bandage any large sores and saturate the bandage with normal fluid. When purpura (characterized by a blue spot on the face) exists, the discoloration cannot be removed. If anything is to be done at all for the discoloration, it must be of the nature of a covering for the spot, such as paint or other cosmetics. For transportation of the body, govern yourself according to the transportation rules.

TETANUS.

— Synonyms. — Lockjaw; Trismus.

Definition. — An acute infectious, non-contagious disease, characterized by painful spasmodic contraction of the voluntary muscles, most frequently those of the jaw, face, and neck; less frequently those of the trunk, the extensors of the spine and limbs.

Cause. — The cause is recognized as the bacillus tetanus.

Pathology. — The infection usually enters by way of a wound, especially of the hands and feet, and a punctured wound rather than an incised one. The post-mortem lesions are not constant.

Treatment. — The body should receive a complete arterial injection using half strength fluid for the first part of the injection, followed by sufficient normal fluid to secure preservation and disinfection. Blood should be drained from the veins and should be disinfected before being disposed of. Wash the wound with 1 : 500 solution of bichloride of mercury and bandage it to avoid infection from it. Inject the cavities of the body. Close the openings. For transportation, govern yourself according to the provisions of the transportation rules.

ACTINOMYCOSIS.

— Synonyms. — Big Jaw; Lumpy Jaw.

Definition. — A specific infectious, non-contagious disease of domestic animals, particularly cattle, communicable to man, and caused by the ray-fungus.

Pathology. — Infection takes place, as a rule, through the mouth, through a cut or abrasion of the skin and rarely through the respiratory tract. The fungus produces a tumor, with a rapid proliferation of the neighboring connective tissue. The disease is not limited to any organ as the name lumpy jaw would imply; we may have actinomycosis of the lung, digestive tract, and of the skin.

Treatment. — Disinfect the outside of the body by washing with a good germicide. Care should be exercised against inoculation through an abrasion of the skin. Give the body a thorough arterial injection, draining blood, and disinfecting the blood before disposing of it. Close all openings. For transportation, govern yourself according to the provisions of the transportation laws.

DENGUE.

*—Synonyms.—*Break-bone fever; dandy fever; broken-wing fever.

*Definition.—*An acute, specific, infectious, non-contagious fever, occurring epidemically in tropical and subtropical climates and characterized by two severe paroxysms of fever, separated by an intermission, great muscular pain, and usually attended by an eruption.

*Cause.—*The nature of the infection or contagion is not known. That it is infectious is shown by the rapidity with which it spreads when once it invades a section. In 1885, within a few weeks, sixteen thousand, in Austin, Texas, were stricken. Neither age, sex, race, nor position exert an influence in staying the disease.

*Pathology.—*As few cases prove fatal, but little opportunity has ever been given to study its pathological character. There has been found infiltration of the tissues about the joints. It is rare for a case to end fatally, only few succumbing to its influence. For this reason the embalmer will not have many of these cases to treat.

*Treatment.—*As this rarely comes excepting in the epidemic form, that form will be treated on. The body should be washed with a good germicide, and all openings should be closed with absorbent cotton. The body should then receive a very heavy arterial injection, with drainage of blood, and cavity injection. As is the case in epidemics, the body should be buried as soon as possible. While the mortality is light, yet the most strenuous treatment should be given to assist in the campaign of the health authorities against the disease and its spread. When more is known about the characteristics of the disease, it is likely that a more definite treatment can be advised.

MALARIAL FEVER.

*—Synonyms.—*Ague; Chills and fever; Intermittent fever; Swamp fever; Marsh fever; Paludal fever.

*Definition.—*A specific, infectious, although non-contagious disease, caused by the hematozoa of Lavaran, and consisting of two distinct parts; first, a succession of exacerbations and intermissions, or a series of short fevers separated by short intervals of health; second, a continued fever made up of exacerbations and remissions, there being but one cold stage.

*Cause.—*The hematozoa of Lavaran.

*Pathology.—*There is a destruction of the red blood corpuscles, due to the action of the parasite. There is an increase of pigment, in the spleen, liver, kidneys, bone marrow, skin, and in fact, in all the tissues, due to the conversion of hemoglobin into pigment granules. The spleen is enlarged as are also the liver and the kidneys. The skin presents a jaundiced appearance in chronic malarial fever.

*Treatment.—*Arterial injection of 64 oz. 1% solution of borax or oxalic acid followed by 64 oz. of half strength fluid and then a sufficient quantity of normal fluid to complete preservation. Drainage of blood and solution to wash stain from capillaries. Application of full strength peroxide hydrogen to face, and massage during injection.

For transportation of bodies dead of this disease, govern yourself according to the provisions of the transportation rules.

YELLOW FEVER.

—*Synonyms.*—Typhus ichteroides; Febris flava; Black vomit; Yellow jack.

Definition.—An acute, infectious, though non-contagious disease of the tropics or sub-tropics, characterized by a high grade of fever, lasting from two to seven days, tenderness over the epigastrium (stomach), vomiting of black, broken down blood, and yellow discoloration of the skin.

Cause.—Not known, although it is definitely known that the infection is spread through the bite of a species of mosquito, the stegomyia fasciata.

Pathology.—The skin and the mucous membranes show a varying degree of jaundice, from a light yellow to a dark brownish or orange color; the color deepening over the course of the blood vessels. The stomach contains more or less of broken down blood, the so-called black vomit. The blood is dark and broken down.

Treatment.—Arterial injection of 64 oz., of half strength fluid followed by sufficient normal fluid to assure disinfection and preservation. Drainage of contents from vein and massage of face with full strength hydrogen peroxide in an attempt to clear the complexion. Full abdominal cavity treatment, and close orifices of the body.

For transportation of bodies dead of this disease, govern yourself according to the provisions of the transportation rules.

DIPHTHERIA.

—*Synonyms.*—Diphtheritis; angina maligna; membranous croup.

Definition.—An acute infectious, contagious disease characterized by a grayish-white, fibrinous exudate, usually located on the tonsils or the neighboring tissues.

Cause.—This is the bacillus diphtheriae, although some still hold that the specific cause has not as yet been determined.

Pathology.—In the severe forms the deeper connective tissues are involved, and there may be extensive destruction of tissue, including the blood-vessels. There is more or less discoloration of the tissues from extravasation of the coloring matter. The kidneys and spleen may be enlarged. The blood is more or less broken down, the fibrin is deficient.

Treatment.—Disinfect the oral and nasal cavities with the embalming fluid. Wash the body externally with 1 : 500 solution of bichloride of mercury. Inject an amount of fluid equaling 10% of the body weight into the arteries, and give cavity injection. Drain blood and inject additional fluid to make up for that which will be lost in drainage. In young persons the strength of the fluid for the first 64 ounces of the injection should be cut to half of the normal strength. Close all openings of the body with absorbent cotton. Dress the body and then place it in the casket, drawing the glass slide and closing it, after which, it should not be re-opened. Abide by the regulations of your district concerning the amount of time to elapse between the time of death and of burial in these cases. For transportation govern yourself according to the provisions of your district rules.

TUBERCULOSIS.

*—Definition.—*An infectious, slightly contagious disease, characterized by the formation of small nodules, tubercles, varying from the size of a millet-seed to that of a mustard-seed or even larger.

Cause.—Tubercle bacillus of Koch.

Pathology.—Any organ of the body may be the seat of the disease. In the adult the lungs are the most frequently affected, while in children the lymph glands, joints, and intestines are favorable seats for the disease. Probably the only form that will give the embalmer any trouble is tuberculosis of the lungs. Here either from the poison, developed by the bacilli, or from some other source, necrosis of the cells occurs, forming a cheesy condition known as caseation. At a later period this breaks down, forming an abscess, the cavity being filled with a purulent material. At other times there is a calcareous deposit, and the tubercular mass is said to undergo calcification.

Treatment.—In pulmonary tuberculosis, give the body a complete arterial injection using half strength fluid for the first part of the injection, followed by three-fourths strength for the latter part. Hohenschuh prefers to drain blood from all cases; the authors prefer to drain blood in tuberculosis, only when it is necessary as a means of preventing discolorations, and that would be in case the blood vessels contained much blood. Massage the face carefully with one of the commercial solutions, or, with water which of course has no bleaching action. For transportation, govern yourself according to the provisions of the transportation rules.

TYPHOID FEVER.

*—Synonyms.—*Typhus abdominalis; Typhus nervosus; Ileo-typhus and Autumnal fever, are the most common terms, although Murchison's list includes forty others.

Definition.—An acute, infectious and slightly contagious disease, derived from a specific cause and characterized by inflammation and generally sloughing of Peyer's glands, swelling of the mesentery, engorgement of the spleen and a rose colored eruption.

Cause.—A specific germ called the bacillus of Eberth or the bacillus typhosus.

Pathology.—The lesions resulting from this disease may be divided into two parts. First, the lesions of the intestinal canal, Peyer's patches, the solitary glands of the ileum and caecum, and more rarely of the colon and the rectum, and changes in the spleen. Secondly, those lesions resulting from sepsis occurring during the long period of fever, and affecting the tissues and organs at large. The first effect of the poison or bacilli is to cause hyperemia (swelling) of the lymphatics, the capillaries become engorged and cell infiltration takes place in the solitary glands of the intestines. Frequently the infiltration is so excessive that the capillaries become engorged and entirely choked with the infiltration. Ulcers form, which are shallow or deep, according to the amount of necrosis (sloughing), and when very deep, perforation of the bowel may follow, although this condition is rare. The spleen is nearly always involved, congestion takes place, followed by softening. The liver becomes hyperemic, swollen and soft, and often shows abscess formation. There is granular degeneration in the kidney, ulceration of the larynx and sometimes congestion of the lung. The heart muscles too often become weakened the result of the poison.

Treatment.—If death occurs early in the disease, the body will not be greatly emaciated, and the following treatment may be followed in detail:

If intense abdominal fermentation exists, relieve the accumulated gas with trocar, aspirate as much serous matter as possible from the pelvic cavity, introduce a strong fluid into the cavity, taking care to have as much of this fluid reach the cavities of the intestines as possible. Open one of the arteries commonly used in one of the drainage processes and inject 64 ounces of half strength fluid, draining blood from the vein simultaneously with the injection. Then inject a sufficient quantity of normal fluid to complete preservation. Close all openings of the body with absorbent cotton. Massage the face with water or a commercial solution during the injection.

If death occurs late in the disease, the abdomen may require a stronger treatment such as we would give in acute peritonitis. The trocar may not prove efficient in reaching the affected parts and in such a case we would make a 4 inch incision along the median line and between the umbilicus and the pubic arch, exposing the ileum and caecum, which should be incised, their contents removed, and then all replaced in the cavity thoroughly surrounded with hardening compound. After this the wound should be closed with stitches. After preservation has been completed in either this form of the disease or the one mentioned above, dust on a good quality of face powder to remove the moist appearance from the skin. When a body dead of this disease is to be transported, consult the state or local transportation rules in addition to these treatments.

LEPROSY.

—*Definition.*—A chronic, infectious, contagious disease, which usually terminates fatally.

Cause.—The bacillus leprae. There are tuberculous growths in the skin, which push outward, form nodular masses, between which are seen areas of ulceration and cicatrization, which in the face, distort the features. These tubercular masses discharge a thick purulent material. The destruction of tissue proceeds gradually, years being occupied in destroying a patient. The deep, ulcerative process may amputate fingers and toes in its progressive march.

Treatment.—The body is rarely presentable for sometime before death, and this should not be a consideration in our treatment. If an arterial injection is possible, give it, using normal fluid for the injection. Work with rubber gloves. Give a complete cavity injection. Wrap the body in absorbent cotton and then in a sheet. For transportation, govern yourself according to the provisions of the transportation rules.

INFLUENZA.

*—Synonyms.—*Epidemic catarrhal fever; la grippe.

*Definition.—*An acute, infectious disease, the contagion of which is questionable occurring pandemically.

*Cause.—*The bacillus influenza.

*Pathology.—*There is no characteristic lesion in the uncomplicated case. When death occurs it is usually from complication.

*Treatment.—*Disinfect the oral and nasal cavities with embalming fluid. Inject as much fluid as you can into the arteries and cavities. The usual 10% of the body weight must be given for transportation. If blood vessels are filled with blood, drain from a large vein, and add more fluid to your injection, to make up for the loss of blood to the blood bottle. Close all openings with absorbent cotton. For transportation, govern yourself according to the provisions of your district rules.

CHOLERA.

*—Synonyms.—*Cholera Algida; Cholera Asiatica; Cholera maligna.

*Definition.—*Cholera is an acute, specific, infectious slightly contagious disease, occurring epidemically and endemically, and characterized by severe vomiting and copious watery stools, violent cramping of the muscles and collapse.

*Cause.—*The exciting cause is now generally recognized as the comma bacillus of Koch, or spirillum cholerae.

*Pathology.—*The tissues after death are shrunken and drawn, and the extremities are inclined to be mottled; in some cases there is a postmortem rise of temperature. Rigor mortis sets in very early. Spasmodic contractions sometimes occur for some moments after death; hence the eyes and jaws have been seen to move after life was extinct. Owing to this marked contraction, the limbs have been distorted and the partial turning of the body is thus accounted for, and is not, as many have supposed, the result of being buried alive. The tissues are dry, having been drained of these fluids before death, hence some time elapses before decomposition begins after death. The chief visceral lesion is that of the intestinal canal. The intestines contain a more or less quantity of rice-water, fluid rich in the comma bacillus. The blood is very dark, but slightly coagulable and robbed of its salts and fluids.

*Treatment.—*Arterial and cavity embalming, closing all orifices of the body. Any discharges from the bowels should be disinfected before being disposed of. In epidemics, cosmetic effect is a non-essential and in that case the most thorough treatment must be given without regard to appearances.

For transportation of bodies dead of this disease, govern yourself according to the provisions of the transportation rules.

BUBONIC PLAGUE.

—Synonyms.—The Pest; Black Death; Plague of Egypt.

Definition.—A specific, infectious, contagious disease, running a rapid course, and characterized by inflammation of the glands (buboes), carbuncles, ecchymoses, and petechiae upon the surface. It is endemic on the eastern coast of the Mediterranean Sea and the Oriental countries adjacent. Epidemics occur when it spreads to other parts of the world, traveling along the great thoroughfares of travel and commerce.

Cause.—To Kitasato belongs the honor of discovering the specific cause, the bacillus pestis. On entering the body, either by inoculation or by way of the digestive or respiratory tracts, it multiplies with great rapidity. It is found in the blood, in the internal organs, in the intestinal canal, lymphatic glands and in great numbers in the suppurating buboes.

Pathology.—Rigor mortis occurs early, and often there is elevation of temperature immediately after death. Petechiae, ecchymoses, and carbuncles are generally found upon the skin. The lymphatic system is generally affected, the lymph glands of the groin and axilla showing evidence of inflammation.

Treatment.—Wash the body thoroughly with a good germicide, close all openings, first however, disinfect the oral and nasal openings. Nothing should be done for the ecchymotic spots, the cosmetic effect in these cases being secondary to disinfection. The arteries should receive a heavy injection of normal fluid, blood being drained from the veins. The blood should be disinfected before being disposed of. The cavities should receive a heavy injection of normal fluid. For transportation of these cases, govern yourself according to the provisions of the transportation rules.

SCARLET FEVER.

—Synonyms.—Scarlatina; scarlet rash.

Definition.—An acute, contagious disease, characterized by a bright scarlet colored eruption, diffused over the entire body, terminating by desquamation of the skin.

Cause.—Not definitely known, although thought by Klein and Gordon to be the streptococcus scarlatinae.

Pathology.—The blood is dark, diffluent, and does not coagulate readily, owing to a defect in the fibrin. The eruption disappears after death, except in those malignant cases where the eruption failed to appear during life, and appears upon the death of the patient.

Treatment.—First protect yourself by wearing a bandage of surgical gauze over your mouth and nose, then enter the room of death and wash the body thoroughly with a 1 : 500 solution of bichloride of mercury. Inject an amount of fluid equaling 10% of the body weight into the arteries and inject into the cavities. Drain blood through one of the drainage processes, and add an amount of fluid to the arterial injection equal to that which is lost to the blood bottle. Close all openings with absorbent cotton, dress the body, and then place it in the casket, drawing the glass slide and closing it, after which, it should not be reopened. Abide by the regulations of your district concerning the amount of time to elapse between the time of death and of burial in these cases. For intra-state and inter-state transportation, govern yourself according to the provisions of your district rules.

VARIOLA.

*—Synonyms.—*Small-pox; German Blattern; French, La Petite Verole.

*Definition.—*A specific, infectious, highly contagious febrile disease, characterized by a dermatitis, in which the eruption passes from the papule to vesicle, and this in turn into pustule, finally dessicating.

*Cause.—*The true nature of the virus is not known, and although certain micro-organisms have been described which are found in the pock, there is no proof that they are responsible for producing the poison. All that is positively known is, that it is developed in the system and reproduced in the pustule.

*Pathology.—*The most marked change occurs in the skin, where an eruption takes place, finally with the formation of scabs or crusts. The blood does not reveal any microscopic changes, although darkened in color.

*Treatment.—*No one but an immune should handle these cases, and he should first wash the body with a 1 : 500 solution of bichloride of mercury. After this has been done, inject an amount of fluid equal to 10 per cent. of the body weight, distributing same by arterial injection. If blood is drained, and it is proper to do so, add fluid to the injection to make up the loss into the blood bottle. Give full cavity injection. Bodies dead of this disease should be buried within a reasonably short length of time, so that the apartments may be rendered safe by fumigation, and under no circumstances should a public funeral be held. After the body has been placed in the casket, the slide, preferably of glass, should be closed and should not be reopened under any circumstances. Govern yourself by the regulations of your district for transportation of these cases.

MEASLES.

*—Synonyms.—*Morbilli; rubeola.

*Definition.—*An acute, infectious, contagious fever, characterized by a general papular eruption.

*Cause.—*The efforts to isolate a specific germ which will produce the disease has thus far failed, though many organisms have been found in the secretions.

*Pathology.—*There is a lack of coagulability of the blood, which is dark in color. The internal organs are congested and softened. The lesion of the skin consists of an acute hyperemia with exudation in the vascular papillae of the corium, the sebaceous and sweat glands.

Treatment.—Bodies rarely die from this cause; the usual immediate cause of death is exhaustion. An injection of half strength fluid for the first part of the injection followed by normal fluid for the balance of the injection, with full cavity injection, closing the orifices is all that is necessary. For transportation, govern yourself according to the provisions of the transportation rules.

PAROTITIS.

—*Synonyms.*—Mumps, epidemic parotitis.

Definition.—An acute, infectious, and contagious disease, characterized by an inflammation of one or both of the parotid glands.

Cause.—The specific cause is a contagion generated during the course of the disease, the exact nature of which is not known, although thought by some to be the tetrad of mumps.

Pathology.—The parotid glands become swollen and hard. Death very seldom occurs from this disease.

Treatment.—Disinfect the oral cavity with embalming fluid. The swelling cannot be reduced, so that the next concern to the embalmer will be to preserve the body. This should be done by injecting 64 ounces of half strength fluid, followed by enough normal fluid to secure preservation. If blood vessels contain much blood, drain from a large vein, and then inject additional fluid to make up for that lost by drainage. Close all openings with absorbent cotton. Abide by the regulations of your state governing the transportation of these cases.

PERTUSSIS.

—*Synonyms.*—Whooping-cough; tussis convulsiva.

Definition.—A specific infectious, contagious disease occurring epidemically, and characterized by a peculiar, spasmodic cough, ending in a whoop.

Cause.—The cause of whooping-cough has always been a matter of conjecture.

Pathology.—In the uncomplicated form there is no lesion which can be said to be characteristic. There might in complications be hemorrhage from the lung.

Treatment.—Disinfect the oral and nasal cavities with embalming fluid. Inject 64 ounces of half strength fluid followed by enough normal fluid to secure preservation. If blood vessels contain much blood, drain from a large vein, and then inject additional fluid to make up for that lost by drainage. Close all openings with absorbent cotton. Discourage public funerals in these cases. For intra-state or inter-state transportation of these cases, govern yourself according to the provisions of your district rules.

TYPHUS FEVER.

—*Synonyms.*—Famine fever; Ship fever; Jail fever; Hospital fever; and Putrid fever.

Definition.—An acute, infectious, very contagious, endemic, and also epidemic disease, characterized by a high grade of fever and a peculiar rash.

Cause.—Not known.

Pathology.—The blood is dark and diffluent the result of the intense fever and rapid work of the poison. The liver is somewhat enlarged and softened, as are also the kidneys and spleen. There is an extravasation into the pericardium which gives it an ecchymotic appearance. There is also a slight engorgement and infiltration of the capillaries. The muscular tissues are of a dark red color. The skin shows a characteristic rash and ecchymotic spots are found on the more dependent parts of the body after death.

Treatment.—Slow arterial injection and drainage of blood. On account of rash, apply bichloride of mercury 1 : 500. In the presence of fermentation, give the abdomen a special treatment.

For transportation of bodies dead of this disease, govern yourself according to the provisions of the transportation rules.

VARICELLA.

—*Synonym.*—Chicken-pox.

Definition.—An acute, specific, and infectious disease, characterized by an eruption that rapidly passes through the stage of papule, vesicle, and pustule, and terminates by dessication.

Cause.—This is not known. All attempts to isolate the microorganisms or the contagium, whatever that may be, have failed.

Pathology.—The only pathological lesion is the eruption that appears on the skin.

Treatment.—These cases should be thoroughly washed with 1 : 500 solution of bichloride of mercury, after which a thorough arterial and cavity injection should be given, consuming for this purpose an amount of fluid equal to 10 per cent. of the body weight in the arteries. Blood should be drained from the veins, and an amount of fluid equal to what is lost to the blood bottle should be injected in addition to the 10 per cent. mentioned above. After the body is placed in the casket, close the slide which should be of glass, and do not reopen again. Public funerals of these cases should be discouraged, to avoid the indiscriminate transfer of the disease.

SEPTICEMIA.

—*Definition.*—A morbid process commonly known as blood poisoning, in which there is an invasion of the blood by bacteria or their toxins.

Cause.—Any bacteria or its toxin.

Pathology.—The blood is found to be dark, diffluent, and rich in bacteria. The liver and spleen are soft, dark in color, and show swelling. The lymphatics are also swollen.

Treatment.—The operator should approach these cases with unbroken skin on his hands, or if that be impossible, with rubber gloves, as the disease is disseminated through abrasions. Take up a large artery and vein, inject half strength fluid for the first bottle and normal fluid thereafter in the arteries, and drain from the veins. Disinfect the blood obtained from the vein before disposing of it. Give the body a complete cavity injection. Massage the face to stimulate capillary circulation while the arterial injection is being made. For transportation, govern yourself according to your district transportation rules.

PYEMIA.

—Definition.—An infectious disease due to the absorption of animal poisons, principally pyogenic organisms, and characterized by the formation, in the various tissues and organs, of multiple metastatic abscesses.

Cause.—One of the forms or a combination of pyogenic micrococci are held to be responsible, for this condition. The streptococcus and the staphylococcus are the forms most common, though it is not uncommon to find the micrococcus lanciolatus, the gonococcus, the bacillus coli communis, bacillus typhosis, bacillus pyocyaneus, and many others.

Pathology.—The body does not undergo putrefaction as rapidly as in septicemia. The first effects of the morbid changes are found in the veins, which result in thrombi. These thrombi are found in the various organs and tissues of the body.

Treatment.—Use the precautions observed in the treatment for septicemia. Give the body a complete arterial injection using half strength fluid for the first bottle of the injection. Drain as much blood from the veins as possible. Thrombi may complicate the drainage, and if none can be obtained from several of the larger veins, tap the heart as a last resort. Disinfect the blood before disposing of it. Streptococcus infection of the embalmer from abrasions of the skin is very dangerous and every possible precaution should be carefully taken. Give the body a complete cavity injection. For transportation, govern yourself according to the provisions of the transportation rules.

CHAPTER XX.

TREATMENT OF SPECIAL DISEASES.—CONTINUED.

DISEASES OF THE RESPIRATORY SYSTEM.
GANGRENE OF THE LUNG.

—*Definition.*—A putrefactive necrosis of the lung.

Cause.—Many putrefactive bacteria thrive in the necrotic soil, but whether they are the cause or the result is not known.

Pathology.—When the gangrene is due to the plugging of one of the large branches of the pulmonary artery, a large part of the lung becomes dark, greenish brown, or a black fetid mass, softening rapidly in the center, forming an irregular cavity, containing a foul-smelling disgusting, greenish fluid.

Treatment.—Give complete arterial injection. Inject the pleural sac on the affected side through the first intercostal space or through the apex of the cavity. Spray fluid into the mouth and nose and close them with absorbent cotton. For shipment of these cases govern yourself according to the transportation rules.

PULMONARY HEMORRHAGE.

—*Synonyms.*—Hemoptysis; Broncho-pulmonary hemorrhage; Bronchorrhagia; Pneumorrhagia.

Definition.—An expectoration of blood, due to hemorrhage from the mucous membrane of the bronchi, trachea, or larynx and from erosion or rupture of capillaries in lung cavities.

Cause.—The hemorrhage may result from congestion of the lungs, due either to pulmonary lesions or from cardiac derangements. It may accompany malignant affections, infectious fevers, scurvy, cancer of the lung, gangrene, and abscess of the lung.

Pathology.—There is, in most cases rupture of the capillaries of the bronchial mucous membranes. If tubercular cavities are formed, a ruptured aneurism is sometimes seen, or large blood vessel eroded by ulceration. If pulmonary apoplexy has existed, the parenchyma may be lacerated.

Treatment.—Some operators wait until fluid passes from the mouth before taking steps to stop the hemorrhage due to the injection of fluid. We prefer to use plaster of paris and cotton, making a paste of them and forcing the paste down upon the epiglottis to prevent the waste of fluid from that source. When the cause of death is known, this operation must be done before the injection is begun or the throat will have to be dried out before the plaster of paris will set properly. Another treatment to prevent the leakage of fluid would be to tie off the trachea just above the upper border of the sternum.

The body is usually emaciated and should be injected arterially with comparatively mild fluid, in order to avoid drying or dessication of the features. Whenever fermentation exists in the abdomen, the cavity should be injected; otherwise it is not usually necessary. The amount of fluid for the injection should be based on the amount that will be taken by the vessels of a body the size of the one being injected. For transportation of these cases the provisions of the transportation rules should be your guide.

PULMONARY ABSCESS.

—*Synonyms.*—Abscess of the lungs; Suppurative pneumonitis.

Definition.—A collection of pus in the lung, accompanied by degeneration of tissue.

Pathology.—The abscess may involve one or more lobules, or engage almost the entire lobe, or the abscesses may be scattered throughout the whole lung.

Treatment.—Should hemorrhage occur, treat this case the same as for pulmonary hemorrhage. If no hemorrhage occurs, give the body a complete injection with a mild fluid and inject the pleural sacs from the first intercostal space or the apex of the cavity. For transportation, govern yourself according to the provisions of the transportation laws.

PNEUMONIA.

—This disease is divided into different subdivisions as follows: Lobar Pneumonia, broncho-pneumonia, and chronic interstitial pneumonia.

(A) *Lobar Pneumonia.*—*Synonyms.*—Croupous or Fibrinous Pneumonia; Pneumonitis; Inflammation of the lungs; and Winter fever.

Definition.—This is an acute infectious disease characterized by an inflammation of the lung tissue in which there is, first, congestion and engorgement, second, exudation or consolidation; and third, resolution or suppuration.

Pathology.—The right lung is more frequently affected than the left, and one lobe, or one entire lung, rather than both lungs at the same time.

Treatment.—Should suppuration occur, turn the body on its side, press on the sternum and cause the suppurative matter to leave the windpipe by purging it into the folds of a towel which should be placed at the mouth. Spray the mouth with fluid and close the oral and nasal cavities with absorbent cotton.

Give the body a thorough arterial and cavity injection, paying especial attention to the pleural sacs, which should be injected independently from the first intercostal space on each side or from the apex of the cavity. Drain blood and disinfect the contents of the blood bottle before disposing of same. For transportation, govern yourself according to the provisions of the transportation laws.

(B) *Broncho-Pneumonia—Synonyms.*—Capillary Bronchitis; Lobular Pneumonia; Catarrhal Pneumonia.

Definition.—An inflammation of the terminal bronchi, air vesicles, and interstitial tissue of a few or many of the lobules.

Pathology.—The interstitial tissue between the air cells and the capillaries are greatly weakened. In most cases the lung will float when placed in water, though the small mahogany-colored nodules found distributed throughout the lung when excised sink in water.

Treatment.—The nature of the disease is such that preservation is comparatively simple, the disease affecting the extremities of the respiratory system. Arterial injection together with special attention to the pleural sacs will suffice for the cases. For transportation, govern yourself according to the provisions of the transportation rules.

(C) *Chronic Interstitial Pneumonia.—Synonyms.*—Cirrhosis of the lungs; Fibroid Pneumonia.

Definition.—A chronic inflammation of the lungs, in which the normal air cells are replaced by fibrous or connective tissue, followed by induration and atrophy of the lung.

Pathology.—The disease is nearly always confined to one lung, though, in very rare cases, both lungs may be involved, while localized areas are the rule. The affected lung becomes atrophied and in extreme cases, may be no larger than the closed hand. As a result of the shrinkage of the lung tissue, the heart undergoes hypertrophy. When tuberculosis exists, cavities of varying size and number are found, and the interstitial tissue between the capillaries and the air cells is very much weakened.

Treatment.—Should this disease be followed by a rupture of the capillaries during the injection, thereby causing a hemorrhage from the oral and nasal openings, treat it as you would a case of pulmonary hemorrhage. Otherwise give the body a thorough arterial and cavity injection with special attention to the pleural sacs. For transportation, govern yourself according to the provisions of the transportation laws.

HYDROTHORAX.

—Synonyms.—Thoracic dropsy; Dropsy of the chest; Dropsy of the pleura.

Definition.—A collection of serous fluid within the pleural cavity without inflammation.

Pathology.—Hydrothorax, unless due to cardiac affections, is usually bilateral. The quantity of fluid varies, and is generally greater on one side than on the other. The fluid is free, and of a low specific gravity, alkaline in character, clear, and of an amber color.

Treatment.—To prevent the formation of blisters on the posterior surface of the thorax, aspirate the serous fluid from the pleural sacs, introducing the trocar through the apex of the cavity, and extending it into the cavity until it has almost reached the diaphragm. This must be done with both the right and left sacs. Give the body a complete injection, using normal fluid throughout the entire injection. Inject the pleural sacs after the serous fluid has been withdrawn. For prevention of post-operative dangers such as bursting blisters, etc., line the casket with rubber for a distance of 3 inches above the bottom. For transportation of these cases, govern yourself according to the provisions of the transportation laws.

CHAPTER XXI.

TREATMENT OF SPECIAL DISEASES.—CONTINUED.

DISEASES OF THE CIRCULATORY SYSTEM.
PERICARDITIS.

—Definition.—An acute inflammation of the pericardium and the serous covering of the heart.

Treatment.—Give the body a thorough injection of half strength fluid followed by normal fluid. Drain from the veins. Inject the abdominal cavity. For transportation of these cases, govern yourself according to the provisions of the transportation rules.

HYDROPERICARDIUM.

—Synonym.—Dropsy of the pericardium.

Definition.—Hydropericardium is a non-inflammatory condition of the pericardium, attended by an accumulation of sero-albuminous fluid.

Pathology.—Hydropericardium is not a disease of itself, but it is always secondary. The accumulated fluid is usually clear, of an amber color, though it may become turbid by the presence of fibrin or red blood corpuscles. The fluid is alkaline in reaction.

Treatment.—As this disease is always secondary to another, the treatment will also be secondary and all that can be said is that the heart sac should be relieved of its accumulated serous fluid, after the body has received the treatment necessary for the immediate cause of death. Transportation will also be covered by the disease causing death.

HEMOPERICARDIUM.

—Definition.—Hemopericardium is an infiltration of blood into the pericardium. It is the result of a rupture of an aneurism of the aorta or coronary arteries, or in rare cases from rupture of the heart. It may also arise from injuries such as bullet wounds, fracture of the ribs, sternum, etc.

Treatment.—This condition is usually secondary to another such as gun shot wound, aneurism of the aorta, etc., so that the treatment must be given under the heading of the immediate cause of death. For transportation requirements also refer to the immediate cause of death and the transportation rules.

PNEUMO-PERICARDIUM.

—*Definition.*—Pneumo-pericardium is an accumulation of air in the pericardium. Although this is a rare disease, it does occasionally occur, either through diseased processes, such as cancerous or tubercular ulceration or through injuries; thus a ruptured pulmonary cavity might result in this condition, or the perforation of the esophagus, by malignant processes would give rise to this lesion. Sometimes pus in the pericardium will generate gas.

Treatment.—As the accumulation of air or gas is secondary to some other process of disease, the immediate cause of death will carry with it the proper treatment. The gas itself should be removed by piercing the pericardium with a small needle or trocar, after which a small quantity of fluid should be injected.

ENDOCARDITIS.

—*Definition.*—Endocarditis is an inflammation of the lining membrane of the heart, and is generally confined to the valves, though other parts may be affected.

Pathology.—The morbid changes are, first, a reddened and injected appearance of the endothelium, which soon becomes opaque and swollen from congestion of the small blood vessels. This swelling or thickening of the membrane furnishes a favorable resting place for deposits of fibrin, and we have small, beady deposits from the size of a pin point to that of a pea, or even larger. These small, beady excrescences may become detached, and floating off in the general current, give rise to embolism in distant parts.

Treatment.—An embolism means the obstruction of a blood vessel by some foreign material. If in the injection of fluid, there is an obstruction in one of the blood vessels, leading to one of the organs, you will never be any the wiser, but if the obstruction is in one of the vessels supplying a certain area of skin, the condition will show up sooner or later, when that certain part will have to be treated hypodermically. Slow arterial injection with drainage of blood should be given and when symptoms of fermentation are present, include special attention to the abdominal cavity.

AORTIC INCOMPETENCY.

—*Synonyms.*—Aortic Insufficiency; Aortic Regurgitation.

Definition.—Inability of the aortic valves to properly close an abnormally large aortic opening, or a change in the segments whereby they are shortened by curling of the leaflets, or by calcification.

Treatment.—Bodies dead of this disease will be found with very much blood, and the elimination of the blood by drainage should be the first consideration along with the injection of fluid. The fluid should be diluted one-half for the first part of the injection, and sufficient fluid used to reach all parts of the circulatory system. It will be well to add fluid equal to the amount of blood and fluid taken from the vein to your normal injection in a body the size of the one to be operated on. A complete cavity injection should be given. For transportation, govern yourself according to the provisions of the transportation rules.

AORTIC STENOSIS.

*—Definition.—*Aortic stenosis is an obstruction of the aortic orifice, due to changes in the segments of the semilunar valves, or arterio-sclerosis, or atheromatous deposits.

*Treatment.—*Give same treatment advised for aortic incompetency, with special care in the injection. Sclerotic conditions may complicate the injection, and in that case as many arteries should be injected as possible together with full blood drainage.

MITRAL INCOMPETENCY.

*—Synonyms.—*Mitral Regurgitation; Mitral Insufficiency.

*Definition.—*This condition is an incomplete or imperfect closure of the auriculo-ventricular opening, permitting the regurgitation of blood during the contraction of the left ventricle, and due to an abnormal condition of the leaflets or an enlarged opening.

*Treatment.—*Give same treatment as advised for aortic incompetency, with special care to remove as much blood as possible, which, with massaging the face downward, should relieve any blood discolorations.

MITRAL STENOSIS.

*—Definition.—*Mitral stenosis is a constriction of the left auriculo-ventricular orifice, usually due to valvular endocarditis.

*Treatment.—*Give this body the same treatment as advised for aortic incompetency, with special care indicated in mitral incompetency.

TRICUSPID INCOMPETENCY.

*—Synonym.—*Tricuspid Regurgitation.

*Definition.—*This condition is an imperfect closure of the tricuspid valves, due to dilation of the right ventricle or to disease of the valves.

*Treatment.—*Drain as much blood as possible from this case. Massage the face downward, and inject the maximum amount of fluid; diluting the first bottle to half strength. In obstinate cases of blood discoloration, open the common carotid arteries and internal jugular veins, inject upward in the arteries and drain from the veins, so as to wash out the vessels of the face. For facial injection use nothing stronger than half strength fluid. Give thorough cavity injection. For transportation, govern yourself according to the provisions of the transportation rules.

TRICUSPID STENOSIS.

—*Definition.*—Tricuspid stenosis is an obstruction of the tricuspid opening, usually congenital, though it may be acquired.

Treatment.—Treat the same as for tricuspid incompetency.

PULMONARY INCOMPETENCY.

—*Synonym.*—Pulmonary Insufficiency.

Definition.—Pulmonary incompetency is an imperfect closure of the pulmonary orifice of the right ventricle due to changes in the pulmonary valves.

Treatment.—Treat the same as for tricuspid incompetency.

PULMONARY STENOSIS.

—*Definition.*—Pulmonary stenosis is an obstruction of the pulmonary opening of the right ventricle, due to congenital defects or to endocarditis.

Treatment.—Treat the same as for tricuspid incompetency.

CARDIAC THROMBOSIS.

—*Definition.*—Cardiac thrombosis is the formation of blood clots in the cavities of the heart.

Pathology.—The blood clots are found most frequently in the right side of the heart. They vary in size, from that of a pin head to that of a hen's egg. When degeneration takes place, softening follows, and sometimes particles become dislodged and float off to set up thrombi in other viscera.

Treatment.—Remove the maximum amount of blood by drainage along with the injection of fluid. The fluid in this case should be not more than half strength for the first part of the injection, to be followed by enough normal fluid to secure preservation. If thrombi have lodged in any of the larger arteries, the circulation to the part reached by the branches of the artery will be affected. This can be overcome by injecting an artery close to the part which is not receiving the fluid. Massage the face downward to assist capillary circulation. Give a complete cavity injection. For transportation, govern yourself according to the provisions of the transportation rules.

HYPERTROPHY OF THE HEART.

—*Definition.*—Hypertrophy of the heart is an enlargement of the organ, due to an increase in the volume of its muscular fibers, and usually also to dilatation of its cavities.

Treatment.—Secure full drainage from the veins. Drainage will be stimulated by an injection of half strength fluid for the first part of the injection and a massage of the face. Follow the first part of the injection with enough normal fluid to secure preservation. Give a complete cavity injection. For transportation, govern yourself according to the provisions of the transportation rules.

CARDIAC DILATATION.

*—Definition.—*Cardiac dilatation is an increase in the size of the cavities of the heart, due either to thickening or thinning of the walls.

*Treatment.—*Treat the same as for hypertrophy of the heart.

CARDIAC ATROPHY.

*—Definition.—*Cardiac atrophy is a decrease in the size, strength, weight, and activity of the heart.

*Treatment.—*Remove blood by drainage, and inject half strength fluid for the first part of the injection. The amount of fluid need not be as great as in the acute disease of the heart. Massage the face downward. Give cavity injection. For transportation, govern yourself according to the provisions of the transportation rules.

ARTERIO-SCLEROSIS.

*—Synonyms.—*Endarteritis; Atheroma; Arterial Sclerosis.

*Definition.—*Arterio-sclerosis is an inflammatory and degenerative condition of the arterial system, primarily of the intima, although later degenerative changes may involve the whole structure. Calcarine deposits are quite common.

*Pathology.—*As a result of proliferation, infiltrated areas begin in the middle and outer coats. These nodules vary in size from that of a small shot to that of a large coin. As they increase in size, the intima loses its smoothness and becomes thickened and rough. As these changes progress, the middle and outer coats are weakened. Calcification may also occur in the wall.

In the diffuse form the change in the coats of the vessels extends throughout the greater part of the arterial system, and in some cases invades the capillaries and veins.

In the senile arterio-sclerosis calcareous deposits occur, which render the vessels rigid. Where these tissue-changes involve the capillaries, there may be complete obliteration of their lumen in some places.

*Treatment.—*In some cases the artery appears to be closed at a point ahead of the tube and will resist the injection of fluid. Usually, however, the injection can be made without resistance. Blood should be drained from these cases so as to allow as full capillary penetration as possible. When no arterial injection can be made, open the internal jugular and several other large veins, drain blood from them and then inject fluid while the tube is within the vessel. If necessary add a complete hypodermic injection to all parts of the body excepting the face. Give the cavities full treatment. For transportation, govern yourself according to the transportation rules.

FATTY DEGENERATION OF THE ARTERIES.

—In the fatty degeneration of arteries the process consists in the gradual replacement of certain parts of the muscular cells by fat droplets. The fat makes its appearance as minute droplets or granules in the cells. These granules, which are characterized by their dark color, gradually increase in number and ultimately the whole of that part of the cell may be transformed. During the process the granules coalesce, and in this manner form distinct drops of fat. As the process proceeds the cell is increased in size and becomes more globular in shape. The cell wall is destroyed and the cell may thus be converted into a mass of granular fat. Ultimately the matter between the granules of fat liquify. The corpuscles break up and the fat becomes distributed in the surrounding tissues. The immediate effect of this fatty degeneration is to produce more or less softening of the fatty part, which will impair or destroy its function. In the case of the artery, the internal, middle and external coats may be affected, but the external is the one usually first attacked. The inner layer or endothelium, and the connective tissue cells in the deeper layers of the inner coat may become affected in various parts of the vessel. The process may involve a great portion of the inner coat, even the whole thickness of the intima may be destroyed. The walls of the artery may be entirely solidified, the canal being closed completely with a soft, yellowish substance as a result of the disease. The artery might appear to be a solid mass when the dissecting knife is passed through. We have seen the anterior and posterior tibial, the popliteal, radial, ulnar, the aorta arteries, and especially the arch of the aorta thus affected. Calcification may be present at many places. These cases are frequently met with in old age.

A body of this kind, where there is fatty degeneration of the arteries, is sometimes hard to embalm. The walls of the artery will be very much weakened, and too much pressure must not be made on them while injecting fluid. Inject the fluid so that it will take several hours to fill the tissues. The pressure should be gentle and regular when the aspirator and injector pump is used. If this precaution is taken often the whole body can be embalmed without a rupture of the arterial system, the fluid reaching all the extremities by means of collateral circulation.

If the embalmer should be so unfortunate as to rupture the circulation then he will have to resort to cavity embalming, and the subcutaneous tissues will have to be embalmed by the hollow needle trocar.

ANEURISM.

—*Definition.*—An aneurism is a circumscribed dilatation of an artery, formed by the giving away of one or more of its coats. A false aneurism is where there is a rupture of the coats, and the blood is found in the adjacent tissues.

Treatment.—Drain blood from a large vein. Inject half strength fluid for the first part of the injection, followed by enough normal fluid to secure preservation. The aneurism itself, will not affect the circulation of fluid to any great extent. Massage the face downward. Give a complete cavity injection. For transportation, govern yourself according to the transportation rules.

CHAPTER XXII.

TREATMENT OF SPECIAL DISEASES.—CONTINUED.

DISEASES OF THE DIGESTIVE SYSTEM.
JAUNDICE.

—*Synonym.*—Icterus.

Definition.—Jaundice is a symptom rather than a disease, and is found in the various affections of the liver. It is characterized by a deposit of bilirubin in the various structures and fluids of the body, which gives them a yellow or jaundiced hue.

Etiology.—Most pathologists agree that all the forms of jaundice can only come from obstruction. The obstruction is due to inflammation tumefaction of the duodenum or bile-ducts; to foreign bodies, such as gall stones or parasites, within the ducts; tumors within the duct or by pressure from without, such as tumors, gravid uterus, or fecal matter; or to stricture or obliteration of the duct.

CATARRHAL JAUNDICE.

—*Definition.*—Catarrhal inflammation of the lining membrane of the biliary ducts, and the duodenum, and attended with discoloration of the skin and tissues from the consequent retention and absorption of the bile.

Pathology.—That portion of the duct lying in the intestines is more frequently and seriously affected, though the inflammation may extend to the cystic and even the hepatic duct. The membrane lining the ducts is swollen and inflamed. The liver is usually congested, slightly enlarged, and of a deep yellow color. The gall bladder is usually distended with bile. The ducts are occluded by the swollen mucosa and plugs of inspissated mucous.

Discoloration of the skin and conjunctiva occurs. The yellow tinge begins in the eyes, forehead, and neck, gradually extending over the body, the color being the deepest in the wrinkles and folds of the skin. The color is generally of a lemon hue, becoming darker and assuming a bronze or greenish tint as the hepatic lesion assumes a graver character.

INFANTILE JAUNDICE.

—*Etiology.*—It is not known positively what causes give rise to temporary jaundice in the new-born. Some say it is due to a reduction of blood pressure in the hepatic capillaries, while others say it is due to a stasis in the smaller bile ducts, which are compressed by the distended radicles of the portal vein. The severe form may be due to congenital closure or absence of the common or hepatic duct, to hepatic syphilis of congenital form, or to septic infection due to phlebitis of the umbilical vein.

In the child the skin becomes a yellowish hue of various shades. In the severe form the hue increases in intensity, the skin assuming a bronze or yellowish-green color. The abdomen becomes full and tumid, owing to the congestion of the liver and spleen. When due to syphilis, there is usually skin eruption.

MALIGNANT JAUNDICE.

—*Synonyms.*—Acute Yellow Atrophy of the Liver.

Definition.—A grave form of jaundice characterized by neurosis of the hepatic cells and atrophy of the liver.

Pathology.—The liver shows marked atrophy, being not more than two-thirds or one-half of the normal size, is thin, flabby. On making a section a yellow or a reddish yellow surface is presented. The hepatic cells are found in every stage of necrosis. Most of the organs are bile stained, as well as the skin, and hemorrhages are frequent.

Treatment for Jaundice.—Since the conditions are similar and since the conditions after death are identical in reference to pigmentation, we will consider the treatment of infantile, malignant, and catarrhal jaundice under one head.

The pigmentation of the skin, no matter how small, is the condition which presents itself most forcefully, and is the most annoying to the embalmer. Much study has been given to the subject, but with little success. It is claimed by some that certain fluids will bleach and bring out the natural color.

A small amount of bile is sufficient to tint the surface of the body. Bile is composed of salts, fats, organic matter, acids, and also coloring matter, called the bile pigments. Bilirubin is the principal coloring matter, and when dissolved in alkali, forms, when coming in contact with the air and also in the dead body, a green precipitate known as biliverdin. The bile pigments in the blood are carried with the serum from the capillaries to the tissues, being deposited in the internal coat or deep layer of the epidermis as well as the papillary of the dermis. The amount deposited regulates the extent of the pigmentation.

One of the most beneficial things to do, where pigmentation is present is to wash out the arterial system, draw blood from the veins, massage the exposed parts. Inject a diluted fluid at first, follow with a fluid of full strength, until complete disinfection and permeation of the tissues has taken place. Keep up constant massaging during the whole course of injection. This may bring fair results, with the addition of face tints and showing the body under artificial light.

Strong solutions of formaldehyde when used at first are deleterious, causing the skin to become green. This greenness is more pronounced when chemicals such as methylene blue have been administered by the attending physician before death. Bilirubin is a red yellow color, and alkalies precipitate the bilirubin and form biliverdin. Biliverdin is a greenish color.

All fluids contain alkalies, and are mostly alkali in reaction, and this may account for the greenish color of the skin after the injection of fluid. Acids do not precipitate the biliverdin and there is a tendency to dissolve it and keep it in solution.

Moadinger suggests that a weak solution of some acid be injected into the arterial system before the injection of embalming fluid. He prefers a two per cent. solution of oxalic acid.

Dhonau prefers the use of a one or two per cent. solution of borax, to be injected into the arterial system, followed by half strength fluid, and this followed by full strength fluid. Dhonau also applies full strength peroxide of hydrogen to the skin while massaging the face.

Eckels prefers the use of a fluid containing a peroxide.

If methylene blue has been administered by the attending physician and you have learned this fact before hand, it is then not advisable to use a formaldehyde fluid. There is a chemical action set up between the methylene blue and the formaldehyde which will give to the tissues a greenish color which is quite objectionable. In this case you would inject some fluid which does not contain formaldehyde. A benzoate of soda or borax, or peroxide solution would do.

A good formula to use, when you know methylene blue has been used by the attending physician is:

Rx	Carbolic acid	5	oz.
	Borax	12	oz.
	Glycerine	1	oz.
	Water, qs.	1	gal.

For transportation, govern yourself according to the transportation rules.

CIRRHOSIS OF THE LIVER.

*—Synonyms.—*Interstitial Hepatitis; Sclerosis of the Liver; Nutmeg Liver; Hobnailed Liver.

*Definition.—*A chronic disease of the liver, characterized by an increased connective tissue, a reduction in the size of the organ, and a degeneration of the parenchymatous constituents.

*Etiology.—*In a great majority of cases the disease is due to alcohol, syphilis, highly spiced and very rich foods. Cirrhosis may result from chronic obstruction of the bile ducts, due to gall stones, or tuberculosis. Cirrhosis frequently occurs between the ages of thirty and sixty years, though it may be found in the extremes of life. Men are more liable to contract the disease, owing to greater dissipations.

*Pathology.—*The liver is increased in size by the increase of connective tissue, and hyperaemic. On the surface it exhibits a knobbed appearance (hobnailed liver) and these knobs present through the capsule a yellowish appearance. The granulations vary in size from a pinhead to a pea. As a rule there is a little jaundice, as there is a decrease in the production of bile, instead the skin takes on an earthy, sallow tint. There is generally ascites, swelling of the feet and legs, which increases until the abdomen and the lower extremities become of an enormous size. The nutrition of the body suffers, the skin is dry and harsh. The blood is altered in quantity, and coagulates quickly. Ecchymotic spots appear on the skin, about the face and nose.

Treatment.—There are probably not many other cases of death, which need greater skill and intelligence in their treatment than does cirrhosis. The condition that presents itself is a distended abdomen with gas and liquid. The limbs are also distended and the upper part of the body is wasted away and is greatly discolored as death was caused by asphyxia.

Place the body on the board, open the femoral vein, and insert your drainage tube. It is better to use this vein as it is larger, and there is more control of the removal of blood, and we would advise in this case the use of the flexible rubber drainage tube, which can be pushed up in the vein till it reaches the right auricle of the heart if you wish. Drain all the blood possible. Use the trocar method, see page 255, or the direct incision, see page 257, to remove the gases and ascitic fluid from the abdomen. Use the bandage method, see page 339 to remove the water from the tissue of the extremities.

Raise the femoral artery and inject slowly a diluted fluid and massage the face gently toward the jugular vein, using some recognized face bleacher. Then follow with an injection of fluid of full strength until you are sure the fluid has permeated every tissue of the body. Do not be afraid to use plenty of fluid. Inject the cavities.

For transportation, govern yourself according to the transportation rules.

CARCINOMA OF THE LIVER.

—*Definition.*—A cancerous growth in the liver.

Pathology.—Jaundice is present in most cases and where the portal circulation is seriously compressed, ascites developes. The liver is greatly enlarged, and the surface is nodular.

Treatment.—As in all chronic affections of the liver, where the skin takes on a yellowish or bronze hue, due to pigmentation, it is almost impossible to bring about the desired cosmetic effects. The pigment is not only in the blood vessel but also in the tissues of the skin.

We would advise the washing out of the tissues, by the use of the oxalic or borax solution, injecting the axillary artery and draining from the femoral artery or raising both the carotid arteries, injecting upward on one side and draining from the other.

For transportation, govern yourself according to the transportation rules.

APPENDICITIS.

—An inflammation, acute or chronic, of the appendix.

Pathology.—The pathology will depend to a great extent upon the degree of the inflammation. Ulceration may take place or there may be perforation.

Treatment.—If, after an operation, reopen the incision made by the surgeon, relieve the gas pressure on the intestines by incising them; surround the intestines with hardening compound; then inject an artery, using half strength fluid for the first 64 oz., followed by enough normal fluid to secure preservation. Drain the blood during the injection by one of the drainage processes.

If no operation has been made, insert a trocar into the caecum to relieve the gas pressure, then inject normal fluid into the same place, using sufficient fluid to neutralize the process of putrefactive fermentation. The trocar can be first inserted in the usual place passing it to the caecum, or through the abdominal wall directly over the caecum. The arterial injection and drainage should be made as is mentioned above. For transportation, govern yourself according to the transportation rules.

PERITONITIS.

—An acute or chronic inflammation of the peritoneum either local or general.

Pathology.—There is nearly always present more or less fluid in the abdominal cavity.

Treatment.—Drain blood from a large vein, and inject half strength fluid for the first part of the injection, following this with enough normal fluid to preserve the tissues of the body. After the arterial injection and drainage have been completed, pierce the abdominal cavity in the usual place and draw off all the fluid that you can reach, paying especial attention to the lower part of the cavity. Then inject normal or supernormal fluid into the cavity to neutralize the process of putrefactive fermentation. Pierce the colons and inject fluid into them as well. If fermentation resists this treatment, make a small incision along the median line and above the umbilicus, examine the stomach and intestines, incising them if they contain the gas. After eliminating the gas, inject fluid directly into them, or, surround the organs of the cavity with good hardening compound; sew up the incision and the body should not deteriorate in any way. For transportation, govern yourself according to the transportation rules.

DROPSY.

—*Definition.*—Dropsy is the accumulation of serous fluid in a cavity or in the tissues.

Dropsy of the abdomen is called ascites.

Dropsy of the chest is called hydrothorax.

Dropsy of the peritoneum is called hydroperitoneum or ascites. General dropsy of the cellular tissues is called anasarca.

ASCITES.

—*Synonyms.*—Dropsy of the Peritoneum; Abdominal Dropsy.

Definition.—An accumulation of serous fluid in the peritoneal cavity.

Etiology.—Any obstruction of the portal circulation is a possible cause of ascites, the most frequent being cirrhosis of the liver. Pressure from tumors or neighboring organs may also give rise to it. Peritonitis and valvular diseases of the heart are also responsible for ascites, and chronic pulmonary affections may impair the portal circulation to the extent of producing it.

Pathology.—The quality and character of the fluid show great variation, from a few pints to several gallons, and from a straw or lemon tint to a brownish or greenish hue. It may be blood stained, and occasionally clean and transparent. It is usually watery in character.

Treatment.—Use the trocar method. Insert the trocar through the umbilicus and draw off all the ascitic fluid from the abdomen, then surround the organs with a quantity of fluid sufficient to preserve them. Or if you desire, use the direct incision and after the ascitic fluid has been drawn off, surround the organs with a hardening compound.

The body in general should be preserved through an arterial injection of normal fluid for the first 64 ounces, then one and one-quarter strength for all subsequent bottles. This, if attended by copious drainage from a large vein, will preserve all portions of the body excepting possibly the epidermis of the posterior abdominal wall, which, by gravitation of the ascitic fluid, will become separated from the derma, producing skin slip, and causing the formation of blisters.

Previously to placing the body on the embalming board for treatment, a rubber cover should be placed over the board so that drippings of all kinds can be made to flow into a bucket at the lower end of the embalming board. When the above mentioned blisters are cut and their contents disposed of by gravitation into the bucket, a strong solution of formaldehyde should be applied to the affected skin to harden it and to prevent any further progress toward decomposition.

In ascitic cases the casket should be lined with rubber or oil cloth to a point three or four inches above the bottom. In addition to this precaution, the use of sawdust is favored so that any unlooked for breaking of blisters may not be attended by a flow of the ascitic liquid from the casket. Many embalmers do not protect themselves against contingencies of this kind and are frequently criticized by the friends and family of the deceased.

ANASARCA.

—*Definition.*—Anasarca is a general dropsy of the cellular tissues.

Treatment.—*Bandage Method.*—Bandage the extremities of the body, commencing at the toes and finger tips, bandaging upward to the hip and shoulder, using a rubber bandage. Relieve the water as you go along, then rebandage, and by the third application you will have removed most of the water from the extremities.

Do not leave the bandage on while injecting.

Bandage Method. —Bandage the lower limbs, commencing with the thighs. Bandage as tight as possible down to the toes and make an incision in the heel, from which drainage of the serous fluid can be secured. In this method no laps are left between the bandaging so that the serous fluid can be forced toward the opening at the heel. (This method is said to be reliable, although we have had but little experience with it.)

Any accumulation of ascitic fluid in the cavities should be removed by aspiration with the trocar, as described in the treatment of ascites and hydrothorax. The rubber cover for the embalming board as described in the treatment for ascites, should not be omitted.

After the water has been eliminated as far as possible, the arterial injection should be made, using 64 ounces of normal strength fluid, followed by enough one-fourth strength fluid to secure preservation. Copious drainage will help to clear the blood vessels and allow a better distribution of the fluid, thereby assuring good preservation of all parts excepting the epidermis, which is practically closed off to the fluid by the accumulation of water in the subcutaneous tissue.

In these cases the skin should receive a good application of strong formaldehyde fluid before and after the principle operation, so as to strengthen it against the putrefactive tendencies of the rete mucosum.

These cases should be watched closely between the time of embalming and the funeral, as the most thorough preparation is sometimes unequal to the task of preserving the entire body in such a way as to prevent the formation of blisters.

For transportation of all dropsical conditions, govern yourself according to the provisions of the transportation rules.

CHAPTER XXIII.

TREATMENT OF ACCIDENT CASES.

Under this head are treated those deaths which are the result of accident.

SPECIFIC TREATMENT OF ACCIDENTS. —BROKEN NECK, HANGING, STRANGULATION.

—The mode of death may possibly cause a separation or dividing of the blood vessels of the neck. If this is the case there will remain in the head and face a large amount of blood, which would soon become coagulated, causing a dark bluish turning black discoloration. The treatment then must be to get this blood from the face, so would recommend the common carotid for injection of fluid and the internal jugular vein for the removal of blood.

Raise both the artery and the vein to the surface, and insert the arterial tube in the artery toward the face, and inject a small quantity of fluid in order to cause a pressure on the venous system, then open the vein, insert the drainage tube and begin to remove the blood, and as the blood drains from the drainage tube inject slowly into the artery. This will help to push the blood out of the capillary system and into the blood bottle and thus clear up the face of its discoloration.

In these cases the raising of only one common carotid would hardly suffice, and it would be far better to operate on both carotids to get the best results. For this reason then the circular incision would be the best operation, and perhaps the use of the Y shaped drainage tube. With the Y shaped drainage tube both sides of the face could be injected at the same time, and the blood could be removed from both internal jugular veins, and the operator could not help but get good results. The removal of blood from the internal jugulars in this direct way will relieve the pressure in the capillaries and smaller veins and induce a better circulation to all the immediate tissues.

BODY SEVERED.

—For these cases one should have a very good idea of the general arterial and venous circulations of the body, for many of the smaller as well as the larger vessels will be cut, necessitating one to tie them off.

If the body is severed below the diaphragm remove and cleanse all the loose and injured organs and tissues, place them in a bucket or pan and cover with fluid. Ligate all the injured arteries and veins in the upper and lower parts.

Inject the lower extremities from inside the abdominal cavity using the common iliac artery, observing the presence of the remaining united arteries and veins, which you can now see, for fluid will leak from them. The lock forceps will enable you to pick them up and with the aneurism needle dissect around the end of the vessel and tie each one tight.

Treat the upper extremity in the same way injecting either from the inside or the outside, according as the severity of the accident may lead you to decide. Inject from the inside upward through the aorta, or from the outside either through the radial, brachial, axillary or carotid.

The trunk may now be sewed together, beginning at the middle of the back. Sew each side up leaving the top open to receive the organs and the tissues which were removed. After these are placed more or less in position sprinkle hardening compound throughout the cavity. Now sew up the front and then place a strong bandage around the body.

THE ARM SEVERED.

—Clean off the parts, and inject the severed part through the radial towards the hand and by means of collateral circulation through palmar arch, the upper part will be embalmed and the arteries that have been severed disclosed, when they can be tied off. If there is a great leakage through the stub end, and all the arteries can not be tied off, plaster of paris may be put on the stub and then a strong and tight bandage drawn around.

The remaining body can then be injected through the opposite carotid, brachial or femoral, and when the leakages begin to occur at the stub end of the arm they can be found and tied off or if the leakage is too great plaster of paris may be used and a tight bandage placed about the stub end.

After both the arm and the body have been injected the arm can now be sewed on in its natural position, plaster of paris put around and a strong bandage placed around or a splint may be used on both sides.

THE LEG SEVERED.

—Clean off the parts, and inject the severed part through the large dorsal toward the foot and by means of collateral circulation through the plantar arch, the upper part will be embalmed and the arteries that have been severed disclosed, when they can be tied off. If there is a great leakage through the stub end, and all the arteries can not be tied off, plaster of paris may be put on the stub and then a strong and tight bandage drawn around.

The remaining body can then be injected through the carotid, brachial, axillary, or the opposite femoral and when the leakages begin at the stub end of the leg they can be found and tied off, or if the leakage is too great plaster of paris may be used and a tight bandage placed about the stub end.

After both the leg and the body have been injected, the leg can be sewed on in its natural position, plaster of paris put around and a strong bandage placed around, or a splint may be used on both sides.

THE HEAD SEVERED.

—Clean off the parts, and inject the head through the stub end of the carotid artery, and by means of collateral circulation through the circle of Willis, the fluid will leak through the other severed vessels and disclose them, so that they can be tied off. If one side of the face should take more fluid than the other side by this method the other carotid can be injected so as to equalize. It would perhaps be impossible to tie off all the tiny vessels that are severed so plaster of paris may be used to cover the stub end.

To inject the body, the four principle arteries to be tied are the two common carotids and the two vertebrals, besides numerous veins and small vessels. If it is impossible to tie all the severed vessels plaster of paris may be used, and then by injecting either through the brachial, axillary or femoral a thorough injection may be obtained. The stub end of the carotid might also be used for injection, but would not advise it as in most cases we find that it would be hard to get especially if the head were cut off close to the shoulders.

When both the head and the body have been injected, bring the two parts together by using a splint in the vertebral column, and having plastered well together sew the skin. Demi-surgery can be practiced to the fullest extent in this case, with great cosmetic effect.

THE HEAD CRUSHED.

—Remove all the coagulated blood and the injured parts of the brain. Cleanse the cavity thoroughly and remould with plaster of paris. Inject the best you can through one or both of the carotid arteries, and complete the injection hypodermically. Inject the rest of the body in the regular way, through one of the carotids raised for the injection of the head. With the practice and use of demi-surgery, all the bruised and torn fragments may be blended together, and the cosmetic effect made almost perfect.

THE FOOT CRUSHED.

—Remove all the coagulated blood by washing, and place all the parts together as nearly natural as possible. Now inject any of the principle arteries used in embalming, watching carefully the flow of fluid and blood. As soon as you see a leakage stop injecting long enough to tie it up, and when all the visible leakages have been thus treated, wrap the whole of the injured part with a bandage saturated with a plaster of paris solution. After this becomes dry and set complete the injection.

THE CHEST CRUSHED.

—Open up the cavity and remove all the injured organs and tissues, which you will place in a vessel containing formaldehyde fluid. With a soft sponge remove all the coagulated blood from the cavity. Now tie up all the visible arteries and start the injection from the inside, using first the innominate to inject the right arm and the right side of the face then the left common carotid to inject the left side of the face and the left subclavian to inject the left arm. It must be remembered though that while one artery is being injected the others should be tied off lest by collateral circulation you would get leakages. The thoracic aorta might be used but it will be found more difficult because of the leakages which would occur through the intercostal arteries. These leakages would not occur nearly as much by the raising of the branches off the arch of the aorta, namely the innominate, the left common carotid and the left subclavian. Any leakage can be stopped by means of the lock forceps and then tied.

The lower part of the body, if it is not injured, can be injected now through the abdominal aorta, but if there has been any damage done below the diaphragm, it would probably be best to further open up the cavity and inject each lower extremity through the common iliacs.

Now replace all the organs and surround them with hardening compound, and sew up the cavity incisions, with great care and neatness. It would be well to practice demi-surgery here, so that you would become more proficient in the art, and thus be able to do more efficient work on the exposed parts, should the occasion ever demand it.

GUN-SHOT IN THE ABDOMEN.

—When death occurs it is generally due to severing or dividing of an artery or decomposition resulting from the injury done the intestines. The operator should open the body cavity, from the end of the sternum bone to the pubic bone, and cleanse the cavity of all the coagulated blood and other putrid matter. Locate and tie up the injured vessels. The injection can then be started from one of the principle arteries which will aid in locating the other injured vessels. Puncture the stomach and inject inside, so as to prevent the formation of gas, and after the body has been injected place hardening compound inside the body cavity and sew up carefully and neatly.

BURNS AND SCALDS.

—A burn is an injury to the body produced by the application of a flame or of a substance heated above a certain temperature.

A scald is an injury produced by the application of a liquid heated above a certain temperature.

Injuries resulting from corrosive liquids such as sulphuric acid, nitric acid, caustic potash, carbolic acid, etc., are properly termed burns. A heated solid such as iron may produce a burn of great intensity from the blistering of the skin to the charring of the underlying tissues. Metals heated above 212 degrees Fahrenheit will produce redness, vesication and coagulation of the blood. Molten metals cause burns or scalds very similar to those produced by heated solids. Boiling oil produces severe burns. If a part is severely scalded with boiling water, the skin may appear sodden, blistered, and of an ash grey color, but never produces blackening or charring of the cuticle. Phosphorous burns are usually very severe and of great depth, while the area of skin destroyed is usually small. Gunpowder burns caused by explosions are often of great superficial extent, extensive scorching and numerous carbon particles are commonly found imbedded in the true skin. Petroleum burns are generally severe, as usually all or nearly all the body is scorched and blackened. Burns from flame, extensive scorching with burnt hair is a usual feature in a flame burn. Burns from explosions of fire damp in coal mines are frequently of great extent and present the appearance of great scorching, and very often a quantity of coal dust will be found imbedded in the true skin. There are six degrees of burns as follows: (a) Simple hyperemia of the skin, (b) dermatitis, with vesicles or bullae, (c) necrosis of the superficial layer of the skin, (d) complete necrosis of the skin, (e) necrosis of the skin, superficial fascia and muscles, and (f) complete carbonization of the part.

Treatment.—The embalmer does not treat these cases according to the cause as much as to what is left of the part after burning has been accomplished. After observing the part to note whether the condition can be bettered by a replacement of tissue by artificial means and finding such to be the case, I would use a form of paste commonly used for filling in cuts and restoring the features and with this paste thoroughly cover the burned part. If the affected part covers the entire face or most of it, an entire new surface will have to be built up with the paste. If the burning of the skin has left particles of epidermis adhering to the derma, I would use sweet oil and bath the entire face with it, thus softening the skin and allowing the removal of the small particles. Any small desiccated spots should be covered with the paste. After carefully blending the paste with the skin so as to produce a smooth even complexion, which can best be done by the use of a brush to smooth it with, apply a good quality of face powder (flesh color) to the part. If the color is too striking, or too white, destroy the contrast with carmine rouge. This form of operation is commonly known as demi-surgery. We find that the face powder is best applied with a pad made of surgical gauze especially when applied with a patting movement. This gives a good imitation of the pores of the skin, and if any further smoothing is necessary the brush can be used again. The principal result wanted is a good imitation of the natural parts. If the operator will use the utmost care to give the parts gentle, fine touches here and there, a most artistic effect will be produced. If the eye brows have been destroyed, imitate them with charcoal, carbon, or dark theatrical paint. A good make-up outfit is indispensable for an embalmer handling many railroad cases during the year, and as such can be had at any dealer in theatrical supplies, we advise the securing of a few varieties of pastes, and some good face powder together with carmine rouge.

If the face is damp or moist, the theatrical paste above mentioned will not adhere properly, and in that case alcohol applied to the skin will cause it to dry. One of the most important considerations in these cases, is the placing of the body in the casket. The body should be placed as low as possible, the silk slide should be closed and a view of the body only secured through it, the light in the room should be tempered so that no striking rays of light serve to distort any portion of the features. Wonderful work has been accomplished by the authors and by others in rescuing cases of this kind from non-presentability to presentability, but in all cases, the ingenuity of the operator is taxed to the utmost, and the case never looks just right until the last touch is applied. With the above information, you have only the rudiments of the work. Your success or failure will depend upon how hard you try to make good in each individual case, and your success in matching colors, which can only be acquired with much patience.

Give burned bodies a very thorough arterial injection, using half strength fluid for the first part of the injection. The cavities should also receive a good injection of normal fluid. The peculiar odor present about a burned body can be lessened by the use of false deodorizers such as flowers, perfume, etc.

CHAPTER XXIV.
TREATMENT OF POSTED CASES.

CRANIAL EVISCERATION.

—By this term is meant the complete removal of the brain. To do so the scalp is cut from ear to ear, the front part is pulled forward over the nose and the back part over the occipital bone. A skull clamp is placed in position and with a saw take away the calvarium. When the calvarium or skull cap has been removed the brain is in full view and can be easily removed by cutting the arteries at the circle of Willis and the ligaments at the base of the skull.

THORACIC AUTOPSY.

—By this term is meant the complete removal of all the organs of the thoracic or chest cavity. To do so the skin is cut on either side from the sterno-clavicular junction to a point where the ninth rib joins to its costal cartilage. The ribs are cut on either side at the costochondral articulation, which will permit the entire front chest wall to be taken away. The heart and lungs are now in full view and can be easily removed.

ABDOMINAL POST.

—By this term is meant the complete removal of all the organs of the abdominal cavity. To do so the skin and muscles are cut on either side from a point where the ninth rib joins its costal cartilage vertically downward to about an inch above Poupart's ligament and from there to the top of the pubic bone. When the anterior abdominal wall has been removed all the organs will be in full view and can easily be removed.

POSTED CASES.

—By this term is meant those cases on which an autopsy has been held and all the internal organs of the body have been removed. Here all the internal circulation has been destroyed.

Treatment.—Place the body on the cooling board and undo all the stitches made by the physician in sewing up the body after the post-mortem. Remove all the organs, that have been previously removed by the physician, and place same in a bucket or other container. Clean out thoroughly all the blood from the cranial, thoracic and abdominal cavities. Now try to tie off the arteries in the cranial cavity which will be the vertebrals or the basilar and the common carotids. If these have been cut too short to be tied, then mix up some plaster of paris and cover them securely so that there will be no leakage. While the plaster of paris is setting raise the common iliac artery, which you will find at the back of the abdomen just over the ilio-psoas muscle, represented by a line drawn from the body of the fourth dorsal vertebra to the center of Poupart's ligament. Inject the right and left common iliac arteries downward which will take care of the lower extremities. Here the only artery you need to tie off is the deep epigastric artery which is a branch of the external iliac just a short distance above Poupart's ligament and which takes a course upward over the abdominal muscles finally to anastomose with the deep mammary artery.

By the time you have injected the lower extremities, the plaster of paris will be set. Work from the inside of the thoracic cavity, and tie off the innominate, left common carotid and the left subclavian arteries, and when this has been accomplished inject each one separately. Here the only leakage you will have will be through the mammary or intercostal arteries which you will tie off as the leakage occurs.

Now turn the body over and hypodermic the back, then turn body over again. Fill the cranial cavity with sawdust, place the skull cap in position and sew up the scalp. Wash all the organs and place them back in the cavities in their proper positions or as nearly so as possible and as you do so fill in with hardening compound. Sew up the abdomen and wash the body with a disinfecting solution and apply outward cosmetics.

CHAPTER XXV.

TREATMENT OF MISCELLANEOUS CASES.

ALCOHOLISM.

—*Definition.*—An intoxication, acute or chronic, due to the injection of a sufficient quantity of alcohol to produce muscular inco-ordination, mental disturbances, and finally narcosis.

Pathology.—Where death is the result of acute alcoholism, the mucous membrane of the gastro-intestinal canal is engorged, injected, and dark red in color, and covered with a sticky, mucoid exudate. The brain and the kidneys show the same characteristic changes. In chronic alcoholism, changes of a more permanent character take place, depending somewhat upon the quantity, quality and kind of alcoholics consumed, and the length of time used. While all the bodily tissues are more or less impaired, the brain, kidneys, and digestive system suffer most. There may be connective tissue changes, fatty degeneration, sclerosed kidneys, liver or arteries, and a more or less dilatation of the stomach.

Treatment.—In acute alcoholism, the blood should be drained from a large vein, while fluid is being injected into a large artery. After draining a sufficient amount of blood from the body, the vein tube should be shut off and the arterial injection should continue until the capillaries have been filled to their utmost capacity. This strong treatment is advised on account of the early tendencies toward putrefaction, which is sometimes in an advanced state shortly after death. The cavities should receive a thorough treatment with normal or supernormal fluid. Myers advises the re-injection of the cavity in 6 or 8 hours after removing the fluid remaining in the cavity from the first injection. As a preventive treatment, this last is a wise precaution. While the cavity treatment is being given the stomach should be entered by the trocar, relieved of its contents and injected, thus preventing post-operative purging.

In chronic alcoholism, the greatest circulation difficulties will be encountered. The capillaries will not receive the fluid, the putrefactive processes causing the formation of tissue gas early in the case, which, when coupled to many natural impediments to the circulation in cases of this kind, virtually nullifies the circulation for fluid distribution. Inject as many arteries as possible, and if necessary the veins also. Use the hollow needle or trocar and give the unexposed portions of the body a heavy hypodermic injection. The fluid used in this case should be not less than normal in strength and in most cases should be at least ¼ over normal. Give the cavities a very heavy injection, paying special attention to the food passages. This is one of the cases coming to the attention of the embalmer where every emphasis must be laid upon the injection of a sufficient amount of fluid, through as many channels as possible. Do not count the cost of the fluid in this case, if you value the securing of satisfactory results. Cosmetic effect will be enhanced by injection of the carotids upward with drainage from the internal jugular veins. Finish the case with the use of good face powder, unless a discoloration is present, when this should be obliterated with one of the improved methods mentioned in the chapter on discolorations.

MORPHINISM.

*—Definition.—*A chronic intoxication due to the habitual use of opium, or some of its alkaloids, especially morphine.

*Pathology.—*There are no characteristic tissue changes, other than that due to indigestion and malnutrition. At death the patient is anemic, the skin dry, sallow and inelastic, the heart and blood vessels show the effects of poor nutrition, and the tissues generally present a starved appearance. The blood disintegrates, causing a discoloration of a brownish color, one or two days after death.

*Treatment.—*Drain blood from these cases using half strength fluid for the first part of the injection. The more blood obtained, the less the danger of discoloration will be. Give the body a thorough cavity injection in addition to the arterial injection. If your treatment does not eliminate the blood as a factor, the discoloration will occur and then it cannot possibly be removed. In this case the use of cosmetics, if in the hands of a patient operator, will overcome the color.

PLUMBISM.

*—Synonyms.—*Lead-poisoning.

*Definition.—*A chronic intoxication due to absorption of lead.

*Pathology.—*The muscles are atrophied and pale in color. Arteriosclerosis of the cerebral blood vessels is found. There may be softening of the brain and hemorrhage.

*Treatment.—*Drain blood from the veins while injecting fluid in the arteries. The fluid should be used half strength for the first bottle of the injection. Massage the face downward to help eliminate any discoloration of blood origin from cerebral hemorrhage. Give the body a thorough injection both as to arteries and cavities. If the face is unduly pale from this treatment, carmine rouge, judiciously applied will lessen the paleness.

ARSENICISM.

*—Definition.—*A chronic intoxication caused by the continued absorption of arsenic.

*Treatment.—*Same as for plumbism.

MERCURIALISM.

*—Definition.—*A chronic mercurial poisoning, caused, either by ingestion of the drug, or by inhalation and absorption of the mineral in the industrial pursuits.

*Pathology.—*There is an acute inflammation of the mouth, stomach, and intestines. The kidneys are inflamed and the liver is degenerated.

*Treatment.—*Drain blood from a large vein while the injection is going on. The first bottle of fluid for the injection should be half strength. The cavities should be injected, as intense inflammation takes place in the alimentary tract.

HEAT-STROKE.

*—Synonyms.—*Sunstroke.

*Definition.—*Heat-stroke is the result of exposure to intense heat, either from the direct rays of the sun, or the radiation of blasts or furnaces, or to an overheated atmosphere.

*Pathology.—*Owing to the excessive heat of the body, putrefactive changes occur very early. If a post-mortem examination is made very soon after death, the left heart will be found contracted, while the right heart will be engorged, and the venous trunks filled with dark semi-fluid blood. There is also venous engorgement of the brain, spinal cord, and lungs. Ecchymoses and extravasations of blood are found in the skin and mucous membranes.

*Treatment.—*Drain blood from a large vein during the injection. The first two bottles of the injection should be of half strength fluid. The face should be massaged to assist in the securing of capillary circulation and in the elimination of the blood discoloration. The body should be treated as soon as possible after death, as putrefaction begins early. The cavities should have a very thorough treatment, eliminating the gases and injecting normal fluid therein. Should ecchymosis occur, obliterate the color by an application of cosmetics.

OBESITY.

*—Definition.—*An excessive accumulation of fat, impairing the bodily functions, or rendering one uncomfortable.

*Treatment.—*Drain blood from these cases, injecting the first bottle of fluid half strength followed by normal fluid for the balance of the injection. Massage the face downward during the injection. Inject the cavities, with special attention to the stomach and intestines. For transportation of these cases, govern yourself according to the provisions of the transportation laws.

ELEPHANTIASIS.

*—Definition.—*A chronic disease caused by inflammation and obstruction of lymphatics and marked by great thickening of the skin.

*Treatment.—*Drain blood from these cases and inject normal fluid sufficient enough in quantity to secure preservation. For long time preservation, supplement the foregoing treatment by a special injection into the thickened extremity, either through an artery leading directly to the part or by trocar or hollow needle inserted under the skin. Give the body a thorough cavity treatment, using normal fluid throughout. For transportation, govern yourself according to the provisions of the transportation laws.

DROWNED CASES.

*—Treatment.—*Inject fluid into the lungs by inserting a child's trocar into the windpipe at the upper border of the sternum, making the injection sufficient in strength and amount to fill the lungs. If this is not done, a bloody purging will take place several hours after death. Tap the stomach through the epigastric region, aspirate the contents and inject strong fluid before removing the instrument. Drain blood from the body during the injection, which should be quite heavy and of normal fluid. The last bottle should be made 1¼ strength or ¼ over normal.

FLOATER.

*—Definition.—*A body that has been floating on the water.

*Treatment.—*The body is distended with gases in the cavities, tissues and capillaries, putrefaction is in an advanced state, and a vile odor will be present. If body is to be shipped, aspirate all the gas possible from the tissues with the hollow needle, injecting strong fluid in the same openings. Open the body from the base of the neck to the pubic bone, relieve the gases in the alimentary tract and lungs, and fill cavity thoroughly with hardening compound, after which it should be sewed up. Inject as many arteries as possible with very strong fluid. Dress the body and place it in a metallic casket. Pour the contents of two pound bottles of Platt's chlorides on the underclothing to assist in deodorizing the body. Do not open the casket after it is once sealed.

If the body is not to be shipped, it will be advisable to deodorize it as much as possible and bury it without delay.

MOTHER AND UNBORN CHILD.

*—Mother and Foetus in Utero.—Treatment.—*Before pregnancy has reached the three months stage, the child will receive fluid directly from the circulation connected with the mother.

After the three months stage, the circulation, by direct flow, is stopped and fluid could only reach the foetus by absorption from the placenta. This is naturally insufficient to preserve the child, which by this time is immersed in the liquor amnii (water of the womb) and which is subject to early putrefaction in that situation. The trocar should be directed to the uterus or womb from a point on the median line, half way from the umbilicus to the pubic arch, care being taken to reach the water which surrounds the foetus. Withdraw the water, and inject as much strong fluid as possible so that the foetus will be surrounded with fluid, and in that way preserved. If the trocar enters the body of the child, this will not occur, so the instrument should be carefully manipulated to reach the space between the child and the uterine wall. The mother should receive a very heavy arterial and cavity injection, with full drainage of blood. The vulva should be closed with absorbent cotton. The face should be massaged thoroughly toward the heart.

SENILITY.

*—Synonyms.—*Old age.

*Definition.—*A state of decline in an aged person characterized by progressive atrophy of all the tissues and organs.

*Pathology.—*Excessive shrinking and obliteration takes place among the capillaries. The skin becomes diminished in thickness. When this occurs, it is easily seen why in old age there will follow, after the injection of fluid into the arterial system, greenish, brownish, and soft spots, in the different parts of the body, especially notable in the face, neck and hands. The products of degeneration may accumulate in the tissues and cause them to be thicker than they are in health, as is seen in the vessels, the walls of which are much thicker than normal. The blood contains fewer corpuscles and solid constituents, is more watery, and coagulates more readily; also the total quantity is less. The pericardium, endocardium, and the capsules of the liver and spleen are opaque and toughened. Degeneration of the cardiac substance may lead to a state of asthenia, which generally produces death. Dilatation of the orifices of the heart may be the prominent lesion, or they may be contracted by atheroma, or by thickening of the vales or rings. The lungs are changed more or less, increasing the bronchial secretions, which during life have been attended by severe paroxysms of coughing.

*Treatment.—*Inject half strength fluid for the first bottle, following that with ¾ strength for the second and normal for the third and all thereafter if more be necessary. Blood may be drained from the vein if the operator thinks it advisable. The commercial face solution or water should be used on the face while massaging in order that the skin may be kept moist and to prevent dessication from the action of the fluid. The cavity should be injected as a matter of precaution.

GANGRENE.

*—Synonyms.—*Senile gangrene; mortification.

*Definition.—*Putrefactive fermentation of dead tissue, from various causes.

*Treatment.—*The extremities are affected in senile gangrene. They should be wrapped with absorbent cotton which should then be saturated with fluid. The body itself should receive the same treatment accorded in the paragraph on senility.

INDEX

A

Abdomen *34, 63, 64, 65, 66, 68, 69, 70, 71, 76, 78, 112, 113, 120, 121, 129, 161, 162, 163, 172, 173, 185, 190, 193, 203, 205, 206, 207, 216*

Abdominal Cavity *63, 64, 68, 72, 76, 79, 119, 157, 158, 161, 162, 163, 164, 183, 196, 197, 206, 210, 215*

Abdominal Fermentation *119, 185*

Abdominal Post *215*

Actinomycosis *181*

Ague *182*

Alcoholism *217*

Alimentary Canal *32, 60, 61, 62, 66, 72, 158, 161*

Anasarca *206, 207*

Anatomical Guides *136*

Aneurism *133, 137, 138, 145, 150, 152, 158, 192, 196, 201, 210*

Angiology *17*

Antemortem Staining *124, 125*

Anthrax *25, 177*

Anus *61, 69, 70, 72*

Aortic Incompetency *197, 198*

Aortic Insufficiency *197*

Aortic Regurgitation *197*

Aortic Stenosis *198*

Apnea *104, 105*

Aponeuroses *19, 31*

Appendicitis *70, 119, 206*

Arm Severed *210*

Arsenicism *218*

Arterial System *39, 81, 82, 87, 88, 115, 131, 140, 163, 166, 167, 168, 169, 200, 201, 203, 204, 221*

Artery *11, 14, 24, 28, 29, 30, 31, 33, 34, 35, 39, 54, 55, 57, 60, 68, 69, 70, 74, 75, 76, 82, 83, 84, 85, 86, 87, 88, 89, 95, 98, 99, 107, 108, 133, 135, 136, 137, 138, 139, 143, 144, 145, 146, 147, 148, 149, 150, 151, 152, 153, 154, 155, 156, 158, 160, 162, 167, 169, 170, 171, 172, 173, 174, 179, 191, 192, 199, 200, 201, 205, 206, 209, 210, 212, 216, 217, 220*

Ascites *205, 206, 207, 208*

Asphyxia *105, 111, 116, 205*

Lector House believes that a society develops through a two-fold approach of continuous learning and adaptation, which is derived from the study of classic literary works spread across the historic timeline of literature records. Therefore, we aim at reviving, repairing and redeveloping all those inaccessible or damaged but historically as well as culturally important literature across subjects so that the future generations may have an opportunity to study and learn from past works to embark upon a journey of creating a better future.

This book is a result of an effort made by Lector House towards making a contribution to the preservation and repair of original ancient works which might hold historical significance to the approach of continuous learning across subjects.

HAPPY READING & LEARNING!

LECTOR HOUSE LLP
E-MAIL: lectorpublishing@gmail.com

www.ingramcontent.com/pod-product-compliance
Lightning Source LLC
Chambersburg PA
CBHW051316130726
47987CB00004B/1832